The Peninsular War

To Yolanda, Ferran and Valèria

Visiting archives, researching, reading, writing, editing, proofreading, proofreading again, takes time. In this case, years, and much of this time has been taken away from spending time with my family. I would like to thank my wife and children for their patience, understanding, support, advice and encouragement throughout this time. Thank you for accompanying me on my journey.

The Peninsular War

The Spanish Perspective

J.J. Herrero Giménez

AN IMPRINT OF PEN & SWORD BOOKS LTD
YORKSHIRE – PHILADELPHIA

First published in Great Britain in 2023 by
FRONTLINE BOOKS
an imprint of Pen & Sword Books Ltd
Yorkshire – Philadelphia

ISBN 978-1-39904-785-2

Typeset by Concept, Huddersfield, West Yorkshire, HD4 5JL.
Printed and bound in England by CPI Group (UK) Ltd, Croydon, CR0 4YY.

Pen & Sword Books Ltd incorporates the Imprints of Aviation, Atlas, Family
History, Fiction, Maritime, Military, Discovery, Politics, History, Archaeology,
Select, Wharncliffe Local History, Wharncliffe True Crime, Military Classics,
Wharncliffe Transport, Leo Cooper, The Praetorian Press, Remember When,
White Owl, Seaforth Publishing and Frontline Books.

For a complete list of Pen & Sword titles please contact
PEN & SWORD BOOKS LTD
47 Church Street, Barnsley, South Yorkshire, S70 2AS, England
E-mail: enquiries@pen-and-sword.co.uk
Website: www.pen-and-sword.co.uk
or
PEN & SWORD BOOKS
1950 Lawrence Rd, Havertown, PA 19083, USA
E-mail: uspen-and-sword@casematepublishers.com
Website: www.penandswordbooks.com

Contents

List of Illustrations

Plates

Episode du siège de Saragosse: assaut du monastère de Santa Engracia, le 8 février 1809, by Louis-François, Baron Lejeune.

Portrait of Ferdinand VII, by Vicente López Portaña.

Portrait of Joseph Bonaparte, by François Gérard.

Portrait of Juan Martín Díaz, known as El Empecinado ('The Undaunted'), by Francisco de Goya.

Juan Malasaña avenging his daughter Manuela Malasaña on the streets of Madrid during the Dos de Mayo uprising, by Eugenio Álvarez Dumont.

Battle of Tudela, by January Suchodolski.

Bronze statue dedicated to the Drummer of Bruc by Frederic Marès (1956) in Corinto Street in Barcelona.

The great day of Girona, by César Álvarez Dumont.

The promulgation of the Constitution of 1812, by Salvador Viniegra.

Heroic combat in the pulpit of the Church of San Agustín in Zaragoza during the Second Siege of 1809, by César Álvarez Dumont.

The Third of May 1808, by Francisco de Goya.

Le maréchal Suchet, duc d'Albufera, by Adèle Gault.

Portrait of the ancient General Castaños, by Vicente López Portaña.

Battle of Somosierra, by January Suchodolski.

The surrender of Bailén, by José Casado de Alisal.

Spanish medals of the Peninsular War: two Medals of Bailen, Medal of the Escape of the Division of the North; Medal of Nalda; Medal of Pontesampaio; and Medal of the Siege of Girona.

The Disasters of War: with or without reason, by Francisco de Goya.

The Disasters of War: the same, by Francisco de Goya.

vii

The Disasters of War: And they are fierce or *And they fight like wild beasts*, by Francisco de Goya.

Monument to the Fallen for Spain.

Battle Maps

Acknowledgements

To write this book, I have visited archives and libraries and consulted primary sources such as letters, royal decrees and the press of the time, which I have contrasted with the works of the best specialists in each subject, whether Spanish, British or French. It is a work on which I have spent more than three years, and it would not have been possible without the help, support and trust of many people. First and foremost, I am eternally indebted to John Grehan. His advice and guidance have been essential in getting this book into your hands. John, thank you very much for your trust. I also want to thank all his colleagues from Pen & Sword for the excellent edition of the book. Among my friends, Jaume Boguñà tops the list. Some years ago we started an ambitious project on history and phaleristics that I hope one day we will be able to complete, and the first part of which is this book. I must also thank my friends David Alfaras and Joan Mayans for their support and advice throughout the writing of this book. I would also like to thank Ignacio Pasamar and Francisco Medina of the publishing house HRM Ediciones for the Spanish edition.

J.J. Herrero Giménez
20 September 2022

Introduction

The Peninsular War has been widely studied by Anglo-Saxon historiography, but readers from these countries are probably less familiar with a Spanish perspective on the war. The aim of this book is precisely to explain the war from the Spanish point of view, trying to answer questions such as: what was the real contribution of the Spanish Army during the Peninsular War? Was it really a disastrous army, commanded by useless generals with cowardly troops? What was the real role of the guerrillas? The answers to these questions are not influenced by a nationalist or chauvinistic view. On the contrary, we are going to analyse the virtues, but also the many defects and problems that the Spanish Army had to face when confronting what was probably the best army in the world in 1808.

At the beginning of the nineteenth century the Spanish armed forces were a typical *ancien régime* army. Apart from the invasion of Portugal, which was achieved in a few days in November 1807 by the combined armies of France and Spain, the last wars they had fought in the late eighteenth century had been the War of the Pyrenees (1793–1795), as part of the French Revolutionary Wars, and the War of the Oranges, against Portugal, during a few weeks in 1801. The year before, Manuel Godoy, the first secretary of state and the man who really ruled the country in place of the weak Charles IV, signed the Second Treaty of San Ildefonso, which meant that Spain was no longer allied with Britain but with France. That war saw some of the strengths and weaknesses that would be magnified throughout the Peninsular War. On the one hand, the Spanish forces had excellent artillery troops, but the quality of the infantry and cavalry regiments depended heavily on the officers who commanded them. One of the biggest problems that the Spanish army had to face was the lack of men qualified to become officers; in the first place, to be an officer, they had to be able to read and write, and Spain in the early nineteenth century had an illiteracy rate of 85 per cent of the population (by way of comparison, at the same time in England and Wales the rate was 40 per cent among men and in France 50 per cent). Moreover, the attempts to create military academies during the reign of Charles III (1759–1788) had ended up failing in most cases, with only the Academy of Artillery (1764) being consolidated, so in order to gain access to high positions in the army, personal contacts and family relations were more important than the individual capacity of the commanders, who practically all came from the nobility. During the war we will see how, thanks to these practices, totally incapable generals such as Areizaga, Venegas or Blake were put in charge of large armies, and the pernicious influence of the Palafox family placed its undeserving members in positions of power. But Spain also had excellent generals, such as the Duke of Albuquerque (*see* Chapter 26), the Marquis de la Romana (*see* Chapter 9) and General Copons, among others. This lack of Spanish officers had meant that for decades the Spanish Army had relied on a large number of foreign officers and troops, who fought in the service of the Spanish crown. These troops included three Irish regiments (Ireland, Hibernia and Ultonia), six Swiss regiments (Wimpffen, Bertschart, Traxler, Preux, Reding major and Reding minor) and an elite corps of the Royal Walloon Guard, but also many officers of Neapolitan origin, given the close relations between the Bourbon houses of Naples and Spain. At the beginning of the Peninsular War only a small proportion of the Swiss troops sided with Napoleon, the great majority of them remaining on the Spanish side, contributing valuable officers such as O'Donnell and Reding to the patriot army. In short, at the beginning of the war the Spanish Army had thirty-nine regiments of line infantry (three battalions each), twelve regiments of light infantry (one battalion each), the aforementioned six Swiss regiments (two battalions) and twenty-four regiments of cavalry (five squadrons). But by virtue of the friendship treaties between France and Spain, the best Spanish troops were fighting in Portugal and Denmark alongside the Napoleonic troops.

What happened in Spain in the spring of 1808? Napoleon had a plan and, let's face it, it did not seem far-fetched at first. It was to conquer Spain by occupying it militarily with the excuse of invading Portugal, in order to subsequently install his brother Joseph as king, replacing the decadent Spanish Bourbon branch, and taking advantage of the political instability that arose as a result of the Escorial Conspiracy (*see* Chapter 1). A similar plan worked in the Netherlands, where Napoleon's younger brother Louis had reigned since 1806. Napoleon only needed to complete the plan and obtain the resignation of the crown of Charles IV and Ferdinand VII, who had become the King of Spain after forcing his father to abdicate in mid-March. At first, it seemed that everything was going as planned. On 7 May Napoleon achieved the abdication of the two Spanish kings in Bayonne, but something unexpected occurred. A few days earlier, on 2 May, the people in Madrid had risen up against the Napoleonic troops. This revolt was reproduced in different Spanish cities: a revolution of unforeseeable consequences was under way. As Napoleon had predicted, the Spanish elites (with the exception of the Church) accepted the new status quo. But the people rose up in arms, not only against the Napoleonic forces, but against all political authorities suspected of collaborating with the enemy, the so-called *afrancesados* (literally, Frenchified). To organize this revolution in different cities and regions of Spain, new Juntas were created, government bodies that were responsible for channelling the revolutionary fury and which would soon end up being controlled and dominated by the most conservative elements of society: the Church and the nobility, for in a kind of *avant-la-lettre* gattopardism, everything would change so that nothing would change. These Juntas were responsible for raising and organizing the new army with which they would have to face the fearsome Napoleonic troops. In this book we dedicate a chapter to an analysis of the creation of the Junta de Asturias, one of the first and most important ones (*see* Chapter 3). To coordinate the different Spanish Juntas, in September 1808 the Supreme Central and Governing Junta of Spain and the Indies was created, based in Seville, which organized the available troops into four great armies: the Left, the Centre, the Right and the Reserve. As we have mentioned, one of the functions of these local Juntas was to start up a new army, practically from scratch, a titanic task if we consider that the best units of the Spanish Army were abroad and that some of the officers had gone over to the Napoleonic troops or, in the best of cases, remained in a neutral position waiting to see how events would develop. Initially, these newly created armies had to face myriad problems: to begin with, the endemic lack of officers, the inexperience of the troops, and the lack of weapons, ammunition, uniforms and even food. There was no time to train the troops to face the powerful war machine that Napoleon had created. The lack of officers was partially alleviated by the employment of retired officers and officers from the navy who joined the army. In fact, we will see many Trafalgar heroes fighting and dying on dry land. The newly created regiments, many of them with really bombastic names, such as 'Victory or Death', did not have enough time to train and, especially at the beginning of the war, were easily massacred by the Napoleonic troops; for example, when the dreadful French *voltigeurs* managed to defeat the few Spanish officers, the troops were left without a commander to give them orders or, worse still, they did not know how to form squares in the face of cavalry charges, and consequently suffered appalling casualties when they disbanded. It was worse for the cavalry units, which had to train not only their horsemen but also their horses. Lack of training caused many horses to flee in panic at the first exchange of fire. All of this is discussed in detail in Chapter 10. A large part of these newly created units would end up disappearing due to lack of troops, but those that managed to survive the first defeats, such as the Regiment La Unión, became excellent combat units.

From a Spanish point of view the Peninsular War can be divided into three phases. The first phase, between 1808 and 1810, saw a series of unexpected victories, most notably at Bailen and the first siege of Zaragoza, but it was a period in which the French achieved their greatest victories, as we will see in the chapters dedicated to the battles of Tudela, Uclés and Ocaña (*see* Chapters 11, 14 and 23), but it was also the period in which Moore's army retreated, culminating in the battle of Corunna. Many of Napoleon's victories over the Spanish Army were truly crushing. But even so, despite the fact that the invaders were destroying army after army, probably the greatest virtue of the Spanish Army in this period was its steadfast and almost incomprehensible ability to resist and to present new armies on the battlefield. This will to resist to the utmost and to the last consequences can be seen perfectly in the chapter devoted to the second siege of Zaragoza (*see* Chapter 15), where Marshal Lannes was forced to break the city by dynamiting house after house, fighting for every inch of ground. The Spaniards defied the laws of war. It must be said that this firm will to resist can be most clearly seen in sieges of cities, such as Girona and Tarragona (*see* Chapters 25 and 28). At the end of this period the Supreme Central and Governing Junta of Spain and the Indies went into crisis, coinciding with the Napoleonic conquest of Seville, and was replaced by the Regency Council of Spain and the Indies, which moved to Cadiz and reorganized the Spanish armies, which were numbered from 1 to 7. The latter was the number that the army of frightening guerrillas received (*see* Chapter 31).

The second phase of the war was from 1810 to 1812. In this period the French dominated practically all of Spain, with the exception of Galicia (which they abandoned in mid-June 1809: see Chapter 19); Catalonia, which, despite being practically completely occupied, continued to resist; some strongholds on the Spanish southeast coast; and finally the city of Cadiz, which was subjected to the longest siege of the war between 1810 and 1812. It was in Cadiz that the first liberal Spanish constitution was drawn up.

Wellington's victory at the battle of Salamanca in 1812 initiated the third and final phase of the war, which culminated in the definitive defeat of Napoleon in Spain. The last chapters of the book focus on topics that are not strictly military, but that help us understand the development of the war in Spain, such as, for example, the fate of prisoners of war (Chapter 34), the Spanish Navy in a war that was almost exclusively land-based (Chapter 35) and the stay of Ferdinand VII in his French exile in the Valençay palace, which illustrates his most abject side (Chapter 37). In conclusion, although it is clear that Wellington's victories were decisive for the victory over Napoleon in the Peninsular War, we will see how these victories could not have been achieved without the almost fanatical resistance of the Spanish in their unwavering will to resist the troops of the French emperor.

Of course, the most complete gallery of characters can be none other than the Spanish themselves. Throughout the war certain characters became legendary and have remained in our collective imagination, such as Agustina de Aragón or the drummer of Bruc, and generals who personified the indomitable spirit of the Spanish people, such as Palafox or Álvarez de Castro, even though the reality of the situation indicates that their military skills were questionable. And it is the case that the Fernandine Army suffered some truly incompetent generals, such as Areizaga and Venegas. However, it is worth noting the presence of other outstanding generals who were able to overcome very adverse circumstances and achieved resounding triumphs on the battlefield, such as the Duke of Albuquerque and Copons. There was no shortage of guerrilla fighters, some of them legends, such as Espoz y Mina, and others less well-known but no less daring, such as Rovira. And, alongside them, characters who are difficult to classify, such as Juan van Halen, the intriguing servant of Ferdinand VII, Amézaga and Mayoral, the impostor who made half of France believe that he was a Spanish cardinal. Even a descendant of the prophet Muhammad fought in the Fernandine ranks, and Moctezuma had descendants fighting in both armies.

Chapter One

A Plot in El Escorial

Date: October 1807. *Place*: El Escorial, Madrid.

As a preamble, it seems appropriate to begin with this event that, although it does not strictly belong to the Peninsular War, is nevertheless linked to it, not to mention that many of its protagonists will continue to appear throughout this book. Within the amazing life of Ferdinand VII, one of the most embarrassing episodes was undoubtedly the Plot and subsequent Escorial Process. Ferdinand, dissatisfied with the policy developed by his father and hating the plenipotentiary minister Godoy, began to conspire against them in the spring of 1807. Supporting him, Juan de Escoiquiz and the Duke del Infantado encouraged the Prince of Asturias[1] to carry out his plans. Directly or indirectly, other nobles of Ferdinand's closest confidence and his servants also took part in the intrigue.

At the end of October Charles IV moved to the Escorial[2], where he wanted to spend All Saints' Day. On 27 October the king found an anonymous letter in his chamber warning him of his son's conspiracy. Charles immediately went to his son's chamber, where 'his own eyes served as a guide for Charles IV to proceed with a search that placed in his hands several damning papers'.[3] In these papers the Prince of Asturias called for an insurrection that would bring him to power, overthrowing his father and Godoy. Subsequently, the king delivered the documents to the Marquis of Caballero, Secretary of the Universal Office[4] of Grace and Justice. Godoy, sick, had stayed in Madrid. Charles IV decided to lock up his son in one of the monastery's cells, in addition to writing to Napoleon and publishing the details of the plot in the *Madrid Gazette*. That same night the nine royal guards who had been with the Prince of Asturias that day were arrested.[5] By royal order shortly afterwards they were released and dispersed in different regiments throughout the peninsula. On the 30th Charles IV interrogated his son, but Ferdinand remained evasive. A few hours later the Marquis of Caballero again questioned the Prince and then Ferdinand betrayed all the other participants in the conspiracy, presenting himself as the victim of these schemers who had deceived him, and pointing to Escoiquiz as the mastermind of the plot. Finally, Godoy himself arrived at El Escorial and met with the Prince of Asturias, who received the Minister 'with tears in his eyes and open arms'.[6] He also wrote to his parents, begging their forgiveness and to be allowed to 'kiss their royal feet'. Advised by Godoy, Charles IV pardoned his son, making his mercy public through the *Madrid Gazette*, and ordered to be imprisoned and prosecuted those he had denounced. On 5 November Ferdinand was released, at least in appearance, as from that moment onwards his servants were replaced by Godoy's men.[7] The following day Charles IV appointed a tribunal to judge the conspirators, made up of three members of the Royal Council: Arias Mon, Sebastián de Torres and Domingo Fernández Campomames. Benito Arias de Prada was appointed secretary. The role of prosecutor fell to Simón de Viegas, a person closely linked politically to Godoy. Making some harsh accusations, Viegas demanded the death penalty for treason for two of the conspirators: Juan de Escoiquiz, archdeacon of Alcaraz and canon of Toledo, and Pedro Alcántara de Toledo y Salm-Salm, Duke del Infantado, grandee of Spain, Knight of the Golden Toison and lieutenant general; and lesser penalties for the crime of infidelity to the king for a number of others: Pedro María Jordán de Urríes y Fuenbuena, Marquis of Ayerbe, chief steward of the prince; Joaquín Crespí de Valldaura Leguina, Count of Orgaz, general, and gentleman of the bedchamber to Ferdinand; Joaquín de Haro, Count of Bornos, grandee of Spain, gentleman of the bedchamber to Ferdinand and lieutenant general; Juan Manuel de Villena,[8] gentleman of the bedchamber to Ferdinand and brigadier; Pedro Giraldo de Chaves, brigadier; Andrés Casaña, servant of the Marquis of Ayerbe; José González Manrique, servant of the Duke of Infantado; Pedro Collado, *casiller*[9] of Ferdinand VII[10]; and Fernando Selgas, *casiller* of Ferdinand VII.

The detained service personnel were taken to the Real Sitio gaol, while the patricians were locked up in the cells they occupied at the time of their arrest.[11] The trial became a storm of accusations and counter accusations. While the Prince of Asturias had already been responsible for opening the floodgates (it should be added that although he had accused many of his servants, the accusations were so weak that they were neither imprisoned nor prosecuted), other defendants such as Escoiquiz tried to implicate other notables, such as the Duke of Montemar, the Marquis of Castelar and the Palafox brothers.[12] The trial ended on 25 January 1808. All the defendants were acquitted as no solid evidence had been presented to justify a conviction. The verdict was humiliating for Charles IV, who refused to accept it. Using a royal prerogative, and under pressure from Godoy and the Queen, he sent the defendants into exile in different Spanish cities.[13]

When the king informed his son of the decision, the Prince of Asturias prostrated himself at his feet and, embracing his father's legs, thanked him for his pardon. Later, he hugged affectionately with Godoy. The future King of Spain did not mind humiliating himself in that way before his enemies. He knew that soon he would have the opportunity to take revenge. King Charles and Godoy had reason to be furious. From the first moment Ferdinand had won the day in the eyes of public opinion. In Madrid and even on the outskirts of the Escorial there were demonstrations in his favour.[14] Ultimately, the trial strengthened the *Fernandista* party, which took less than three months to carry out the Aranjuez Mutiny, which resulted in the fall of Godoy and the abdication of Charles IV. On 19 March the Prince of Asturias became Ferdinand VII, King of Spain, but when he arrived in Madrid, Murat's troops had already occupied the city.

Notes

1. This is the title that the heirs to the Crown receive in Spain; its corresponding title in the British royal house would be 'Prince of Wales'.
2. The royal site of San Lorenzo de El Escorial (in short, El Escorial) is a historical residence of the kings of Spain located in the town of San Lorenzo de El Escorial, around 45km (28 miles) northwest of Madrid. It was built during the second half of the sixteenth century by order of King Philip II and is the largest Renaissance building in the world; it includes a monastery, basilica, royal palace and royal pantheon, among other buildings.
3. Padín (2019), citing Morayta.
4. Minister.
5. Campos (2007), p. 287.
6. Padín (2019).
7. Campos (2007), p. 291.
8. His inclusion is surprising, since he was married to Josefa Álvarez de Faria, cousin of Godoy himself.
9. A servant who used to take out and clean the chamber pots and urinals in the palace.
10. Pedro Collado later accompanied Ferdinand VII in his exile to Valençay, along with Escoiquiz and the Marquis of Ayerbe. See Chapter 37.
11. Campos (2007), p. 289.
12. Parra (2010), p. 139.
13. Campos (2007), pp. 294–5.
14. Alonso (2015), p. 61.

Chapter Two

The 2 May Uprising

Date: 2 May 1808. *Place*: Madrid.
Result: Spanish revolt repressed by French troops.

Background

In October 1807 the Treaty of Fontainebleau was signed between Manuel Godoy, on behalf of Charles IV, and Napoleon. It stipulated the joint Franco-Spanish military invasion of Portugal and allowed the passage of French troops through Spanish territory. By virtue of this agreement, in February 1808 French troops were to occupy the fortifications of Figueres, Barcelona and Pamplona without opposition. In the following days the Napoleonic Army occupied other cities such as Burgos and Salamanca, dominating communications not only with Portugal but also with Madrid. Spanish society soon realized the true intention of the French Emperor, which was none other than to invade Spain.

As described in the previous chapter, the Mutiny of Aranjuez resulted in the abdication of Charles IV and the fall of Godoy, and Ferdinand VII was crowned king. The riots against Godoy and Charles had spread through several Spanish cities. In Madrid, for example, there was also an uprising against the *corregidor*[1] José de Marquina Galindo, who was lynched by the mob.[2] As the situation in Madrid was still out of control on 23 March, the city was occupied by Murat's troops, who were welcomed by Ferdinand VII. Napoleon quickly realized the

4

weakness of the Spanish Crown. Charles IV and Ferdinand VII both tormented him with requests, so he decided to put an end to this uncomfortable situation and summoned them to Bayonne. Ferdinand VII arrived on 20 April and his parents ten days later.

The revolt

While the Emperor tried to obtain the abdication and resignation of the Bourbons, on 2 May the people of Madrid rose up against the French troops. That morning, following the orders of the Emperor, the infante Francisco de Paula, the youngest son of Charles IV, was preparing to leave for Bayonne. These preparations were noticed by the palace locksmith, Blas Molina,[3] who, shouting, managed to mobilize an indignant crowd.

Supervising the operation, Murat had placed in the palace one of his aides-de-camp, Colonel Auguste Lagrange, who now unexpectedly found himself surrounded by a mob that wanted to lynch him. His guard of twenty Royal Walloon Guards barely saved him. At that moment a battalion of the Grenadiers of the Imperial Guard appeared, ready to pacify the uproar in the palace by opening fire. But as they cleared out the palace, the rioters spread throughout Madrid shouting: 'Death to the French!' A hunt began through the streets of Madrid for any Frenchmen to be found there, especially the Mamelukes, Murat's personal guard. Even the prisoners of the royal gaol issued a written request to their warden to give them permission to go out and massacre the French, with the promise to return once the revolt was over.[4] Surprisingly, they were given permission and some fifty-six armed convicts headed towards the Plaza Mayor, where they killed as many French as they met. But once the imperial troops organized themselves, the massacre of the Madrid patriots began. As for the regular Spanish Army, the troops were ordered to remain locked up in their barracks; most obeyed. But this was not the case at the Artillery Park, located in the Palace of Monteleón.[5] The artillery officers Captain Luis Daoiz and Lieutenant Pedro Velarde went there, as well as volunteers from other army corps and a large group of citizens. They convinced the French artillerymen to lay down their arms. Shortly after, the Regiment of Westphalia appeared under General Lefranc and a bloody fight ensued, ending in a bayonet charge by the Napoleonic troops. All the defenders of the Palace of Monteleón were killed or seriously wounded. The artillery officers Daoiz and Velarde, who died in the battle, became the first heroes to symbolize the Spanish resistance against the invasion. Another martyr was Manuela Malasaña, a seamstress killed by a French soldier, whose death was depicted in a painting by Eugenio Alvarez Dumont. Once the city was pacified, Murat ordered the execution of all detainees, military or civilian, who had been arrested carrying arms. That same afternoon the executions began in various parts of the city and would continue into the next day, an event that Francisco de Goya immortalized in his painting 'The Third of May 1808'.[6] The revolt in Madrid lit the fuse for various uprisings in the rest of Spain. In the meantime, in Bayonne a few days later both Charles and Ferdinand renounced the throne in favour of the Emperor, who gave the crown of Spain to his older brother Joseph Bonaparte, who was duly proclaimed King of Spain.

Interestingly, of the fifty-six inmates of the gaol, four died in the revolt and one was declared a fugitive, but fifty-one returned as promised to the royal gaol. It was a matter of honour.

Notes

1. The mayors of the Spanish *Ancien Régime*.
2. Marquina was a very unpopular character at the time, due to his undisguised anti-clericalism. He is one of the few mayors of Madrid who does not have a street named after him.
3. Pérez de Guzmán (1908), p. 374.
4. Pérez-Reverte (2007).
5. Property of the descendants of Hernán Cortés, Marquesses of the Valley of Oaxaca and Dukes of Monteleón and Terranova. After 2 May it was reduced to ruins. It was never rebuilt and only an arch remains that forms part of the Daoiz y Velarde sculptural ensemble.
6. Murat (1897), pp. 318–25; Pérez de Guzmán (1908); Hocquellet (2008), pp. 75; Southey (1825), pp. 245–50.

Chapter Three

The Asturian Army of 1808: the Creation of an Army

Date: 1808. *Place*: Asturias.

The creation of an army

The events of early May in Bayonne and Madrid had shocked Spanish society. Thus, while the elites hesitated, waiting for events to unfold, in most Spanish towns the people rose up as they received the news of the massacre of 2 and 3 May in Madrid. The two main cities in Asturias, Gijón and Oviedo, were no exception.

On 9 May riots broke out in Oviedo when the people were informed of the massacre in Madrid. In the afternoon, fearing a general revolt, the Junta General[1] agreed on various provisions to appease the masses. Among them, it was decided to commission Joaquín de Navía-Ossorio, Marquis of Santa Cruz de Marcenado, José María Queipo de Llano y Ruiz de Sarabia, Count of Toreno,[2] and Manuel de Miranda Gayoso to organize the future Asturian army. The patriotic drift of the Junta General of Asturias collided with the will to obey the laws and provisions coming from the Real Audiencia,[3] which reacted by informing Murat of everything that happened and distributed edicts describing the penalties to be faced by those who disobeyed the new laws dictated by Napoleon. A few days later, and in the midst of great tension in the streets, the Junta General of Asturias gave in to the pressure from the Real Audiencia and acceded to the latest orders sent by Murat, which included, among other things, the appointments of José Pagola as the new Regent of Asturias and of Juan Crisóstomo La Llave as Commander General of Asturias. In addition, Murat sent a unit of Royal Carabineers and the Regiment of Hibernia to Oviedo to ensure compliance with his orders.

At the same time clandestine groups were preparing an uprising. On the night of 24/25 May groups of volunteers from several towns arrived on the outskirts of Oviedo to support the revolt. While the judge José María García del Busto forced Juan Crisóstomo La Llave to convene an extraordinary meeting of the Junta General, the peasants attacked the weapons factory in the town, seizing a large quantity of rifles, pistols and ammunition. The Junta, which was presided over by La Llave, ended with his dismissal (and later, imprisonment), being replaced by the Marquis of Santa Cruz de Marcenado and, since Ferdinand VII was captive, sovereignty fell to the People. This was a true revolution. In addition, the Junta agreed to declare 'war on the tyrant of Europe'[4] and to sign peace treaties with the United Kingdom and Sweden. It was decided to send the Count of Toreno to London to report on the revolt and to request the shipment of arms. And, as a result of the efforts of the Marquis of Santa Cruz de Marcenado, Count Toreno and Miranda Gayoso, the 1st Division of Volunteers of Asturias was created, based on the Provincial Regiment of Oviedo. This unit was subsequently renamed the Regiment of Covadonga. On the 26th a squadron of the Royal Carabineers arrived from Valladolid and decided to join the patriotic cause *en masse*. However, the unit major, Manuel Ladrón de Guevara, did not support the revolt and was imprisoned. A few days later the 1st Battalion of the Regiment of Hibernia arrived from Bilbao. Likewise, the men of this unit decided to rebel and their colonel, Carlos Fitzgerald, was also imprisoned.

In mid-June the Marquis of Santa Cruz de Marcenado, after completing the enormous job of organizing the volunteers who had come from all over Asturias, resigned as Captain General of the Army of Asturias, being replaced by Vicente María de Acevedo. The new regiments created between June and August were:

- Avilés, with Colonel José Valdés Solís, retired captain.
- Villaviciosa, with Colonel Carlos Rato Ramírez, lieutenant of the Navy.
- Llanes, with Colonel Sancho Victorero de Junco
- Gijón, with Colonel Pedro Castañedo, lieutenant of the Navy.
- Castropol, with Colonel José María Navía-Ossorio, son of the Marquis of Santa Cruz de Marcenado.
- Oviedo, with Colonel José María Queipo de Llano, Count of Toreno.
- Salas, with Colonel Gregorio Cañedo.
- Siero, with Colonel Menendo de Llanes Cienfuegos.
- Luarca, with Colonel José Jove, *Caballerizo Mayor* (Great Equerry) of the king.
- Mountain Chasseurs, with Colonel Gregorio Jove.

- Covadonga, with Colonel Pedro Celestino Méndez de Vigo, captain of the Regiment of Oviedo
- Navía, with Colonel José Gabriel Trelles.
- Cangas de Tineo, with Colonel José Pesci, captain of the Regiment of León.
- Guard of Honour of the Junta, with Colonel Guillermo Livesay, captain of the grenadiers of the Regiment of Hibernia.
- Cangas de Onís, with Colonel Salvador Escandón y Antayo, lieutenant of the Navy.
- Candas and Luanco, with Colonel Juan Cienfuegos, Viscount of San Pedro Mártir.
- Ribadesella, with Colonel Juan de Dios Bernaldo de Quirós.
- Lena, with Colonel Juan Dringold, captain of the grenadiers of the Regiment of Hibernia.
- Infiesto, with Colonel Juan Galdiano.
- Pravia, with Colonel Sancho Valdés, retired captain.
- Colunga, with Colonel Francisco Martínez Casavieja.[5]

The enthusiasm of these volunteers cannot hide the many shortcomings suffered by these regiments: their numbers were small for a regiment (indeed, in most cases they were little more than a battalion); a lack of suitable commanders, and none with experience of commanding a regiment; a serious lack of equipment; and, above all, a lack of time to properly train troops of brave citizens who would have to face one of the best armies in the world. Also, all these regiments were infantry units. They were too few horses to organize cavalry squadrons, whose military training, of both horses and horsemen, is more complicated and requires even more time. They also had no artillery detachments.

The first regiment to set off was Covadonga, which was sent to the town of León at the end of May to promote the revolt against the French. With León rising up in favour of the Fernandine cause, Covadonga's colonel, Méndez de Vigo, offered his unit to General García de la Cuesta to join his Army of Castile. The general gladly accepted the offer and the regiment went to Valladolid, where the Castilians had their headquarters. Here, the Asturian forces were integrated as a light infantry force and were renamed as the Volunteers of Asturias. However, now the unit began to suffer losses. Many married soldiers asked permission to return to Asturias, and the first desertions also took place. The men who left were replaced by soldiers from the Royal Spanish Guards and the Regiment of the State Volunteers. The regiment was made up of 28 officers, 103 non-commissioned officers and 514 soldiers, for a total of 645 troops – much smaller than a battalion. It was not long before they were in action. Their baptism of fire came on 14 July at the battle of Medina del Rioseco in Valladolid. The battle ended in a complete defeat of the Spanish Army, and the Asturians, part of the vanguard division, suffered a total of 90 casualties, with their company of *voltigeurs* being totally destroyed. Only four of its fifty-five men survived. After the battle many other soldiers decided to desert and the regiment returned to Asturias to reorganize.

The Asturian case is typical of events that took place in many of the Spanish regions that were free from a Napoleonic presence, or in which the invaders occupied just a few cities, such as in Galicia, Castile and Andalusia.

Notes

1. The governing body of the Principality, created in 1388.
2. The father of José María Queipo de Llano (1786–1843), 7th Count of Toreno, who would later write one of the main works about the Peninsular War entitled *Historia del levantamiento, guerra y revolución de España* (*History of the uprising, war and revolution of Spain*).
3. The Real Audiencia (literally, Royal Audience) was responsible for the administration of justice and compliance with Royal Orders. It was presided over by a governor and was made up of a variable number of oidores (judges). In the event that the post of governor was vacant, as was the case in Asturias at the time, his functions were carried out by the senior judge.
4. Sala Valdés (1908), p. 38.
5. García Prado (1947a), pp. 104–5.

Chapter Four

The Battles of El Bruc

Date: 6 and 14 June 1808. *Place*: Bruc, Catalonia.
Result: Spanish victories.

Order of battle

First battle of El Bruc

Spanish Army: commanders: Major Justo de Bérriz and Lieutenant of the Swiss Franz Krutter Grotz; troops: Regiment Wimpffen (1st Swiss Regiment), 2nd Battalion, Royal Walloon Guards, Somatén[1] of Igualada, Manresa, Sampedor, Sallent and Esparreguera; some soldiers from the Regiment of Extremadura. In total, around 900 men.

Napoleonic Army: General Schwartz's Brigade: Regiment Wimpffen (1st Swiss Regiment,[2] 2 coys), 1st Regiment of Line Infantry of Naples (2 bns), 2nd Regiment of Line Infantry of Italy (2 bns), 1st Regiment of Mounted Chasseurs of Naples (2 sqns) and the 11th Artillery Company of Italy. In total, around 3,800 men.

Second battle of El Bruc

Spanish Army: commander: Colonel Joan Baget; troops: Regiment Wimpffen (1st Swiss Regiment), 2nd Battalion, Royal Walloon Guards, Somatén of Igualada, Manresa, Sampedor, Sallent and Esparreguera; some soldiers from the Regiment of Extremadura. In total, around 1,800 men.

11

Napoleonic Army: General Joseph Chabran's 1st Division, comprising the Goullus[3] Brigade with the 7th Regiment of Line Infantry (2 bns) and the 16th Regiment of Line Infantry (1 bn) and the Nicolas Brigade with the 2nd Regiment of Line Infantry (1 bn), the 37th Regiment of Line Infantry (1 bn), the 56th Regiment of Line Infantry (1 bn) and the 93rd Regiment of Line Infantry (1 bn). In total, around 5,600 men.

Background

Catalonia is the northeastern region of Spain. Due to its border with France, the war in this territory had special characteristics, given that the hatred felt towards the French here was particularly intense. The history of Catalonia with France, or rather against France, goes back to the Middle Ages, when Catalonia was one of the federated states of the Kingdom of Aragon. During this period the rivalry with France was especially intense, with constant wars that culminated in the Treaty of the Pyrenees (1648), by which Philip IV of Spain ceded to France the Catalan territories north of the Pyrenees (Roussillon, Conflent, Vallespir, Capcir and Cerdagne). Thus, for example, the city of Girona, before the Peninsular War, had already been besieged by French troops in 1285, 1694 and twice during the War of the Spanish Succession, at the beginning of the eighteenth century. Moreover, given that Catalonia had been the main battlefield of the relatively recent War of the Pyrenees (1793–1795), it is no surprise that animosity towards the French was much greater here than in other territories where the French, in the past, had been distant enemies. In addition, geographical proximity meant that Catalonia was the first territory to be occupied and the last to be abandoned by the Napoleonic forces. In fact, as we will see later, the 'Catalan problem' was of such magnitude that the Napoleonic administration chose to incorporate Catalonia into French territory, thus separating it from Spain.

The Napoleonic occupation of Catalonia began in early 1808. In mid-February General Duhesme's troops peacefully occupied the castle of St Ferdinand in Figueres (in the far northeast of Catalonia) and Barcelona. As in the rest of Spain, initially the attitude of the Spanish authorities was passive in most cases. In fact, in Barcelona only Brigadier Álvarez de Castro, commander of the Montjuich castle, refused to obey the Napoleonic authorities and fled. But it didn't take long for the first riots to begin, the most important one taking place in Lleida on 28 May; Tortosa rose the next day and Tarragona on the 31st. The General Captain of Catalonia, the Count of Ezpeleta, ordered Brigadier García Conde, commanding a small army, to leave Barcelona to put down the uprising in Lleida. On 1 June he reached Tárrega, where the city declared itself in rebellion, and García Conde's column joined the patriot side. During the following days the trickle of Catalan towns joining the revolt continued. General Duhesme, in command of the Napoleonic forces in Catalonia, realized that he had a serious problem: his Eastern Pyrenees Observation Corps was too small an army to deal with a general uprising. But it seemed that all of Spain had taken up arms against the French and Duhesme received orders to send reinforcements to Valencia and Zaragoza. To impose order in the latter, he sent General Schwartz's brigade, which left Barcelona on 4 June. Although they numbered some 3,800 troops, most of them were inexperienced soldiers with no combat experience, but they trusted that it would not be difficult for them to prevail against an improvised army made up mostly of civilians. Duhesme had no precise information on what was happening in the interior of Catalonia, although he knew that some cities had rebelled. So he also entrusted Schwartz with the mission of carrying out punitive operations in Manresa and Lleida on his way to Zaragoza.

It will become clear throughout this book that land communications in Spain at the beginning of the nineteenth century were extremely complicated. The early Bourbons' attempts to improve the road network had had little influence in peripheral regions, where many of the main roads were still those established by the Romans two millennia earlier. Thus, the route from Martorell to Manresa passed along a steep road surrounded by forests and gorges: ideal places to ambush an army.

The First Battle of El Bruc

On 5 June Schwartz's brigade arrived in Martorell, where they spent the night in the midst of heavy rain. In Igualada, which would not officially rise up against the Napoleonic forces until 12 July,[4] an anti-French atmosphere was developing and the Royal Walloon Guards and a detachment of the Wimpffen Swiss Volunteers, who had deserted, were warmly received. The Walloon major, Justo de Bérriz, and the Swiss lieutenant, Franz Krutter Grotz, decided to ambush Schwartz's troops. They would not lack for volunteers among the *somatenes* of the neighbouring towns to help them in the attack.

The 6th dawned with a tremendous downpour of heavy rain that slowed down the advance of the Schwartz column. It was not until midday that they reached the town of Bruc de Dalt. Shortly afterwards, moving through very thick forest near Can Maçana,[5] the Napoleonic soldiers came under attack and began to receive volleys of rifle fire. After the initial surprise, Schwartz ordered his men to clear the forest, a mission they successfully completed. However, the general did not order his men to continue in pursuit of the rebels, since he must continue on his way. In any case, Bérriz and Grotz's soldiers have dispersed, one group heading north towards Manresa, another returning to Igualada to the west. Along the way both groups met dozens of *somatenes* from nearby towns who had come to join the attack. With these reinforcements, they decide to resume the attack on the French.

Schwartz's men were occupying the farm on the outskirts of Bruc de Dalt when they were again attacked from the nearby woods. The Italo-Swiss troops formed a square and defended themselves, but the large number of enemies and the sound of drums made Schwartz fearful that he was facing the experienced Regiment of Extremadura. Adzerias points out that this is the moment when the legend of the Bruc drummer was born, whose identity remains a mystery. It is also worth mentioning the fierce combating that took place between the Swiss troops of the Regiment Wimpffen who were fighting on opposite sides. After a few hours of combat, the German general decided to withdraw. His men responded with order and discipline, heading south along the highway to the town of Esparraguera. The people there, aware of the fighting at the Bruc, placed barricades at the entrance to the town, rendering the road impassable. Schwartz, unable to break the town's resistance, divided his troops into two columns, intending to bypass Esparraguera and return to Barcelona, where the survivors arrived, humiliated and terrified after being harassed throughout their journey by *miquelets*[6] and *somatens*.

Among the survivors who reached Barcelona was Colonel Pietro Foresti, who was in command of the 2nd Regiment of Line Infantry of Italy. This officer became famous, not only for always showing blind courage in combat, but also because, thanks to theft and corruption, he arrived in Spain miserably poor and amassed a lavish fortune in a very short time. He would die the following year, during the siege of Girona.[7]

The Second Battle of El Bruc

Chabran was at the gates of Tarragona when he received the order from Duhesme to return immediately to Barcelona. The defeat at Bruc could not go unanswered and his brigade would be in charge of carrying it out. On the way back, they encountered some resistance, especially in the town of Arboç, which they looted and burned. In Vilafranca del Penedès the Provençal general enjoyed the complicity of the governor of the village, Colonel Juan de Toda, who just days before had refused to hand over weapons to the *somatenes* of Igualada ahead of the first action of the Bruc. On the 10th, when Chabran's troops had departed, the city rose up and Toda, his wife and other *afrancesados* were killed.

On the 13th Chabran and the remnants of Schwartz's troops spent the night in Martorell. On the Spanish side, the Swiss soldiers, the Walloons and a reinforced contingent of *miquelets* and *somatenes* awaited the French once again in the Bruc forests, under the command of Joan Baget i Pàmies, a notary from Tàrrega, who had become their chief. They no longer had the advantage of surprise, but this time there were more than 1,800 men and four cannon ready to prevent the Napoleonic troops from crossing the mountains of Montserrat.

Chabran ordered his troops to arrange themselves in four columns; the largest travelled along the main road with the artillery and baggage, while a second column advanced along the Collbato path. The action began as shots were fired at the second column as it was passing through one of the thick forests that line the road. As planned, the patriots withdrew, luring the French troops to the position where they had placed the four cannon and the bulk of the riflemen. The pursuers fell into the trap and were slaughtered. The surviving Frenchmen fled in the direction of the main column, which was then in the town of Bruc de

Baix. Chabran organized the defences, but when night fell he decided to retreat towards Barcelona.

Although the Bruc actions were no more than skirmishes, their importance lies in the fact that they were the first Spanish victories over the Napoleonic Army. Effective Fernandine propaganda quickly spread word throughout Spain of the feat that had been achieved in the Bruc gorges. And the mysterious drummer, who was said to be a boy who had managed to terrify a Napoleonic column and make it flee, was exalted to the point of becoming a legend, with statues erected to him, books written and films made. In reality, the mysterious drummer of the Bruc had no more impact on the combat than any other drummers on the battlefield, but the need to find new heroes to serve as examples to the rest of the Spaniards to encourage them to rise up against the Napoleonic troops turned him into a mythical character. We do not even know his name. Local historians have contributed studies on his possible identity, but I fear we will never know who he really was. But what is certain is that his legend inspired many Spaniards in the war that was just beginning, and that now, for the first time, they had optimism.

Notes

1. The *somatén* was a sort of local militia from Catalonia. It was an armed body intended for civil protection, separate from the army, for the defence of their own territory.
2. This is not a mistake. At the beginning of the war there were six Swiss regiments that fought for the Spanish Kingdom. After the Spanish uprising, the Swiss regiments divided their loyalties: some of them remained on the Spanish side while others fought under Bonaparte's flag.
3. Usually spelled Goulas, though his actual surname was Goullus.
4. Cahner i Gallastegui (2009), p. 152.
5. *Can* and *Masia* are types of rural construction common in Catalonia. Some of them were fortified.
6. *Miquelet* were similar to *Somaten*, but would also fight far from their home, and very occasionally far from Catalonia.
7. Moliner Prada (2005), p. 17.

Chapter Five

The Battle of Poza de Santa Isabel

Date: 9–14 June 1808. *Place*: Cádiz bay, Andalusia.
Result: Spanish victory.

Order of battle

Spanish Army: Ships of the line: *Príncipe*, *San Justo*, *Montañés*, *Terrible*, *San Fulgencio* and *San Leandro*. Artillery from Cádiz, and several smaller ships.

French Army: Ships of the line: *Neptune*, *Herós*, *Algeciras*, *Argonaute* and *Plutón*, plus the frigate *Cornélie*.

Background

After the events of May in Madrid, the majority of the Andalusian cities remained on high alert. It was not until 26 May that the Junta of Seville rose, sending an emissary to Cádiz to support the uprising there. The governor of the city, Francisco Solano, fearing that the populace was rioting, chose to maintain a cautious attitude and continued to wait to see how events would evolve. Meanwhile, the French squadron anchored in Cádiz bay, which comprised the surviving ships of the battle of Trafalgar, fearing a Spanish attack, sandwiched its ships of the line between the Spanish ships, which would make an attack by artillery on the coast more difficult. They could do no more, as a British fleet held them blockaded.

The Battle

On 29 May events were precipitated when one of Solano's assistants, José Luquey, urged the crowd gathered in front of the governor's palace not to attack the French ships. In the event he only succeeded in further unnerving the masses. Solano himself went out to the balcony to offer them an explanation, but the crowd ended up storming his palace and lynching Solano under the accusation of being *afrancesado*.[1] He was stabbed, and his body dragged away and hanged. His successor, General Morla, and the chief of the Spanish squadron, Admiral Ruiz de Apodaca, decided to join the rebellion and asked the experienced sailor Joaquín Moreno D'Houtlier to prepare a plan of attack. He designed a detailed plan which included sinking a number of old ships at the mouth of the port to hinder the ability of the French ships to manoeuvre. The presence of various light vessels (12 bombers and 25 gunboats), combined with the batteries on the coast, persuaded the Spanish that they must achieve victory. The attack began at 4.00pm on 9 June, and Moreno's plan went well. The next day there was a stand-off as both sides played for time: Rosily, head of the French squadron, was waiting for the arrival of the army of Dupont de l'Étang, while the Spanish only had sufficient gunpowder for one more day of intense combat. A Napoleonic landing would put Moreno in an extremely difficult situation. While Rosily asked to be allowed to leave with his unarmed ships, Moreno placed more cannons on the coastline, although there was no ammunition for them. Finally, Moreno rejected Rosily's request, and the French commander decided to surrender on the 14th in exchange for their lives and baggage being respected. The victory was Spanish.

On the Spanish side the casualty count was 12 killed and 31 wounded. Among the French, there were 13 dead and 51 wounded, and in addition, their entire fleet was taken, resulting in the capture of 3,676 prisoners and 442 cannon, together with their supplies.

Note

1. The people of Cadiz also wanted to lynch another of his assistants, Captain José de San Martín, a future leader in the Spanish American Wars of Independence, but he escaped. A few days later San Martín would put up a courageous performance in the Battle of Bailén, under Reding's orders.

Chapter Six

The Battle of Mengíbar

Date: 15 July 1808. *Place*: Mengíbar, Andalusia.
Result: Strategic Spanish victory.

Order of battle

Spanish Army: Major General Theodor von Reding's 1st Division of the Andalusian Army, comprising Venegas' Vanguard Brigade, Reding's Brigade and Colonel Naughten's Irish Brigade in reserve.[1]

French Army: Liger-Belair's Brigade, and later General Gobert's Division, including Dufour's Brigade and Lefranc's Brigade. Two squadrons of cavalry under the command of General Fresia.[2]

Background

On 24 May 1808 Joseph Bonaparte ordered General Dupont de L'Étang to save the French fleet trapped at Cádiz, and incidentally to occupy the cities of Seville and Córdoba. Like a plague of locusts, the French spread throughout Andalusia. After looting Andújar, where he established his headquarters, Dupont de l'Étang headed towards Córdoba, which his troops occupied after the battle of Alcolea Bridge on 7 June. The French army, full of confidence after a series of quick and easy successes, were amusing themselves by looting Cordoba and Jaen when news reached them of the loss of the French fleet after the battle of Poza de Santa Isabel.

18

Dupont ordered his generals to return and take control of the Despeñaperros pass,[3] since their mission in Andalusia had no purpose once the Cadiz fleet had surrendered. Vedel's column returned to Mengíbar from Jaén on 13 July. The bulk of the division continued on its way to Despeñaperros, while the town was occupied by the Liger-Belair Brigade. At the same time, following the plan designed by General Castaños, on 14 July the vanguard of the Spanish Reding Division also arrived in Mengíbar, under the command of Brigadier Venegas.

It should be noted that the situation for the French army was far from idyllic. Most of the troops were inexperienced and poorly fed, and dysentery had begun to take its toll. Lafon[4] reports that an average of 22 per cent of the French troops were out of action because of illness. Moreover, they knew that if they fell behind or became separated from the main body of the army, they would fall victim to the relentless *guerrillas*, who harassed them incessantly. The Napoleonic soldiers were terrified of them, and with good reason. The paradigmatic case was that of Brigadier Jean Gaspard Pascal René, who was captured at the end of June by a group of *guerrillas*, along with his officers. They were subjected to terrible torture and then burned alive in a cauldron of boiling oil. The guerrillas weren't interested in the niceties of prisoner exchanges. Days later, a second encounter with the *guerrillas* took place in the La Mancha town of Villarta de San Juan, where a convoy of eighteen carriages carrying some 120 sick and wounded men from the fighting at the beginning of July, along with a meagre escort, was discovered by the *guerrilla* of Tío Camuñas; as the French crossed the bridge over the Gigüela river, they were ambushed and massacred.[5]

The Battle

Arriving in Mengíbar, Venegas did not think twice and immediately launched his troops against the French. The attack by the squadrons of Numancia and the Dragoons of the Queen, the light infantry battalions of Texas and Barbastro and the Walloon Guard was so forceful that the men of Liger-Belair's Brigade hardly had time to cross the Guadalquivir. This was presumably a severe blow for the French, since they left behind their stores of food. Later that same night the bulk of Reding's troops arrived and immediately took up positions. In the palace of the Duke of Montemar they found a large number of Roman lead sarcophagi, which they immediately melted down to make more ammunition. Meanwhile, Liger-Belair had asked for help from General Gobert, whose troops were closer to Mengíbar than Vedel's.

On the 15th Reding began to move his men. He distracted Gobert's units by shooting at them from the left bank of the Guadalquivir, using a battalion from the Ceuta Regiment and a cavalry detachment from the Regiments of Bourbon and Spain, plus two pieces of artillery, while John Naughten's Irish Regiment crossed the river at a ford a few miles upstream and opened fire on the French left flank. Vedel understood the strategy and asked Gobert for help. But in the meantime Reding's men had already crossed the Guadalquivir. Liger-Belair had no choice but to retreat towards the Guadiel river line in the face of the unstoppable Spanish push. Reding launched his horsemen from Farnesio, Olivenza and the *garrochistas*,[6] but the French of the 7th Regiment were a disciplined cadre and repelled the attack; this slight success was used by Gobert to launch his cuirassiers in a counterattack. Their numerical and technical superiority destroyed the Spanish cavalry and left the Tiradores de Barbastro in serious trouble. The rest of the day unfolded with an exchange of blows between the two armies, with charges and counter-charges, which achieved little more than further casualties. The two generals themselves, Reding and Gobert, even led some of the charges. In one such action General Gobert was shot in the head, leaving him badly wounded. He was transferred to Guarromán, where he died a few days later. General Dufour replaced him. Meanwhile, after 7 hours of fighting under a scorching sun and with his troops now exhausted and thirsty, Reding ordered his men to withdraw from the battlefield, fording the Guadalquivir in good order and maintaining a defensive position in the town of Mengíbar. Dufour and Liger-Belair, euphoric after their success, believed that the Spanish were retreating towards the Despeñaperros pass. Thus they set off towards the pass at a forced pace, instead of joining up with the bulk of Dupont's army, which had left Andújar for Bailén. Days later, Dufour and Liger-Belair would not arrive in time to rescue Dupont. Thus, on that day in Mengíbar the battle of Bailén began to be won.[7]

Notes

1. Diego Garcia (2020), p. 12.
2. Vidal Delgado (2015), p. 234.
3. The Despeñaperros pass was the only road that connected Castile with Andalusia, separated by the impassable Inner Plateau. Whoever dominated the pass controlled the road between Madrid and the Andalusian cities.
4. Lafon (2020), p. 28.
5. For details on this ambush, see: https://josemunozvillaharta.blog/2018/03/17/jose-perez-el-practicante-escribio-en-un-programa-de-paces-hace-ya-mas-de-treinta-anos-por-jose-munoz-torres/ (accessed 10 December 2021).
6. The *garrochistas* were a typically Andalusian cavalry unit, made up of ranchers who used long sticks to herd large cattle, such as bulls and cows. In military documents they are usually called Lancers. They were volunteers, countrymen, mostly ranchers, and many of them participated in bullfights. They barely had fifteen days of military training. Unfortunately, Reding, in his detailed casualty reports, always forgot to mention this unit. However, the Swiss general never tired of praising their uncompromising courage in combat. On this topic, see Molero (2020).
7. Lafon (2020), pp. 26–32; Mercurio de España (1815), pp. 118–28; Vidal Delgado (2015), pp. 249–64.

Chapter Seven

The Battle of Bailén

Date: 19 July 1808. *Place*: Bailén, Andalusia. *Result*: Spanish victory.

Order of battle

Spanish Army: Commander-in-chief Major General Theodor von Reding with the 1st Division under the command of Reding himself, comprising the Royal Walloon Guards (1 bn), Regiment of the Queen (2 bns), Regiment of the Crown (3 bns), Regiment of Jaén (2 bns), Irish Regiment (3 bns), Regiment 'Reding the Elder' (3rd Swiss Regiment), Barbastro's Volunteers Regiment of Light Infantry (½ bn), Militia of Jaen's Province (1 bn), 1st Regiment of Granada's Volunteers (2 bns), Regiment of Chasseurs of Antequera, Tercio of the Expeditionary Corps of Texas. Cavalry: Squadron of Montesa, Regiment of Farnesio (3 sqns), Squadron of Dragoons of the Queen, Squadron of Dragoons of Numancia, Squadron of Mounted Chasseurs of Olivenza, *Garrochistas* of Utrera and *Garrochistas* of Jerez. Artillery: 8 cannon.

Major General the Marquis of Coupigny's 2nd Division, with Regiment of Infantry of Ceuta (2 bns), Regiment of the Military Orders (3 bns), Militia of the Provinces of Granada (1 bn), Trujillo (1 bn), Bujalance (1 bn), Cuenca (1 bn) and Ciudad Real (1 bn), 2nd Regiment of Volunteers of Granada (1 bn), 3rd Regiment of Volunteers of Granada (1 bn), 2nd Regiment of Light Infantry Volunteers of Catalonia (½ bn). Cavalry: Regiment of Bourbon (2 sqns) and Regiment of Spain (1 sqn). One company of artillery with 6 cannon. In total,[1] around 18,000 men.

Napoleonic Army: General Dupont de L'Étang's II Corps d'Observation de la Gironde, comprising General Barbou's 1st Division and General Pannetier's 1st Brigade, with 3rd Legion de Reserve (2 bns), 1st Regiment Garde de Paris (1 bn) and 2nd Regiment of the Garde de Paris (1 bn). General Chabert's 2nd Brigade, with 4th Legion de Reserve (3 bns), 4th Regiment of Swiss Line Infantry (1 bn) and Marines of the Imperial Guard (1 bn). General Frére's 2nd Division, with General Schramm's 1st Brigade, with Regiment 'Reding the Younger' (3rd Swiss Regiment, 2 bns) and Regiment 'Preux' (6th Swiss Regiment, 2 bn), and General Rostolland's 2nd Brigade, with 2nd Legion de Reserve (3 bns). Cavalry: General Fresia's 2nd Division, with Duprès's Brigade, including the 1st and 2nd Regiments of Provisional Mounted Chasseurs (4 sqns each); Prive's Brigade with 1st and 2nd Regiments of Provisional Dragoons; Boussart's Brigade with 6th Regiment of Provisional Dragoons; also attached was Rigaux's Brigade with the 2nd Regiment of Provisional Cuirassiers. Artillery: 38 cannon. In total, near 9,500 men.

Background

In order to save the French squadron anchored in Cádiz, Napoleon sent Dupont with the II Corps of the Army of the Gironde to Andalusia, as well as to occupy Córdoba, Seville and Cádiz. After looting Córdoba for a week, on 16 June Dupont was informed that the naval squadron had surrendered, so he withdrew to Andújar, intending to muster his troops there and return to Madrid.

In early July Castaños met with his generals in Porcuna to draw up a plan of attack. The plan required him to divide his forces into three columns: he himself would command one column that would attack Dupont at Andújar; Coupigny would lead another that would cross the Guadalquivir through Villanueva de la Reina; and Reding and his column would cross this same river through Mengíbar. In the event, Reding would encounter Gobert's 3rd Division on 15 July, and in the resulting battle the French general was killed.

Dupont ordered Vedel and Dufour (who replaced Gobert) to leave their respective camps in Andújar and Bailén and go to take control of the Despeñaperros pass, since Cruz Murgeón's troops were close to Linares and were threatening to close the pass. By 18 July Vedel was at La Carolina and Dufour at Santa Helena. Dupont himself remained in Andújar, where he had no choice but to abandon some 300 wounded and sick men who could not move, trusting in the goodness of the people of Andújar for their safety. With his troops went a convoy of some 500 wagons carrying 1,500 wounded and sick men who were well enough to travel.

That same day Reding and Coupigny's troops occupied Bailén, which the French had hastily abandoned, and arranged their troops in an arc ready for battle. For his part, Dupont left Andújar to go to Bailén, pursued by the troops of Castaños.

The Battle

Dupont knew that he could not evade battle. Reding had closed the route ahead and the French commander had to hurry to start the battle before the troops commanded by Castaños attacked him from the rear. He was counting on Vedel's division to come to his aid by making a pincer movement to trap the Spanish troops, who were well positioned around Bailén. If we may make a comparison, the situation would be like a kind of Waterloo *avant-la-lettre*, as Vedel would take the role of Grouchy arriving late to the battle, this being one of the causes of the French defeat.

The Spaniards, with Bailén behind them, positioned themselves on the hills called Cañada de Marivieja and Cerro Valentín, while the French, in front of them, occupied some heights covered with olive trees, called Cerrajón, Zumacar Grande and Zumacar Chico. The first stages of the battle took place around 3.00am on the 19th. General Chabert, without waiting for Dupont to join the battlefield, sent his vanguard, made up of elite troops under the command of Major Teuler, against the advanced Spanish posts occupied by the Royal Walloon Guard; the Walloons retreated, allowing Teuler to occupy a hill called Cruz Blanca, but there he was stopped and driven back by units commanded by Brigadier Venegas. The Spanish troops then deployed to the outskirts of Bailén, occupying the high ground known as Cerrajón and Cruz Blanca (*see* Map 1).

Around 5.00am Dupont ordered Fresia, his cavalry general, to send a brigade to retake the Cruz Blanca hill. Duprés's Brigade, composed of approximately 500 dragoons, was sent. The dragoons managed to disperse the Regiment of Farnese horsemen, and then went beyond the Cruz Blanca and fell on the Spanish artillery located in the centre of the line. The Spaniards reacted by counterattacking with the battalions of Ceuta, the Queen's Infantry and a squadron of Farnese reinforcements. After taking heavy losses, the dragoons were forced to retreat, massacred throughout by the Spanish artillerymen. It is believed that the French lost about 100 men during the action. Then Dupont ordered his artillery to begin shelling the Spanish lines and the town of Bailén. The cannon fire was answered immediately by the Spanish side, which had more and larger calibre cannon. Once again, the Spanish artillerymen distinguished themselves, wrecking various French guns.

Around 6.00am Dupont's troops began to arrive, and were immediately ordered to make their first assault. Following the French line, Duprés's Brigade attacked on the left (flanked by mounted chasseurs), with Chabert's Brigade in the centre and Privé's Brigade (flanked by cuirassiers and dragoons) on the right. Reding countered by sending Venegas and Coupigny to threaten the French flanks. Venegas's troops, the Regiment of Military Orders and the Chasseurs of the Royal Walloon Guard, collided with Duprés's cavalry, who were returning to their initial positions on the Valentín hill. However, the French had also suffered heavy casualties, so they did not pursue the Spanish infantry. In the centre

Chabert's disciplined infantry advanced undaunted, despite being decimated by Reding's artillery. They were no more than 100m from the Spanish lines when the squadrons of Bourbon and Farnese and the *Garrochistas* from Utrera and Jerez appeared; their arrival overwhelmed the French troops, who fought a somewhat disorderly retreat. The hardest fighting took place on the left flank, where Coupigny's infantry were attacked by Privé's cavalry, forcing the Spanish general to commit his reserve infantry, a squadron of the Regiment Farnese and the *Garrochistas*. The Spanish troops were decimated, especially the Regiment of Jaén, which lost its colonel, Antonio Moya, and its flag, among many other casualties. The Spanish right flank was now in serious danger of falling apart. Coupigny had no choice but to throw into the fray everything he had left, namely the Provincial Regiments of Trujillo, Cuenca and Bujalance, which, together with effective artillery fire, managed to drive Privé's horsemen to retreat. It was at this point that the heroic charge of the legendary *Garrochistas* of Utrera and Jerez probably took place; in pursuit of dragoons and lancers, they ended up getting into the French lines, where they were massacred. Of the 150 reckless Andalusian horsemen involved, some 75 per cent were killed or wounded. Among the first casualties was their commander, Miguel Cherif, who was a descendant of the prophet Muhammad himself.[2] Dupont's first assault had failed.

Around 8.30am Reding ordered Venegas's troops to launch an assault against Napoleon's left flank. Dupont countered with Pannetier's Brigade, which had just returned from a long and gruelling march, so the French soldiers, exhausted, were unable to stop the Spanish advance. Then Privé's Brigade carried out a vigorous counterattack that drove back Venegas's troops. The Regiment of the Military Orders, an elite unit, protected the retreat, suffering heavy casualties in the process. Around 10:00 am Dupont ordered a new attack, this time focused on the middle of the Spanish line, using Chabert's and Duprès's brigades. This time, the French infantry were halted by the fusillades and cannon fire from the Spanish artillery, which tore them apart. It was then that General Duprès led all his remaining cavalry, barely 150 horsemen, in a charge against the enemy batteries. But the guns smashed his cavalry, leaving a trail of dead and wounded horsemen and horses. Duprès himself, seriously wounded, was withdrawn from the battlefield and died two days later.

By midday Dupont might well have been on the verge of a nervous breakdown. The heat was already suffocating. His exhausted men were dying from the heat, wearing heavy cloth uniforms that were not at all suitable for the sultry day (their cuirassiers would have been torture enough), and from thirst, since they had no source of water. The San Lázaro waterwheel was the only source they could access. It stood in no man's land, but was overlooked by the Spanish troops, who massacred any French detachment that dared to approach. The lack of water also affected the cannon, which, as they could not be cooled, lost their effectiveness, as became evident as the day went on. In contrast, the Spanish, with the town of

Bailén behind them, throughout the morning received water and provisions from the people of Bailén, whose actions were, in many cases, simply heroic, disregarding the danger to themselves of walking with their water jugs along the battle front. In this context we must mention the performance of María Bellido, known as *Culiancha*, who was hit by a bullet as she was offering General Reding a drink from a pitcher. Far from panicking and running away, the brave woman picked up one of the fragments of the vessel that still contained water and offered it to the commander of the Spanish troops.[3]

In desperation, Dupont ordered a new assault. It would be the last one. In the centre he placed the Marines de la Garde,[4] an elite unit. Next to them was everything that was left of the brigades of Pannetier and Chabert. On both flanks were just fifty horsemen from Duprès' brigade, the rest having been killed or wounded. At the head of his men marched Dupont and all his generals. Once again, Spanish rifle and artillery fire smashed into them. Despite orders to continue advancing with their iron discipline, some units began to falter, but not the Marines de la Garde. They were being massacred but still they advanced without complaint. Finally Dupont himself was wounded, which demoralized his troops. Many of the French soldiers, desperate from thirst, broke ranks, hunting for water.

At one point in the combat the Swiss troops from 'Reding the Elder' who remained loyal to Spain clashed with their counterparts fighting on the Napoleonic side under General Schramm. Recognizing each other, they decreed a ceasefire and began to parley, each trying to convince the other to join the opposite side. Failing to reach an agreement, the Swiss troops returned to their respective lines and resumed firing, but as the Spanish gained the upper hand in the battle, a large proportion of the officers and troops of the 'Reding the Younger' and 'Preux' regiments deserted, going over to the Spanish side. After the battle the two Swiss colonels, Charles von Reding and Charles de Preux, were captured and imprisoned in Seville.[5]

An hour later Dupont sent a messenger to the Spanish commanders requesting an end to hostilities. Reding gave the honour of negotiating the French surrender to his superior, General Castaños, who had arrived around 2.00pm with almost 10,000 fresh men. At 5.00pm General Vedel arrived with his division. He had not hurried, despite hearing the noise of battle. Little did he know that the invincible French eagle was being roasted (literally) in an olive grove in Jaén. The Monegasque general refused to believe that Dupont had been defeated, so he organized an attack. After more than an hour of fighting, an emissary from Dupont ordered him to lay down his arms. Accepting the defeat, Vedel ordered his men to march towards Despeñaperros, but his division had been included in the surrender negotiations. Spanish emissaries warned him that if he did not return and surrender, Dupont's troops would be killed, so Vedel, in a gesture that did him credit, turned around and surrendered. The capitulation was not signed until 22 July. It is said that at the time of the signing, Dupont handed his sword to General Castaños, stating: 'I give you this sword, victorious in a hundred battles';

to which Castaños replied, with a certain humour, 'Well, this is the first one I have won.' The casualty count on the Spanish side was 940 men (240 of them dead). On the French side, there were 2,600 casualties (with 2,200 dead, including General Duprès) and 18,600 prisoners, including no fewer than eighteen generals! This seems a disproportionately high number of generals, but as Vidal Delgado indicates,[6] it may have been due to the fact that one of the French objectives was to leave military governors in the main Andalusian cities or create new military units.

We cannot ignore the ugly affair of the prisoners of Bailén. According to the terms agreed in the so-called Capitulations of Andújar, all the prisoners were to be fed, protected and sent back to France. There must have been some tension on the Napoleonic side, since there were several generals who refused to sign the surrender. Certainly, the Spanish did not fulfil their part of the deal. A large proportion of the prisoners were sent to the island of Cabrera in the Balearic Islands, where they were abandoned to their fate, being annihilated by dysentery, typhus and starvation in a veritable hell on earth. Others were sent to the Canary Islands, where their fate was much better. A third group was imprisoned on pontoons in the Bay of Cadiz. The generals were returned to France, where they met different fates, since although some of them were immediately rehabilitated, others had to suffer Napoleon's fury. It was the first time that one of his armies had capitulated on the battlefield and the humiliation reverberated throughout Europe. So, when the generals came home to France, he rehabilitated those who had refused to accept or sign the surrender, namely Rouyer, Schramm (wounded), Rouger de Laplane, Rigaux, Cavrois, Rostollant, Cassagne (who was wounded in Jaén and had not participated in the battle), Liger-Belair, Faultrier, Fresia, Dabadie de Bernet, Barbou des Courières and Boussart. Dufour was captured and sent to England for the rest of the war. But the generals who had accepted it were imprisoned in the gloomy prison of l'Abbaye in Paris,[7] demoted, their Legion d'Honneur withdrawn, and put on trial.[8] Vedel and Marescot were imprisoned until 1812. The former would be rehabilitated by Napoleon himself in 1813, while the second remained in prison until Louis XVIII came to power. Chabert was acquitted but stripped of his command. In 1814 Napoleon reinstated him, and he remained loyal to the Emperor during the Hundred Days. As for Legendre, he retired from the army but was imprisoned in 1812, being released and rehabilitated by Louis XVIII. Ultimately, Dupont de l'Étang was demoted and retired from the army. He was imprisoned in l'Abbaye, but for health reasons was sent to a hospital in Clichy. His trial was held in 1812 and although all his generals testified in his favour, he was found guilty and sent to Joux prison, considered to be one of the most inhospitable and highest security prisons in France. He would not be rehabilitated until the return of the Bourbons, who restored his positions and honours and appointed him to important political positions. It is interesting to note that Dupont de l'Étang was one of the soldiers on whom Joseph Conrad based his renowned novel *The Duellists*, along with the French general Fournier-Sarlovèze.

The main consequence of the French disaster at Bailén was that Napoleon ordered the evacuation of Madrid, establishing the line of the Ebro river as a point of defence for his armies. For a few weeks it seemed that the war had already been won by the Spanish Army.

Notes

1. This refers only to the units that participated in the battle, and ignores the other two divisions that were part of the Andalusian Army, namely the 3rd Division, under the command of General Félix Jones, and the Reserve Division, under the command of Lieutenant General Manuel de la Peña. Their presence would have doubled Reding's strength on the battlefield.
2. Miguel Cherif, reportedly misquoted as 'Nicolás', was the grandson of the Sherifes of Tafilete, a family of notables from Morocco who settled in Spain. For Muslims, the surname Cherif (or its variants Cherife or Sheriff) indicate that they are descendants of the prophet Muhammad.
3. María Bellido was from Porcuna. She was married to a farmer from Bailén and they had no children. At the time of the battle she was 65 years old. She died a few months after the battle, as did her husband. When French troops returned in 1810, their graves were desecrated. Still today, María is a beloved local legend.
4. This is the unit that appears in Goya's 'The Third of May 1808', depicted shooting at the Madrid patriots.
5. Both would be released in January 1810 when Soult conquered the city. They were promoted to generals and Joseph Bonaparte awarded them the title of Knights of the Royal Order of Spain. Reding retired to Marseille, where he died in 1817. For his part, de Preux, who reached the venerable age of 72, was appointed military commander of Seville, Toledo and, finally, Guadalajara, where he was captured again, this time by *el Empecinado*, in August 1812. Deported to England, he was imprisoned in Bridgnorth, where he died the following year. The rest of the Swiss soldiers who remained loyal to Napoleon joined the Swiss Regiment 'Traxler'.
6. Vidal Delgado (2015), p. 50.
7. A former religious building, it was a military prison in 1631. In 1792 it was one of the scenes of the September Massacres during the French Revolution. The prison was demolished in 1854.
8. On this process see Saint-Maurice Cabany (1846) and Houdecek (2016). Army paymasters Lerembourg and Plauzoles were also imprisoned for having embezzled the money seized in Córdoba, distributing it among the high command instead of allocating it to the army.

Chapter Eight

The First Siege of Zaragoza

Date: 15 June–13 August 1808. *Place*: Zaragoza.
Result: Spanish victory.

Order of battle

Spanish Army: under the command of José de Palafox, together with his brother, the Marquis of Lazán, and José Obispo; Volunteers of Aragon, Dragoons of the King, five *Tercios* of Countrymen, two *Tercios* of Fusiliers, the Company of José Obispo. Artillerymen, engineers and sappers. In total, 8,963 men.[1] It should be added that throughout the siege numerous fresh troops managed to enter the city, including 3rd Battalion of the Royal Spanish Guards, Battalion Fernando VII, Battalion Extremadura, *Tercio* of Gerónimo Torres, five Aragonese Volunteer *Tercios*, *Tercio* of Barbastro, *Tercio* of Huesca, Regiment of the Swiss of Aragon, Foreign Companies of Casamayor (mostly Portuguese deserters from the French army), two Companies of *Miquelets* of Lleida, *Tercios* de Monzón, Cerezo, San Pablo and Tauste, Lancers of Almunia and Company of Benaven. In total, 13,375 men.[2]

French Army: Lefebvre-Desnouettes's 1st Division, with 4th/15th Regiment of Line Infantry, 3rd/47th Regiment of Line Infantry, 3rd/70th Regiment of Line Infantry and 2nd Regiment of the Legions de Reserve. Cavalry under the command of General Habert, with 5th Squadron of Chasseurs de Marche, Colonel Józef Chłopicki's Regiment of the Legion of Vístula (3 sqns), and 36th Regiment of Line Infantry Spanish of Calatrava. After the siege began there arrived both Verdier's 2nd Division, including 3rd/14th Regiment of Provisional Infantry, 5th Regiment of Line Infantry of Portugal, 11th Battalion of Portuguese Chasseurs, 13th Squadron of Cuirassiers de Marche, 8th Squadron of Hussars de Marche (2 coys), and General Grandjean's Brigade, with 12th/2nd Regiment of Vístula and 6th Battalion de Marche, as well as a company of Engineers under General Lacoste. Later also came a column under the command of Colonel Piré, Napoleon's aide-de-camp, with 3rd Regiment of Vístula, 9th Squadron de Marche and 1st Battalion of Chasseurs and Grenadiers de la Garde of Bordeaux. In total, 13,000 men.[3] Verdier, as senior officer, remained as commander-in-chief, while Lefebvre-Desnouettes remained in command of his 1st Division and the Portuguese Gomes Freyre led the 2nd Division.

Background[4]

On 24 May 1808 news of the popular uprising in Madrid reached Zaragoza, the capital city of Aragon. Two movements had long been brewing in the city, one comprising aristocratic elements and the other led by popular classes, but on that day it was the latter who took to the streets demanding that the Captain General of Aragon, Jorge Juan Guillelmi, hand over weapons to the people to face the Napoleonic Army. Guillelmi, a man of order, refused to arm the mob but his refusal led to his palace being stormed and the lieutenant general was dismissed. He was lucky not to be lynched and ended up sleeping that night in the prison of Aljafería castle, at that time the only fortified point in the city. His lieutenant, Carlos Mori, agreed to hand over weapons to the people, and on an interim basis held the position of Captain General, while trying to find a new man to lead the resistance against Napoleon. The chosen man was José de Palafox, the third son of the old Marquis of Lazán and a brigadier in the Royal Guard of Ferdinand VII. At that time he was in La Alfranca palace,[5] just 15km (9.5 miles) from Zaragoza. In the absence of high-ranking commanders, and with his clear anti-Godoyist past (i.e. loyalty to Ferdinand VII), he seemed the right candidate. Or at least, that was what the people of Zaragoza thought. Palafox was already debating whether to return to Madrid and rejoin the new Royal Guard of Joseph Bonaparte, or to lead the uprising in Aragón, and when a group of countrymen went to look for him on 25 May, he initially thought he was going to be arrested; instead, to his surprise, they wanted to hand over command of Aragon to him. His entry into Zaragoza was tremendous. Accompanied by Jorge Ibor, known as Tío Jorge, one of the leaders of the popular sector, he met with Carlos Mori and shortly afterwards his leadership of the resistance against the invaders was formalized. On 31 May war was declared against Napoleon.

Until then, Zaragoza had been of no military relevance. It was an open city, with very weak defences and a small garrison. But the uprising there convinced General Lefebvre-Desnouettes that he had to subjugate the city, so he sent a division to do so. It should have been a mere formality for a force of professional soldiers almost 6,000 strong, which included the fearsome Polish cavalry. The French were equipped with six 4-pounder campaign guns, which would surely suffice to subdue the city. After all, Zaragoza had barely 220 soldiers and hardly any guns. This problem worried the Aragonese leaders, who needed to mobilize all the defenders they could find. But how were they to do so in a territory where there was not a single regiment of the Spanish Army? The answer was to carry out a general conscription of men between the ages of 16 and 40. The reaction of the Aragonese people was enthusiastic and by mid-June some 10,000 men had already enlisted. But volunteers do not make an army *per se*. They needed professional officers, weapons, discipline and, above all, training – four essential elements if they were to face an army like the Napoleonic one – as they would soon discover.

News soon arrived that General Lefebvre-Desnouettes had left Pamplona with his division. The town of Tudela, which had also taken up arms, seemed the right place to try to stop the French, so Palafox sent troops there under the command of his older brother, Luis de Palafox, Marquis of Lazán, who joined forces with those commanded by Colonel José Obispo, adding a total of about 5,000 men. The first battle of Tudela took place on 8 June and the Napoleonic victory was complete. The first volleys of the French soldiers and the charges made by the Polish cavalry caused terror among inexperienced Aragonese volunteers, who broke ranks and fled in panic. The Polish horsemen massacred them as they ran, and if they did not annihilate them it was because many horses were sick and their riders did not want to force them in pursuit. Fresh troops under the command of Lazán confronted Lefebvre-Desnouettes on 13 June at Mallén, around 60km (37.5 miles) northwest of Zaragoza. Once again the Aragonese soldiers fled in panic, and once again the Polish cavalry massacred them, causing some 600 deaths and the virtual dissolution of Lazan's army. Nevertheless, the people of Zaragoza chose to fight again, so that new troops came out to meet the invaders. This time the battle took place in Alagón, about 30km (18 miles) northeast of Zaragoza, with the defenders under the command of José de Palafox himself. The result was no different. The simple rumour that the Polish cavalry was going to surround the Aragonese troops caused the collapse of the front and as the inexperienced troops fled they were saved from another massacre thanks to the fact that the Battalion of the Volunteers of Aragon and some companies of the Regiment of Extremadura were able to cover their withdrawal.

After these effortless victories for the Napoleonic Army, Lefebvre-Desnouettes assumed it would be easy to conquer a city that had almost no defences and a population wracked with terror. On 15 June Lefebvre-Desnouettes ordered his troops to leave for Zaragoza. The next day was Corpus Christi and the Parisian general planned to celebrate it in the city.

The Siege

That same day, the 15th, at around 9.00am José de Palafox rode around the city, encouraging the people of Zaragoza to resist the invaders. Approximately an hour later, to the astonishment of the citizens, Palafox, together with Tío Jorge and his entire general staff, left the city. Officially, he was going to look for reinforcements in other towns. Shortly afterwards, his brother, the Marquis of Lazán, and a large proportion of the senior officers, including Colonel José Obispo, also abandoned the city. Vicente Bustamante was the new commander of the defences, while civil power fell to Lorenzo Calvo de Rozas. Towards mid-morning General Lefebvre-Desnouettes arrived at the gates of the city with his troops. Before him he saw an open city, its paltry fortifications defended by the same men he had just defeated in Alagón. According to all the classic laws of war, Zaragoza was indefensible. The French general knew that he did not have sufficient artillery for a lengthy siege, but in the circumstances it was inconceivable that the city would not quickly surrender. But seeing that the defenders seemed willing to fight, he prepared for the assault. At midday the French easily captured some defensive positions outside Zaragoza. But the fighting here allowed the Zaragozans a little time to prepare their defences for the battle that was about to begin.

Lefebvre-Desnouettes organized his assault on the city in three columns that would each assault the so-called Eras del Rey, an esplanade located to the southwest of the city. The first column, comprising the 15th and 47th Regiments of Line Infantry, would attack the Portillo Gate; the second, under the command of Colonel Chłopicki with the 1st Vistula Regiment, would go to the Carmen Gate; and the third, under the command of General Habert, would head to the Santa Engracia Gate. The first column failed in its attempt to capture the Portillo Gate, thanks in large part to crossfire from the defenders of the Aljafería castle. Far from retiring, the French skirted around the Augustinian convent and saw that the cavalry barracks had unprotected windows, so they sneaked inside. But that building was to became a death-trap for the invaders, who learned at first-hand that the Aragonese were going to resist at any price. It was a brutal indication of the hard fighting for the city that would follow, and the French began to realize that those men who had fled from battle in the open were a very different proposition when they were defending their homes and their families. This time it was the French who fled from the fighting. Chłopicki's proud Polish infantry of the second column fared no better. Determined fire from the defenders of the Carmen Gate left them pinned down and unable to advance. The third column had better luck, at least briefly. Habert's men managed to open the Santa Engracia Gate and penetrate the city. But behind the gate there was a barricade, which the Polish cavalry jumped over without difficulty, moving forward into the city until they were stopped by rifle fire. Suddenly, the dreaded Polish horsemen found themselves surrounded by a mob of Zaragozans armed with knives, pike blades and any sharp object they could find, and not a single one was left alive. Meanwhile Habert was stuck at the Santa Engracia Gate, unable to advance. The final blow came when the men of Lieutenant Colonel Marcó del Pont and Colonel Renovales outflanked Habert's men, forcing them to withdraw. Lefebvre-Desnouettes retreated, leaving behind some 700 dead, hundreds wounded and

30 prisoners. This triumphant day for the Spaniards became known as the 'battle of the Eras'.

The following days were spent by Zaragozans and French alike preparing for the next onslaught. Lefebvre-Desnouettes obtained numerous reinforcements and the Aragonese worked hard to reinforce their defences. The echoes of the Spanish success had resounded throughout the region and would soon do so throughout Spain. Learning of the unexpected victory, José de Palafox sent his brother, the Marquis of Lazán, to lead the defence of the city. He arrived on 18 June to find the city in turmoil. The citizens of Zaragoza had managed to beat off the French without any high military command and with no real plan of defence, and it seemed that now everyone wanted to wage war on their own, despite the strenuous efforts of Bustamante and Calvo de Rozas to organize them. In addition, conflicts between citizens and professional soldiers were constant.

In the French camp, artillery reinforcements arrived, as did General Grandjean's brigade and Colonel Pépin's 4th Regiment de la Marche. On 26 June the experienced General Verdier arrived to command all the troops. The chief engineer, Colonel Lacoste, also selected points from which to bombard the city. The chosen sites were the height of Bernadona and the neighbourhood outside the walls of Torrero, still defended by Lieutenant Colonel Vicente Falcó and his command of 500 men. Thus, on 28 June a column under the command of General Habert, made up of four battalions, a detachment of Polish cavalry and four guns, set out to take over the position. The superiority of Habert's force was manifest and defence of the site impossible. After a brief fight, Falcó and his men withdrew into the city, where they were greeted with accusations of cowardice; to appease the mob's desire to lynch Falcó, he was arrested and court-martialled, and ultimately condemned to death. He was in fact shot after the siege was lifted. Meanwhile, Palafox continued to travel around Aragón in search of reinforcements. On the night of 23 June he was in the vicinity of Épila, where he had managed to gather some 4,000 men. His intention was to attack the French lines of communication between Tudela and Zaragoza. Lefebvre-Desnouettes was informed of this plan and sent Colonel Chłopicki in command of approximately 2,000 men to counter the threat. On the evening of 23 June the two armies clashed. Once again, it was an easy battlefield victory for the French.

The first massive bombardment of the city was carried out on the night of 30 June/1 July. The shock was overwhelming and panic flooded the streets. The following night José de Palafox re-entered the city. This time he was here to stay, and to set an example. His presence filled the frightened city with courage in the face of the imminent assault on the city, which they did not yet know Verdier had planned for 2 July. On this occasion, the attack would be made at two different points: on the right, under the command of Lefebvre-Desnouettes, three columns advanced towards the convent of San José and the Santa Engracia and Carmen Gates. On the left, the Portuguese general Freire led three other columns in the direction of the Sancho Gate, the Aljafería and the Portillo. In total, some

3,000 men, out of the 13,000 that Napoleon had gathered around the city, were advancing. Despite the fact that Lacoste's artillery had already opened numerous practicable breaches, the attackers again hit all their targets except two: the convent of San José, which was consumed by fire, and the Portillo Gate. By this point, the French artillery had taken great pains to punish the defences, now practically in ruins. By the time Lefebvre-Desnouettes's men approached, there were no defenders left at Portillo. The few men who had survived the accurate gunfire of the artillerymen had fled. The French had a clear passage to enter the city. Portillo was practically deserted. The assailants did not need to take many precautions, as there did not seem to be any defenders left alive. But suddenly a flash of lightning brought down hundreds of them. A 24-pounder cannon had spat out a deadly charge of shrapnel that massacred the French line, causing them to disband immediately. Beside the cannon was a 22-year-old girl from Barcelona, was Agustina Saragossa i Domènech. From then on, she would be known as Agustina of Aragon, giving rise to a legend that has survived to the present day. Just at that moment, Palafox appeared at the head of a column desperately rushing to defend the Portillo Gate. Verdier's men were now retreating from all fronts. Zaragoza remained impregnable. The city was making a mockery of all the laws of war. What was happening was unheard of.

It was Napoleon himself who told Verdier to attack from the southeast corner of the city, in the area of Torre del Pino and Santa Engracia, instead of from the southwest, where strong points such as Aljafería made it difficult for the invaders to carry out their attack. As the days went by, Verdier tightened the siege of the city, while continuing to receive reinforcements, such as a column under the command of General Bazancourt that arrived on 1 August, increasing the Gallic and Polish troops to 15,000 men. That same night, he began a bombardment of the city with his eighty-six artillery pieces, it being the heaviest since the beginning of the siege and focusing on the area suggested (in fact, ordered) by Napoleon himself. The bombardment continued until 4 August, when a new assault was planned.

Three breaches had been opened in the Santa Engracia area. All three were practicable. Each was to be assaulted by a column of Napoleonic soldiers, eager to put an end to the city's sturdy resistance that defied all the parameters of Cartesian reasoning: war was not like this. The columns were commanded by Generals Habert, Bazancourt and Grandjean. This time they had everything on their side to subdue the city. At around 2.00pm Habert's men entered through Santa Engracia and Grandjean's troops through the Carmen Gate. They were already in the city. That afternoon it seemed unlikely there would be further heroic deeds to save the city. There were hardly any soldiers left defending that sector and many soldiers and civilians, including José de Palafox himself, abandoned the city, considering it lost. A mass of Spaniards ran towards the Puente de Piedra (Stone Bridge) to flee. That area, however, was defended by the retired cavalry lieutenant Luciano Tornos, who ordered his cannon to be turned towards his fellow citizens, threatening to shoot them if they fled the city. The fight was not yet over. But that was not what the Napoleonic soldiers thought as they spilled out into the city, which they believed to be theirs, and had begun to plunder. They entered houses and engaged in looting and other crimes of the moment. Nor did they think that the people of Zaragoza would want to go on fighting. Not for a moment did they imagine that, divided as they now were into small groups, they would fall victim to the invincible will of the Spaniards to fight for their homeland.

Everywhere, small groups began to organize themselves to resist. Some gunmen followed Francisco Ipas; Captain Simonó gathered another group of civilians and soldiers; friar Santa Romana led a group of farmers. As they moved through the city, the small groups of French invaders they met were massacred. All sorts of objects were thrown down from the windows, the streets become rattraps and the victory that the Frenchmen had taken for granted seemed likely to be snatched away from them. Verdier, from his headquarters, issued a laconic surrender proposal: 'Santa Engracia HQ: Peace and Capitulation', to which the *corregidor* Calvo de Rozas replied curtly: 'Zaragoza HQ: War by the Knife'. Now Verdier knew what to expect. All over the city there was brutal fighting: in the monasteries of San Diego and Santa Fe, on various bridges and even house to house. The French had entered the city, but they were surrounded by angry massed who rushed to attack them. The battle involved children, monks, old men and every citizen who could stand and fight. Verdier had no choice but to order a retreat, the French suffering 15 per cent of the siege's total casualties that day. The invaders managed to hold a number of strategic points in the city, but at the cost of a dizzying number of casualties: 2,000 men, almost 500 of them dead. Among the wounded were Verdier himself and the newly arrived Bazancourt. The fighting continued, but with only small gains in exchange for a huge number of casualties. On the 5th the French suffered 500 more casualties. By now the morale of the Napoleonic soldiers was at rock bottom. On 9 August Palafox returned with *Tercios* of Catalan Volunteers. The French lost almost all the ground that had cost them so much blood.

To make matters worse for the French, news now reached them that large masses of soldiers and militiamen were coming to Zaragoza from all over Aragon. They feared being overrun and ending up like Dupont's army at Bailén. So on the 13th Verdier and Lefebvre-Desnouettes decided to lift the siege. Before the French pulled out, they laid several mines in the cellars of the monasteries of Santa Engracia and San José, as well as in a number of private houses, which were reduced to rubble the following morning. Their flight was so swift that dozens of fallen French soldiers were left behind to be buried in the monastery of Santa Engracia. On the 14th, after setting fire to the monastery of San Francisco, they retreated towards Tudela.[6] They had suffered a total of 3,500 casualties and an undeniable humiliation.

Notes

1. Alcaide Ibieca (1830), p. 325.
2. Ibid., p. 326.
3. Sorando (2010).
4. This chapter is fundamentally based on Daniel Aquillué's *Guerra a Cuchillo* (2021), which is, without doubt, the best work written to date on the siege of Zaragoza.
5. The Alfranca Palace was built at the end of the 18th century and in those times belonged to the Palafox family, who used it as a summer residence.
6. Hugo (1837), pp. 87–91; Pérez Francés (2017).

Chapter Nine

The Escape of the Division of the North

Date: 21 August–8 October 1808. *Place*: Denmark.
Result: Spanish victory.

Order of battle

Spanish Army: commander: General Pedro Caro y Sureda, Marquis de la Romana; units: Regiment of Line Infantry of Zamora, Regiment of Line Infantry of Guadalajara, Regiment of Line Infantry of Asturias, Battalion of Light Infantry Volunteers of Catalonia, Battalion of Light Infantry Volunteers of Barcelona, Cavalry Regiment of Algarve, Cavalry Regiment of the King, Cavalry Regiment of the Infante, Cavalry Regiment of the Princess, Dragoons Regiment of Villaviciosa, Cavalry Regiment of Almansa, Artillery. In total, 13,355 men.

Background

Until the forced abdications of Charles IV and Ferdinand VII, Spain was one of France's main allies. Accordingly, under various international treaties, such as the Aranjuez Treaty of 1801 and the Fontainebleau Treaty of 1807, Spain undertook to help Napoleon Bonaparte in his campaigns to conquer Europe. For this reason, Manuel Godoy, the prime minister of Spain, who was also the commander-in-chief of the army, had sent the best Spanish regiments to fight for Napoleon abroad. Thus, at the beginning of the Spanish uprising against Napoleon, there were three Spanish armies in Portugal and one in Denmark. The armies in Portugal were commanded by Generals Francisco Taranco, then Captain General of Galicia, Juan Caraffa della Roncella, then Captain General of Extremadura, and General Solano, Marquis of Socorro, Captain General of Andalusia. In March Taranco died of illness in Oporto, and was replaced by General Domingo Ballesta.

As was the case with most Spanish elite families, the three generals initially accepted the abdications of the Spanish Bourbons, but when they heard that several Spanish cities had risen up against the Napoleonic invasion, many soldiers and low-ranking officers set out to return to Spain, against the advice of their generals. The latter, seeing that the situation was untenable, agreed to participate in the plans to return to Spain, despite the opposition of the French army in

Portugal, commanded by Marshal Junot. Ballesta managed to return to Galicia, taking General Quesnel, his staff and his escort of dragoons prisoner as far as Corunna. Solano and Caraffa managed to reach Cadiz with a large part of their troops. However, the future held bitter surprises in store. Their hesitant and indecisive attitude in Portugal led them to be accused of being *afrancesado*. Caraffa was imprisoned and put on trial, at which he was acquitted, but he never managed to obtain another military command. As for Solano, as mentioned above, he ended up being lynched by the crowd.[1]

The origin of this dispersal of the Spanish armies lay in the Treaty of Aranjuez, under the terms of which Spain was forced to transfer some of its troops to the newly created Kingdom of Etruria, where Louis I of Bourbon-Parma, Charles IV's son-in-law, ruled because of his marriage to Charles's daughter Maria Luisa. But Napoleon's war needs forced him to transfer most of these troops, along with new regiments from Spain, to the war he was waging in northern Germany. The Spanish troops, with their generals Marquis de la Romana and Juan Kindelán, were placed under the command of Marshal Brune, and were particularly outstanding in the conquest of the city of Stralsund in 1809. After this victory numerous Spanish soldiers received the Legion of Honour for their heroic deeds. Napoleon himself awarded the gold badge of this prized decoration to the two Spanish generals in command.[2]

The Escape

Marshal Bernadotte, Prince of Pontecorvo and General-in-Chief of the Army of the Elbe, was impressed by the actions of the Spanish at Straslund, so much so that he took them to the north of Denmark (a country allied with France) to prepare for the proposed invasion of Sweden. In addition, he chose for his personal honour guard 100 Spanish grenadiers from the Regiment of Zamora, plus a detachment of 30 King's cavalrymen.[3]

In June, Bernadotte, who had been informed of the uprisings in several cities in Spain against the proclamation of Joseph I as King of Spain, judged that it would be best to disperse the Spanish forces throughout the region to prevent an uprising. He was no fool. Thus, the troops were distributed as follows:

- On the Jutland peninsula, under the command of General Kindelán: the Zamora Regiment, the Algarve Regiment, the King's Regiment and the Infante Regiment.
- On the island of Fyonia, under the command of de la Romana: the Princess Regiment, the Villaviciosa Regiment, the Almansa Regiment and part of the Artillery.
- On the island of Svedenborg, the Battalion of Catalan Volunteers.
- On the island of Langenland, under the command of the French colonel Gauthier: the Barcelona Volunteer Battalion and the rest of the Artillery. This island also had a large French-Danish contingent.

- On the island of Seeland, under the command of the French general Fririon: the Guadalajara and Asturias Regiments.

Finally news reached Denmark of the change of regime that Napoleon was trying to impose in Spain, which caused protests and even a few attempts at revolt among the Spanish soldiers, that de la Romana tried to neutralize. Bernadotte, fearful that the situation would get out of his control, met with de la Romana and, in accordance with Article 7 of the Treaty of Bayonne, informed him that all Spanish officers and troops must swear allegiance to Joseph I.

A few days later de la Romana was dining at his hotel in the town of Nyborg when he was approached by a mysterious gentleman who slipped him a sheet of paper. De la Romana looked carefully at the intruder and then read the paper. A fragment of the 'Cantar del Mío Cid' was written on it. This was a masterpiece of medieval Castilian literature that de la Romana, a highly cultured man, adored, and which he had discussed at length with John Hockman Frere, the British ambassador at the court of Charles IV. The strange gentleman was a British agent named James Robertson,[4] a Scottish Benedictine monk who, thanks to his excellent command of German, was posing as a Teutonic merchant. Robertson urged de la Romana to raise his soldiers against the French, with the help of the British, who offered to evacuate them from the Danish islands.[5] Unsure, de la Romana did not commit himself to anything and said goodbye to the curious spy.

Meanwhile, on 22 July Bernadotte ordered the Spanish troops to finally swear allegiance to Joseph I. In Jutland Kindelán managed by trickery to get his troops to swear, but not without great scandal and disturbance, so much so that General Kindelán abandoned his men that very night. In Seeland the Asturias and Guadalajara Regiments refused to take the oath and revolted. They attacked a French detachment and marched on Copenhagen, but were captured by other units of the French army on the way. Meanwhile, de la Romana tried to swear in the soldiers from Fionia and Langeland, but protests from the troops prevented the oath from being carried out. On 1 August Lieutenant Fàbregues of the Catalan Volunteers, obtained a boat, by trickery, with which he was able to approach a British ship, telling the captain of the willingness of the Spanish troops to be evacuated. Fàbregues stayed on the boat for a few days until the arrival of Rafael Lobo, a representative of the Junta of Seville, who gave him letters for de la Romana, asking him to embark his troops on the British ships. Fàbregues returned to Langeland on 6 August. Events now began to move quickly. While Fàbregues went to meet de la Romana, the Battalion of Catalan Volunteers from Langeland took control of the island, disarming Colonel Gauthier and the Franco-Danish detachment. De la Romana, now determined to return to Spain, informed Bernadotte that he would bring all his troops to Nyborg to finish taking the oath to Joseph I at once, and sent the officers of his general staff to the commanders of his regiments to inform them of the forthcoming move. All units prepared to march to Nyborg. The only problems were with the Algarve Cavalry Regiment, as some of its officers were openly pro-French. There were also some issues with the Villaviciosa Dragoons, but these were logistical. However, through a daring act of deception, their colonel, Baron de Armendáriz, managed to embark his squadrons to Langeland.

Between 9 and 12 August all the Spanish troops except the Asturias and Guadalajara Regiments and the Algarve Cavalry were between Nyborg and Langeland ready to embark. However, Bernadotte had already been warned of the Spanish intentions. José de Kindelán, under the orders of his father, had informed him of General de la Romana's plans. For the Spanish, there was no time to lose. They must embark without wasting any more time. But the situation for Bernadotte was not easy either. The sea was dominated by the British fleet and he could not risk an amphibious assault on Langeland, since the superiority of the Spanish in their defensive position was all too evident. And yet the transport ships still did not arrive, their progress delayed by strong northerly winds in the Baltic Sea. Finally, on 19 August, part of the transport fleet arrived. In order not to delay any longer, as many troops as possible embarked on theses ships, while the rest re-embarked on the Danish ships they had used to reach the island of Langeland. These were unsuitable for a long voyage, but were hopefully sturdy enough to reach the Swedish port of Goteborg. Finally, on 9 October the Spanish troops disembarked at Santander, Santoña and Ribadeo. A total of 8,981 men had been rescued and brought safely home. They were quickly incorporated into the army to begin the fight against the French.

But not all were so fortunate. One of the most famous of those who did not make it back to Spain was Antoni Costa, captain of a cavalry squadron from the Algarve, originally from the Catalan Roussillon. He finally managed, with his squadron and other horsemen, to escape from his barracks and head for a beach in Fionia where they waited for a Danish ship to take them to Langeland. What they encountered, however, was a French infantry battalion. When the French threatened to shoot all the officers and decimate the troops, Costa stepped forward and exclaimed: 'I am the only one to blame, because my soldiers have done nothing but obey me. I am the one who seduced them!' Grasping one of the pistols that hung from the saddle of his horse, and turning to his subordinates, he added: 'I have deceived you and I must die. Memories to Spain from Antoni Costa,' and he shot himself in the temple.[6]

Thus there remained in Denmark the troops of the Algarve Cavalry and the Line Infantry Regiments of Guadalajara and Asturias, as well as officers of other units that for different reasons could not leave the country. They were taken as prisoners to Avignon, where they were forced to form part of the new Joseph I Infantry Regiment, together with other Spaniards who had been captured. In 1811 they were divided into four battalions, and all participated in the invasion of Russia. Always in the vanguard, they fought at Borodinó and were the first unit to enter Moscow, always in the midst of fierce fighting that cruelly decimated their numbers. Murat himself requested a new batch of Legion of Honour medals for various Spanish officers and NCOs, including Captains Mariano Vázquez (from the Zamora battalion), José Hernández (Guadalajara) and Domingo Tierra (Asturias), Adjutant Matías Cardona (Guadalajara), Lieutenant José Corbalán (Guadalajara) and Sergeants Manuel López and Antonio Laborda.[7] However, the price that had to be paid in human lives was very high, and included a number of officers. For example, the commander of the 2nd Battalion, Ramón Ducer, was killed in action, while the commander of the 3rd Battalion, Rodrigo Medrano, was wounded and captured. During the retreat the José I Regiment was part of the French rearguard, being constantly harassed by Russian troops. It was during this phase, around the town of Vilna, that Lieutenant Colonel Alejandro O'Donnell organized a mass desertion. Some 300 Spanish soldiers, led by their commander, turned and joined the Russian army. O'Donnell, from St Petersburg, tried to attract more deserters and prisoners, from whom he formed the Alexander Imperial Regiment. This was kept by the Tsar himself to serve as the imperial guard of honour for the Tsarina and the Tsarina Mother, until October 1814, when they were shipped to Santander.[8] For his part, O'Donnell was invited by Tsar Alexander to accompany him on his triumphal entry into Paris that same year.[9]

Not all the Spanish troops deserted with O'Donnell. The remainder of the army, under the command of Rafael de Llanza, arrived in Germany, where the soldiers continued to distinguish themselves in the battles of Lützen, Bautzen and Leipzig. But by now the regiment, despite the addition of a fifth battalion, was a shadow of its former self. Its last months were spent in France before the regiment was dissolved on 25 December 1813.[10] At the time the colonel's post (as well as most officer posts) was vacant. José de Kindelán was the unit's commander, with 2,048 troops. The men were disbanded into various other units, most of them going to the 14th Line Regiment. Once the war was over, some officers, such as Rafael de Llanza,[11] chose to return to Spain and left the army. Many others decided to join the French army, such as the aforementioned Manuel López, who became an officer in the Legion of Honour and retired from the French army in 1855.[12] José de Kindelán and his son, despite the pardons offered by Ferdinand VII, remained in France. Their military record is littered with splendid decorations, such as the Legion of Honour, the Royal Order of Spain, the Order of Saint Louis and, oddly enough, the Order of Saint Ferdinand and the Order of Saint Hermenegildo.

Of the returnees, the vast majority were reintegrated into the army. Among those who had been awarded the Legion of Honour, Francesc Agustí de Comas took part in the battle of Talavera, Francesc Camilleri i Gomis was in Pontesampaio, and Antoni Maria de Sesespleda was taken prisoner by the French in Bilbao. Joan Antoni Caballero ended up becoming French and placing himself at the service of Joseph I, who awarded him the Royal Order of Spain.[13] Meanwhile, Armando de Armendáriz, the colonel of the Villaviciosa Regiment, was seriously wounded and taken prisoner in the battle of Alcabán. He was imprisoned in

Pamplona until the liberation of the city.[14] At the battle of Espinosa de los Monteros[15] many of the men who had shared the Danish journey were reunited, but met different fates. The former colonel of the Regiment Princesa, Joaquín de Miranda Gayoso y Trelles, Count of San Román, one of the officers most appreciated by the Marquis de la Romana, was killed during the battle. José O'Donnell D'Anethan also fought at Espinosa de los Monteros and went on to play an important role on various fronts on the peninsula.[16] Joan Francesc Vives, colonel of the Battalion of Volunteers of Catalonia, was taken prisoner, while his major, Ambrosio de la Cuadra y López de la Huerta, managed to escape and ended the Peninsular War with a military record full of battles and heroic actions, including Tamames, Medina del Campo, Alba de Tormes and the siege of Cadiz. In 1833 Ferdinand VII awarded him the Grand Badge of the Order of San Fernando. Another of the battalion's veterans was the intrepid Lieutenant Joan Antoni de Fàbregues-Boixar Talarn, Baron de la Font de Quinto. After surviving the Espinosa de los Monteros disaster, he continued fighting, taking part in various battles, such as Igualada and Vilafranca del Penedés. He fought bravely in the siege of his hometown, Tortosa, where he was taken prisoner. He escaped and went on to fight in the siege of Tarragona. After the fall of the city, he joined the Ultonia Regiment, of which he became colonel. In 1812 the Regency Council sent him to Córdoba, where he married and spent the rest of his life.[17] Perhaps the most outstanding career of this 'wild bunch' was that of Francesc Dionís de Vives i Planes, who received an extraordinary number of decorations throughout the war: the Cross of the Army of the Left, Medal of Action of Tamames, Medal of the Battle of Medina del Campo, Cross of the Battle of Albuera, Cross of the Blockade of Pamplona, Cross of the Siege of Bayonne and Cross of Distinction of the North; in addition, he was awarded the Orders of St Ferdinand, St Hermenegildo, Isabel la Católica and Charles III, and was appointed Gentleman of the Chamber of Ferdinand VII. After the war he was sent to the United States on a diplomatic mission. From 1825 to 1831 he served as Captain General of Cuba. Upon his return, Ferdinand VII made him Count of Cuba.[18]

As for Pedro Caro y Sureda, Marquis de la Romana, we will have much to say about him in this book. The general who was presented with the Legion of Honour by Bernadotte himself, who had hesitated to swear obedience to Joseph I or to embark his men on this immortal epic, would end up being one of the most popular and admired generals of the Spanish army, whose legend lives on to this day.

Notes

1. See Chapter 5.
2. Ceballos-Escalera (2002), p. 16.
3. Qadesh (2017).
4. James Robertson (1758–1820) was a Scottish Benedictine monk who lived in his order's monastery in Regensburg, Bavaria. He came secretly to Nyborg posing as a tobacco and chocolate merchant. After this mission, he lived for a time in Dublin, until when Wellington called on him

to carry out some diplomatic missions in Spain in 1813. In 1815 he retired to his Bavarian monastery, on a generous pension from the British government, where he wrote a book that would become a best-seller at the time: *Narrative of a Secret Mission to the Danish Islands in 1808*. Brown (2006), p. 92.

5. Calpena and Junqueras (2003), p. 121.
6. Pérez de Guzmán y Gallo (1909), p. 99. In this report to Alfonso XIII, the author recounts a complete biography of the captain of the Algarve. It was a story that could not be overlooked by Pérez-Reverte, who dedicated an article to him in 2010 entitled 'A grave in Denmark'.
7. Bonne (1899), pp. 162, 215; Ceballos-Escalera y Gila (2002), p. 16.
8. CISDE (2014).
9. O'Donnell (2017), pp. 45–6.
10. Bonne (1899), pp. 245–8.
11. César Alcalá in the Biographical Dictionary of the Royal Academy of History. His full name was Rafael de Llanza de Valls Perpintie and Hurtado de Mendoza.
12. Bonne (1899), p. 172.
13. Ceballos-Escalera y Gila (2002), p. 16.
14. Pérez (2015).
15. See Chapter 10.
16. O'Donnell (2017), pp. 44–5.
17. Salvador J. Rovira Gómez, entry in *Biographical Dictionary of the Royal Academy of History*.
18. Vicente Alonso Juanola, entry in *Biographical Dictionary of the Royal Academy of History*.

Chapter Ten

The Destruction of the Army of the Left

Date: 14 July–11 November 1808. *Place*: Medina de Rioseco, Zornotza, Güeñes and Espinosa de los Monteros.
Result: Napoleonic victories.

Order of battle[1]

General-in-Chief Lieutenant-General Joaquín Blake, with the following units: Vanguard Division, under the command of General Gabriel de Mendizábal with: Grenadiers of the Regiments of Majorca, Zaragoza, Aragon and the Battalion of Volunteers of the Crown (8 coys), Regiment of Zaragoza (1 bn), Battalion of Volunteers of Gerona (½ bn), 2nd Battalion of Volunteers of Catalonia (½ bn); Regiment of Cavalry of Montesa (1 sqn), Dragoons of the Queen; artillery and engineers' companies. 1st Division under the command of General Felipe Jado Cagigal, with: Grenadiers of the Militia of Galicia (2 bns), Regiment of the King (2 bns), Regiment of Hibernia (2 bns), Regiment of Majorca (1 bn), Regiment of Buenos Aires (1 bn), Volunteers of Barbastro (½ bn), Militia of Salamanca (1 bn), Militia of Mondoñedo (1 bn), Militia of Tuy (1 bn), artillery and engineers' companies. 2nd Division under the command of General Rafael Martinengo, with: Volunteers of Vizcaya (1 bn), Regiment of Navarra (2 bns), Regiment of Naples (2 bns), Regiment of Seville (2 bns), Militias of Segovia (1 bn); artillery and

43

engineers' companies. 3rd Division under the command of Admiral of the Royal Navy Francisco Riquelme, with: Volunteers of Navarra (4 coys), Marine Infantry (3 bn), Volunteers of the Crown (2 bns), Militias of Monterrey (1 bn), Militias of Compostela (1 bn); artillery and engineers' companies. 4th Division under the command of General Marquis del Portago, with: Grenadiers of the Prince, Toledo, Navarra, Seville and Naples (2 bns), Literary Battalion of Santiago, Regiment of the Prince (2 bns), Regiment of Toledo (2 bns), Regiment of Aragon (2 bns); artillery and engineers' companies. Independent units under the command of Colonel Marquis of de Valladares, with: Regiment of León (1 bn and 2 coys), Regiment of the Prince (2 coys), Regiment of Ourense Province (1 bn). Garrison in Corunna: Regiment of Aragon (1 bn), Dragoons of the Queen (1 sqn). Garrison in Valença do Miño: Regiment of León (1 bn). Total number of men: 28,613 infantry and 450 cavalry.

Background

The Galician uprising culminated in the creation on 31 May 1808 of the Supreme Junta of the Kingdom of Galicia, which assumed all the powers of the kingdom, including the military, although these functions were delegated to a War Junta presided over by military personnel. Its function was to recruit and arm an army with which to confront the invader. This was not an easy task, given the lack of vocation for the military among those called up. However, after much effort, the Junta managed to enlist sufficient volunteers, including a variety of units, such as the Literary Battalion, made up of university students and professors, and the so-called Battalion of the Exiles, created by the initiative of the Commander of the Navy Manuel Miralles and whose members were former corsairs or sailors from the prisons of the Royal Navy, who were serving sentences for indiscipline, i.e., halfway between a punishment battalion and a sort of *avant-la-lettre* Foreign Legion. Later, this battalion would be renamed the Voluntarios de la Victoria (Victory Volunteers) and performed so well during the war that the Count of Clonard considered it to be among the best in the Spanish Army.[2]

In September the Supreme General Junta ordered the unification of the three armies operating in the north of Spain, that is, the Army of Galicia, the Army of Asturias and the troops arriving from Denmark with the Marquis de la Romana, in a new unit that would become known as the Army of the Left. This was under the command of Lieutenant General Joaquín Blake.

The rest of this chapter describes the most important battles in which the armies participated and which led to their destruction.

Battle of Medina de Rioseco

Date: 14 July 1808. *Place*: Medina de Rioseco, Castile-Leon.
Result: Napoleonic victory.

After the defeat of Cuesta and his Army of Castile at the battle of Cabezón on 12 June, the French had seized Valladolid and all of eastern Old Castile. From his new headquarters in Benavente, García de la Cuesta asked the Junta of Galicia to support him with its army in his goal of reconquering Valladolid and expelling the French from Castile. Galicia was aware of the seriousness of the situation, but did not accede to all of García de la Cuesta's requests. They sent only half of their available men and kept their troops on the fringes of the Castilian troops. On the one hand, it can be assumed that most of the Galician recruits had not yet received adequate training to face a force as professional as the Napoleonic Army, but on the other hand, Blake and Cuesta each claimed for himself the command of both armies and, as neither wanted to give up their command, they agreed to act separately.

The two Spanish armies, totalling some 25,000 men,[3] linked up in the vicinity of Medina de Rioseco on 13 July. Upon learning of this, Marshal Jean-Baptiste Bessières advanced from Palencia towards Medina de Rioseco, although he had only about 14,000 troops. Arriving at the battlefield, the Duke of Istria was pleasantly surprised to see that the Spanish armies had taken up absurd positions: in the north, before the town of Medina de Rioseco, was the Army of Castile, forming a line of infantry, with a small reserve contingent, while the Army of Galicia had its troops facing south, towards Valladolid, occupying the high point of Mount Monclín; between them they had left an incomprehensible chasm 1.5km wide in which the Napoleonic marshal could manoeuvre at will. Bessières knew the die was cast. His plan was relatively simple: he would send Mouton's division to account for the Army of Castile, while the rest of his army would crush the Army of Galicia. The latter, seeing the French arriving from the east instead of the south, did change their positions on the Monclin, but remained in three irregular vanguard lines, with a reserve in the rear. Needless to say, the Spanish cavalry was conspicuous, if not by its absence, then by its dramatic scarcity.

With the Castilians fixed on the battlefield, Bessières launched Merle's division against the centre and right flank of Blake's line at a place called the Valdecuevas moor, which surrounds the Monclín. The Galicians withstood the first Napoleonic attack well, but could do nothing when Bessières moved on to the next phase, taking advantage of the gap between the two Spanish armies to attack Blake's left flank with General Lasalle's impetuous cavalry. This was too much for the Galician infantry. Its soldiers were mostly peasants, many lacking uniform, with no skills in the handling of weapons and little training. In contrast, Lasalle was one of Napoleon's best cavalry generals and his division could be considered among the elite. Blake's lines fell apart and their retreat was chaotic. Fortunately, General Jado Cagigal managed to form a cadre with the Regiment of Navarre, one of his few regular units, which held firm and at great cost saved most of the infantry of the Army of Galicia. Jado Cagigal[4] survived the day, albeit with a serious leg wound, and was subsequently awarded the order of San Fernando 3rd class. The same cannot be said of the other Spanish commanders. Once Blake's infantry were fleeing in disarray, Bessières completed his plan by attacking Cuesta's army; seeing what had happened to their Galician compatriots, his men too soon fled the battlefield in panic. The day ended in a bitter defeat for the Spanish armies, with some 500 dead, 1,000 wounded and more than 1,000 taken prisoner or missing (many of them had deserted). Joseph I, who had been held up in Burgos, now had the way open to enter Madrid.

Battle of Zornotza

Date: 31 October 1808, *Place*: Zornotza, Basque Country,
Result: Napoleonic victory.

This was a minor battle compared to those of Medina de Rioseco and Espinosa de los Monteros. After the unexpected setbacks suffered in some of the summer battles of 1808, which caused the French to withdraw from practically all of Spain, during the month of October that year Napoleon himself took command of his Grande Armée to put an end to the Spanish War and establish his brother Joseph as King of Spain. In the Basque Country the Army of the Left stood in his way. General Blake had some 25,000 troops stationed in the towns of Bernagoitia and Muniketa, on the left bank of the Ibaizabal river, as well as an undetermined number of guerrilla fighters from Biscay. For his part, Marshal Lefebvre-Desnouettes, who was in Durango, took the initiative to crush Blake's troops without consulting Napoleon. Thus, on 31 October he sent Villate's division against Blake's positions in Bernagoitia. The battle was very short, as the Malaga general was completely taken by surprise and could do little more than give the order to retreat; this, at least on this occasion, was carried out in an orderly fashion. Subsequently, the French descended on the towns and villages of the region like a plague of locusts, destroying everything in their path. Amorebieta and Elchano were completely razed to the ground, and murders and looting raged unchecked. Hundreds of civilians fled their homes, seeking the protection of Blake's troops.

Battle of Güeñes

Date: 7 November 1808, *Place*: Güeñes, Basque Country,
Result: Napoleonic victory.

Following the game of cat and mouse as the two armies manoeuvred around the country, on 5 November, surprisingly, Blake turned his retreating army around at the height of Valmaseda and attacked, and defeated, General Villate's division, which was at the forefront of the French pursuit. Far from intimidating the French, however, this tactical victory only served to speed up their pursuit. The next encounter took place two days later in Güeñes. As in the action at Zornotza, Blake could do little more than organize an orderly retreat, while leaving the 1st Division under General Genaro Figueroa, with Galician troops, to cover the retreat of their compatriots. In this battle the Literary Battalion especially distinguished itself.

Battle of Espinosa de los Monteros

Date: 10–11 November 1808. *Place*: Espinosa de los Monteros, Castile-Leon.
Result: Napoleonic victory.

On the 10th Blake reached Espinosa de los Monteros. Realizing that he could no longer flee from the French, he sought a suitable terrain for the battle to come. To his rear he left the Trueba river and the town of Espinosa de los Monteros, while he deployed his troops in an arc as follows: on the left were the Asturian units, before the foothills known as Las Peñucas that gave access to the Cantabrian mountain range; in the centre were the Galician divisions of Generals Figueroa and Mahy, together with the artillery; on the right, on what would be known from that day on as the Loma del Ataque, was the Marquis de la Romana's Northern Division with, behind it, General Martinengo's Galician division. In total, Blake had some 23,000 men. Advancing towards them was Victor's Army Corps, which had a similar number of troops, although as usual the French came to the battlefield with more cavalry and artillery units than the Spaniards could muster, and, needless to say, with much more battle-hardened and better-quality units.

Around 1.00pm Victor's vanguard appeared on the road to Quintana de los Prados. The French were divided into two columns. Six battalions were launched in an assault on the Loma del Ataque, while another three were positioned in front of the Asturian troops at the other end of the Spanish line. The fighting on the Loma del Ataque was fierce. Here, the French troops faced the veteran Northern Division, which forced them to pay in blood for every step they took. Even so, the French gained ground and even managed to conquer the hill momentarily, before a counterattack by the Galician battalions forced them to retreat to their initial positions. However, this Spanish victory came at a high price: Pontevedra Colonel Miranda y Gayoso, Count of San Román[5] and Royal Navy Brigadier Francisco Riquelme[6] were both seriously wounded. Both had to leave the battlefield and died shortly afterwards from their wounds. The day ended at Loma del Ataque with the arrival of French reinforcements, which allowed them to recover part of the lost ground. At the other end of the line, in Las Peñucas, three battalions took positions in front of the Asturians, who went on the offensive, forcing the French to retreat. As it was close to nightfall, the French withdrew to their positions (*see* Map 2).

Blake is often criticized for not taking advantage of the night to break camp and cross the Trueba. But it must be remembered that his troops were moving more slowly than the Napoleonic Army, which would have caught him in a few days. Moreover, he could feel confident here in his men, who had withstood the first onslaught with remarkable resilience. Thus, on the morning of the 11th, Victor saw with some satisfaction that he had before him the chance to finish off the Spanish army. He had realized that the Spanish left flank, that is, the Asturian divisions on Las Peñucas, was the weakest area of the enemy line, so he sent to attack there the six fresh battalions of the Lapisse division, with Brigadier General Maison's[7] three battalions the vanguard. Meanwhile nine battalions held the position of the Loma del Ataque and another six held the centre of the Spanish line. Maison realized that the Asturian troops were inexperienced and that at all times they did nothing more than obey the orders of their commanding officers, who, precisely for that reason, were forced to expose themselves more than was prudent. Maison sent out his best *voltigeurs* to eliminate the Spanish high command. Within minutes, the Divisional General Gregorio Bernaldo de Quirós fell dead and the General-in-Chief of the Asturian forces, Vicente Acevedo, was seriously injured, as were General Cayetano Valdés[8] of the other division and Colonel José Pesci, among other officers. Thus, the inexperienced Asturians were left without commanders to tell them what to do; seeing the French lines advancing, they abandoned the battlefield. Subsequently the centre of the Spanish line lost its cannons to the French advance, so the Napoleonic forces were able to enter and loot Espinosa de los Monteros. Finally, seeing that the troops from Loma del Ataque were going to overrun his own lines, Blake had no choice but to order a retreat towards Reinosa, but this was carried out in complete disorder. In fact, the following day Blake could only muster about 12,000 of his men, meaning that more than half of his army was lost, although in the following days he managed to recover a significant number of dispersed men. Even so, some 3,000 Spanish soldiers remained on the battlefield, either dead or taken prisoner.

Notes

1. Cabanes (1815), pp. 17–18. Order of battle in August 1808 with the army quartered between Manzanal and Fuencebador. The column of the Marquis of Villadares was quartered in Portugal. Throughout the battles described in this chapter this battle order was modified. As far as possible, modifications will be detailed in the text.
2. García Fuertes (2009), p. 11.
3. Around 15,000 men from the armies of Galicia and Asturias, and near 10,000 men from the Castilian army.
4. Like many Galician army chiefs, Jado Cagigal came from the Royal Navy. His record was full of heroic acts, the highlight being his participation in the Battle of Trafalgar, commanding the ship of the line *San Agustín*. Villeneuve's erratic disposition on that day saw Cagigal's ship in the centre of the Franco-Spanish line ahead of *Santísima Trinidad*. The first part of the combat was spent trying to protect *Santísima Trinidad*, but when it had surrendered, *San Agustín* was surrounded by five English ships, which punished it mercilessly. When it neither surrendered nor sank, the English tried to board the vessel. Their first two attempts failed. On the third, Jado Cagigal barely had enough men to defend the ship, so he had no choice but to surrender, on the condition that the Spanish flag was not lowered. Jado Cagigal and the survivors of *San Agustín* were sent to Gibraltar, where they were properly treated for their injuries. The ship itself, seriously damaged by five hours of combat, soon sank.
5. A veteran from the escape of the Division of the North.
6. Riquelme was another of the distinguished sailors who was forced to fight on land during the Napoleonic Wars. Among his many heroic deeds, his service record also includes his participation in the Battle of Trafalgar, being the third in command of the ship of the line *Santa Ana*. When his superiors, Álava and Gardoqui, were seriously wounded, he was given command of the ship, which

continued fighting for more than two hours until it was forced to surrender. However, while he was being taken to Gibraltar, he escaped and returned to Cádiz. To honour his memory, there is a plaque in the Pantheon of Illustrious Sailors in San Fernando. Unfortunately, they made a mistake on the plaque when they entered his first name.

7. Maison was a brave man and, above all, a man of honour. After fighting in Spain, he was sent to Russia, where he fought under the command of Marshal Ney. On one occasion Ney personally saved his life, in what was a compromising situation for both of them. In 1816 Maison was appointed one of the judges who were to try Ney for high treason. Maison preferred to resign from his post rather than be forced to condemn his former superior officer and friend, which cost him demotion and several years of political ostracism.

8. Valdés was another of the outstanding sailors of the late eighteenth and early nineteenth centuries who fought with the army. During the battle of Trafalgar, Valdés had commanded the ship of the line *Neptuno*. His behaviour on that day was heroic, trying to save both *Santísima Trinidad* and *Bucentaure*. His ship ended up being surrounded by four British ships. The survivors were sent to Gibraltar. Captain Cayetano Valdés ended that day with 117 separate wounds.

Chapter Eleven

The Battle of Tudela

Date: 23 November 1808. *Place*: Tudela, Navarre.
Result: Napoleonic victory.

Order of battle[1]

Spanish Army: under the command of General Francisco Javier Castaños, the Army of the Centre or Andalucia,[2] with the following units: 2nd Division of General Grimarest, with: 1st Regiment of Line Infantry of Burgos (1 bn), Regiment of Provincial Militia of Bujalance (1 bn), Battalion of Shooters of Cádiz, Regiment of Line Infantry Fijo de Ceuta (2 bns), Regiment of Provincial Militia of Ciudad Real (1 bn), 1st Regiment of Provincial Militia of Cuenca (1 bn), Battalion of Shooters of Spain, 2nd Regiment of Provincial Militia of Granada (1 bn), 1st Regiment of Line Infantry of Volunteers of Madrid (1 bn), Regiment of Line Infantry of the Queen (1 bn), Regiment of Provincial Militia of Trujillo (1 bn), Regiment of the Royal Walloon Guards (1 bn) and 2nd Regiment of Line Infantry of Volunteers of Seville (1 bn). Cavalry: Regiment of Dragoons of Lusitania (4 sqns), Regiment of Mounted Chasseurs of Seville (3 sqns), Regiment of Bourbon (4 sqns), Regiment of Spain (2 sqns). Artillery: 1 Company of Mounted Artillery. 4th Division of General La Peña: Regiment of Line Infantry of Africa (2 bns), Grenadiers of Provincial Militia of the Army of Andalucia (2 bs), 1st Regiment of Line Infantry of Burgos (1 bn), Regiment of Light Infantry of Campo Mayor (1 bn), Regiment of Line Infantry of Murcia (2 bns), Regiment of

Line Infantry of the Military Orders (3 bns), Regiment of Chasseurs of Navas de Tolosa (1 bn), Regiment of Line Infantry of Zaragoza (1 bn), Regiment of Provincial Militia of Sigüenza (1 bn), Battalion of Chasseurs of Bailén, Regiment of the Royal Spanish Guards (2 bns), Regiment of Line Infantry of Ireland (1 bn). Cavalry: Regiment of Lancers of Jerez (1 sqn), Regiment of Dragoons of Pavia (4 sqns). Artillery: 1 Company of Mounted Artillery and 1 Company of Artillery. 5th Division of General Roca: Regiment of Line Infantry of America (2 bns), Regiment of Provincial Militia of Ávila (1 bn), Battalion of Volunteers from the Arsenal of Cartagena, Regiment of Line Infantry of Liria (1 bn), 2nd Regiment of Provincial Militia of Murcia (1 bn), Battalion of Chasseurs of Orihuela, Regiment of Line Infantry of Saboya (2 bns), Regiment of Line Infantry of Valencia (2 bns), Battalion of Volunteers Chasseurs of Valencia. Cavalry: Regiment of Chasseurs of Olivenza (2 sqns) and Regiment of Chasseurs of Maestranza (1 sqn). Artillery: 2 Companies of artillery. Cavalry: Regiment of Dragoons of Castile (2 sqns), Regiment of Royal Guard Corps (1 sqn), Regiment of Dragoons of the Queen (2 sqns) and Regiment of Dragoons of Madrid (3 sqns). Army of Aragon or Reserve[3]: 1st Division of O'Neill: 1st Battalion of Light Infantry Volunteers of Aragon, 2nd Battalion of Light Infantry Volunteers of Aragon, Regiment of Line Infantry of Swiss of Aragon (2 bns), 4th Tercio of Volunteers of Aragon (1 bn), Regiment of Line Infantry of Volunteers of Castile (1 bn), Battalion of Shooters of Doyle, Regiment of the Royal Spanish Guards (1 bn), Regiment of Line Infantry of Extremadura (1 bn), Battalion of Chasseurs of Aragon, 1st Tercio of Volunteers of Huesca (1 bn), 1st Regiment of Line Infantry of Volunteers of Murcia (2 bns), 2nd Regiment of Line Infantry of Volunteers of Murcia (2 bns), 2nd Regiment of Line Infantry of Valencia (1 bn), 1st Regiment of Light Infantry of Zaragoza (1 bn). Cavalry: Regiment of Dragoons of the King (1 sqn). 2nd Division of General Saint Marcq: Regiment of Light Infantry Volunteers of Alicante (2 bns), Regiment of Light Infantry Volunteers of Bourbon (1 bn), 2nd Tercio of Calatayud (1 bn), Regiment of Line Infantry of Volunteers of Castile (1 bn), Battalion of Volunteers of Chelva, 2nd Battalion of Chasseurs of Valencia, Battalion of Chasseurs of Segorbe, 2nd Regiment of Provincial Militia of Soria (1 bn), Regiment of Line Infantry of Turia (3 bns) and 2nd Regiment of Line Infantry of Valencia (1 bn). Cavalry: Regiment of Dragoons of Numancia (2 sqns). 3rd Division of Villalba: 3rd Regiment of Line Infantry of Volunteers of Murcia (1 bn), 5th Regiment of Line Infantry of Volunteers of Murcia (1 bn), 1st Battalion of Shooters of Murcia, 2nd Battalion of Shooters of Murcia, Battalion of Shooters of Florida Blanca, Regiment of Line Infantry of Peñas de San Pedro (1 bn) and 3rd Tercio of Volunteers of Huesca (1 bn). Cavalry: Regiment of Mounted Chasseurs of Fuensanta (2 sqns). Artillery: 4 Companies of artillery. In total, near 47,000 troops (although only around 20,000 men actually fought).

Napoleonic Army: under the command of Marshal Jean Lannes, Duke of Montebello, the following units: III Army Corps under the command of Moncey, with Maurice Mathieu's Division, including: Buget's Brigade, comprising 14th Regiment of Line Infantry (4 bns) and 44th Regiment of Line Infantry (3 bns); Habert's Brigade with 2nd Regiment of Infantry of Vistula (2 bns), 3rd Regiment of Infantry of Vistula (2 bns) and 70th Regiment of Line Infantry (1 bn). Musnier's Division, comprising Brun's Brigade with 114th Regiment of Line Infantry (4 bns) and Razout's Brigade with 115th Regiment of Line Infantry (4 bns). Morlot's División, with Augerau's Brigade, including 116th Regiment of Line Infantry (2 bns) and Regiment of Infantry of Ireland (1 bn); and Aubre's Brigade with 117th Regiment of Line Infantry (4 bns). Grandjean's Division, including Leval's Brigade with 1st Regiment of Infantry of Vistula (2 bns) and 2nd Legion (3 bns). Artillery: 8 Companies (approx. 50 guns). VI Army Corps. Lagrange's Division with Bardet's Brigade: 27th Regiment of Line Infantry (3 bns) and 25th Regiment of Light Infantry (3 bns); Labasse's Brigade: 50th Regiment of Line Infantry (4 bns) and 59th Regiment of Line Infantry (3 bns). Artillery: 3 Companies (around 20 guns). Cavalry under the command of Lefebvre-Desnouettes, with: Wathier's Brigade (III Army Corps): 1st Provisional Regiment of Cuirassiers (1 sqn), 5th Regiment of Hussars (2 sqns) and 1st Legion of Vistula (3 sqns); Colbert's Brigade (VI Army Corps): 3rd Regiment of Hussars (3 sqns), 15th Regiment of Mounted Chasseurs (3 sqns) and 1 Company of Mounted Artillery (6 guns). Digeon's Brigade (VI Army Corps): 20th Regiment of Dragoons (3 sqns), 26th Regiment of Dragoons (3 sqns) and 13th Regiment of Cuirassiers (3 sqns). In total, near 33,000 men.

Background[4]

After the defeat at Bailén, the Napoleonic troops withdrew to a defensive line north of the Ebro river. But the war was not over. Napoleon had dissolved the Fourth Coalition after the battle of Friedland (14 June 1807), and decided to personally end the Spanish resistance himself, leading his *Grand Armée* to pacify Spain once and for all.

Meanwhile, on the Spanish side, the Central Supreme Junta had met on 5 October to devise a plan to fight Napoleon. The main resistance would be led by General Castaños, the victor of Bailén (with the permission of Theodore von Reding), commanding the Army of the Centre, a re-foundation of the old Andalusian Army which, together with new divisions, would have a strength of about 80,000 troops, with which he hoped to contain the Napoleonic forces on the Ebro line, with the help of the Reserve Army under the command of General José de Palafox. The Junta also planned an offensive with the Army of the Left, commanded by General Blake. But as usual, nothing went as planned. Castaños did not receive the promised troops and, having delayed his departure from Madrid, reached the Ebro line with only about 28,000 men.

On 18 October, in Zaragoza, Castaños and Palafox agreed that the Reserve Army should move forward across the Ebro to Caparroso (Navarre). At the same time Grimarest, commanding the 2nd Division, crossed the river with the intention of occupying Lerín and establishing a bridgehead, through which the entire army could cross and reach Pamplona. At Lodosa, on the northern bank of the river, he awaited the rest of his division. But Moncey was aware of the strategic value of the Spanish movements and attacked with three brigades. Surrounded, and unable to receive reinforcements from outside, the Spanish were forced to surrender after two days of fierce fighting.[5] Meanwhile, Ney had attacked Grimarest in Lodosa; abandoning the city, Grimarest left the bridge-head in the hands of the French. With hardly any effort, the French had turned the strategic tide.

That same day the French advanced towards Logroño, which Castaños hastened to evacuate, planning a new defensive line on the Queiles river, where the Reserve Army was ordered to go as quickly as possible. There were serious logistical problems, however, especially in terms of footwear and food for the troops. From that moment on, the problems between Castaños and Palafox worsened. Up until then their relationship had remained cold but polite, but now they no longer bothered to conceal their mutual antipathy. To try to resolve the issue, the Supreme Central Junta sent two delegates, but they were hardly neutral: one was José de Palafox's brother, Francisco de Palafox, and the other was his cousin, Eugenio Eulalio Palafox Portocarrero, Count of Montijo. Unsurprisingly, the Junta delegates sided with Palafox.

On 21 November, faced with the unstoppable advance of the Napoleonic Army, and overwhelmed by the circumstances, Castaños distributed his forces in a front some 20km long. To the south, in Tarazona, was Grimarest with three divisions; in the centre, in Cascante, was the 4th Division, commanded by La Peña; while to the north was the 5th Division in Ablitas. Meanwhile Castaños ordered General O'Neill, who was incidentally in command of the Reserve Army, to take up position in Tudela. But O'Neill refused to obey Castaños, stating that his superior officer was José de Palafox and therefore, in accordance with the line of command, he only obeyed him. Eventually, however, after a delay, he set off. The following day, the 22nd, another meeting between Palafox and Castaños in Tudela ended in insults, reproaches and counter-accusations. It was a shameful spectacle. The army was unprepared, and the generals would not collaborate – a catastrophe was looming. That same night O'Neill's troops arrived in Tudela, but without deploying or preparing for battle. On top of that, Palafox had gone to Zaragoza, leaving his men entirely in O'Neill's hands.

The Battle

On the morning of 23 November O'Neill's troops, some 18,000 men, were in Tudela, while the 4,000 troops of the Roca Division of the Army of the Centre were stationed on the Santa Bárbara hill. Early in the morning Castaños left for Cascante, in search of General La Peña's 4th Division. Between the troops in Tudela and those of Cascante there was a gap some 10km wide, where Lannes's troops were preparing to attack the Cabezo de Malla hill, to the south of Tudela.

On the Santa Bárbara hill the Roca Division bravely resisted the divisions of Generals Maurice Mathieu and Habert, made up of experienced men who had fought in the battles of the Fourth Coalition. At this point the battalions of Caro and Pinohermoso were especially brilliant, but after a few hours of fighting they retreated towards the ruins of the medieval castle that crowns the hill (*see* Map 3).

Towards midday Lannes decided to occupy the top of Cabezo de Malla, from where he could dominate Tudela and cut off the communications route between this town and Cascante, and so he sent Morlot and Grandjean's divisions towards the hill. Meanwhile, the French cavalry circled the town on the right. Castaños did not appear. In fact, the 4th Division was still held in Cascante, where it was being attacked by Digeon's cavalry. La Peña, believing he was being attacked by the bulk of Lannes's army, held his position. For his part, O'Neill, faced with the danger of being overrun, ordered a brilliant manoeuvre: while the bulk of his troops attacked Morlot's troops from the front, he sent his battalion of the Royal Walloon Guards to envelop the French on his left, managing to drive them off with the bayonet. But these soldiers, already exhausted and hungry, could not hold out for the whole day. La Peña was still in Cascante, and Grimarest, in Tarazona, showed no signs of coming to the rescue, even though he could doubtless hear the din of the battle taking place just a few miles north of his garrison.

Around 2.00pm Lannes struck the final blow. He ordered Morlot to occupy the height of San Juan de Calchetas, breaking the Spanish line, while Maurice-Matthieu achieved the *coup de grâce* at the summit of Santa Bárbara. The French, through an encircling manoeuvre, managed to get part of their forces to advance through steep terrain to the rear of the Roca Division; seeing themselves surrounded, the Spanish troops disbanded, fleeing towards the city and spreading their panic to the rest of the forces still billeted in Tudela. O'Neill's forces, now faced with the risk of being overrun, followed the men of the Roca Division and made a desperate escape. Castaños, who had finally returned from Cascante, was unable to halt their flight.

The afternoon was a disaster for the Spanish troops, who lost some 3,000 dead and wounded, and a similar number of prisoners. The losses would have been greater still had not O'Neill and Saint-Marcq managed to organize the Numancia Cavalry Regiment and the Valencia Battalion, which heroically stood their ground. At around 3.00pm La Peña finally decided to leave Cascante and head in the direction of Tudela. Shortly afterwards, his men began to come across the survivors of Tudela's defenders, who were fleeing in panic. As for Grimarest, he was finally reunited with La Peña in Cascante. Together they marched towards Borja, where that night Generals Castaños, Roca, Caro and O'Neill would converge with the men who were able (or willing) to follow them. But the next day, however, the disbandment continued. Contravening Castaños's orders, the men of Roca's and O'Neill's troops left, following in Palafox's footsteps, to defend Zaragoza from the imminent siege. Castaños, for his part, regrouped what forces he could and headed south to defend Madrid. When he was dismissed by the Supreme Central Junta, his command passing to the Duke of Infantado, there were barely 10,000 men left of the former Army of the Centre. As for the French, the way was now clear for them to re-enter Madrid.

Notes

1. See https://elgrancapitan.org/portal/index.php/articulos3/historia-militar/1132-la-batalla-de-tudela-23-de-noviembre-de-1808-ii (accessed 20 July 2022).

2. The following divisions were also part of this army: the 1st Division of Lieutenant General Joaquín de Riaño y Orovio, Count of Villariezo, and the 3rd Division of General Carvajal, but they did not participate in the battle since they were positioned at other points in the defensive line.

3. The Reserve Army was under the command of General Palafox, although for this battle Castaños claimed the supreme command of all the armies (Palafox was in Zaragoza on those days); this caused harsh discussions between the two generals. As we shall see, the generals under Palafox's command at the beginning of the battle refused to obey Castaños.

4. Iribarren (1942); Aquillué (2020).

5. The troops involved in the defence of Lerín were the Battalion Tiradores de Cadiz (Cruz Morgeón), the Catalan Volunteer Company (Juan Bascourt) and 30 cavalrymen from the Regiment of Bourbon (Pedro Loscertales), a total of between 900 and 1,200 troops. Moncey, who admired their courage, allowed the survivors to surrender with full honours, and days later they were exchanged for a group of French prisoners. On the action of Lerín, *see* Forcada Torres (1966), pp. 143–7; Toreno (1838), p. 282; VVAA (1820), p. 191; Hugo (1837), p. 102; Cobbett (1808), p. 928.

Chapter Twelve

The Battle of Somosierra

Date: 30 November 1808. *Place*: Somosierra, Madrid.
Result: Napoleonic victory.

Order of battle:

Spanish Army: under the command of General Benito San Juan, the following units: Royal Walloons Guards, Regiment of the Queen, Regiment of Cordoba, Regiment of the Crown, Regiment of the Prince, Regiment of Badajoz, Regiment of Jaen, Provincial Militia of Toledo, Provincial Militia of Alcazar de San Juan, Volunteers of Seville, 1st Regiment of Volunteers of Madrid, 2nd Regiment of Volunteers of Madrid. Artillery: 16 cannon and 200 artillerymen.

Napoleonic Army: under the command of Emperor Napoleon Bonaparte, Ruffin's Division with the 9th Regiment of Light Infantry, the 24th Regiment of Line Infantry and the 96th Regiment of Line Infantry, together with the 3rd Squadron of the 1st Regiment of Polish Light Cavalry. Later the 1st Squadron of the 1st Regiment of Polish Light Cavalry and the 3rd Regiment of Hussars (1 sqn). Artillery: 2 cannon.

Background[1]

The defeat at the battle of Tudela had wiped out the Centre and Reserve Armies, clearing the way for the French troops to enter Madrid. The remnants of the

Spanish forces had been divided into three and dispersed: some in Zaragoza under the command of Palafox; some in Cuenca under the Duke of Infantado, who had replaced Castaños; and a small force of the former Army of the Centre which headed for Madrid. In the capital the Supreme Central Junta assembled as many forces as it could under the command of General Benito San Juan. Like the Duke of Infantado, he was related to the all-powerful Palafox family and was an experienced soldier who, at the end of 1808, held the post of commissary general of the light cavalry. On the 28th, in Sepúlveda, the vanguard of his troops, under the command of Colonel Juan José Sardeñ, fought a French division, managing to contain it. However, as his position was indefensible, Sardeñ abandoned it, retreating towards Segovia.

The task facing San Juan was not an easy one. Confronting him was Napoleon Bonaparte himself and his *Grand Armée*. San Juan had only a handful of volunteers and inexperienced recruits, as well as some remnants of the old Army of the Centre, although these men were already demoralized by the defeat at Tudela. However, the terrain was favourable for defence. The gorges of the Somosierra pass could be made impregnable. The French troops had to cross a bridge that was overlooked by the Spanish artillery and its riflemen. San Juan knew it would be a difficult fight, but he had a chance.

The Battle

On 30 November the troops woke up to a thick fog. San Juan arranged his men along the only pass through Somosierra. In the first line he had approximately 400 infantrymen and the first battery of guns in front of a small narrow bridge, which was the only practicable passage for the French. Behind them were another four batteries. As for the French, early in the morning Napoleon deployed the 24th Regiment of Line Infantry on the left flank of the bridge and the 9th Regiment of Light Infantry on the right. The 96th Regiment of Line Infantry was to lead the attack, supported by the only two guns that Ruffin had managed to bring up to the battlefield.

At around 9.00am the French began their advance. Despite the thick fog, they were detected by the Spanish front line, which unleashed a hail of bullets and shrapnel. The French 96th Infantry halted, decimated by dozens of casualties, including their colonel, Jean Chrysostome de Cales. Their route forward seemed impassable. Around 11.00am, as the fog began to lift, Napoleon ordered his artillerymen to try to destroy the Spanish batteries. But the Spanish guns were of larger calibre and their experienced and accurate gunners defeated their Gallic opponents. Napoleon could think of no other way to break San Juan's doughty line than with a cavalry charge. At his disposal was the 3rd Light Cavalry Squadron. This was a fledgling unit, which had not yet faced its baptism of fire, although many of its officers had proven experience and courage. It was an entirely Polish unit, although at the time it was under the command of Pierre d'Autancourt (or Dautancourt). At this time the 3rd Squadron was in the rear of the French lines with the other three squadrons of the regiment. Napoleon called for the squadron leader, Jean León Hippolyte Kozietulski, and ordered him to make the charge. The Emperor's general staff were stunned: surely this was suicide? But the Pole was already haranguing his horsemen. What happened next has become a legend, as the group of 216 horsemen made one of the most glorious cavalry charges of all the Napoleonic wars. Some say that Kozietulski exclaimed: 'Forward, my horsemen! Long live the Emperor!', others that his speech was a little ruder: 'Come on, you dogs! The Emperor is watching you!' Whatever the truth of it, the Polish horsemen charged towards the bridge under a hail of bullets and shrapnel. The Spanish fought back desperately, but the Poles crossed the bridge and reached the first Spanish battery. This had not been foreseen, and the guns were not protected by ditches or barricades. An all-out fight ensued in the first battery line, and Sergeant Jakub Dabczewski pounced on the first cannon. It was a massacre, and the Poles had succeeded in silencing the Spanish forward guns. They paid a high price for their success, with dozens killed or wounded. Among the latter was Squadron Leader Kozietulski himself. Command passed to Captain Dziewanowski, along with the order to charge the second battery. Dziewanowski did not hesitate. Sabre in hand, he rushed the second battery with the horsemen he could muster, and once again, after fierce resistance, the battery was overrun. In attempting to assault the third battery, Dziewanowski was seriously wounded, and command passed into the hands of Captain Pierre Krasinski. Finally, only the fourth and last line of batteries remained. Here Krasinski was one of the first to fall. Command fell to Lieutenant Niegolewski, but there were only about 30 horsemen left to beat the last four guns. It was a Herculean task, but one that the lieutenant threw himself into. The first gun was captured. But suddenly Niegolewski found himself alone with his sergeant, Sokolowski. The lieutenant asked where the men were, to which the sergeant replied laconically: 'They are all dead.' Moments later, Niegolewski himself was shot down and the artillerymen bayoneted him nine times, leaving him for dead. The Spaniards recovered the lost battery, but only just. Immediately, fresh horsemen arrived, sent by Napoleon, from the 1st Squadron of the Light Cavalry and a squadron of the 3rd Hussar Regiment. This new wave of cavalry overwhelmed the artillerymen and infantrymen defending the last line, who retreated. The battle was over. The road to Madrid was finally free and clear.

The Polish horsemen paid a heavy price. The 3rd Squadron was practically annihilated. All eight of its officers were killed or wounded. Among the former were Lieutenants Rowicki, Rudowski and Krzyzanowski. Captain Dziewanowski was wounded and his leg was amputated, but he died a few days later. Among the wounded were Squadron Leader Kozietulski, Captain Krasinski and Lieutenants Roman and Niegolewski, who miraculously survived his nine wounds. Captain Arnoud van Zuylen van Nyevelt, a Dutch Hussar officer, should be added to this list.

On the Spanish side, things were going badly for General San Juan. At first, he withdrew with the rest of his troops to Segovia, where he met with Brigadier Juan Heredia. From there they planned to help Madrid, but it was all too late. As they prepared for the march, fugitives from the capital began to arrive in Segovia. The Spanish generals, with their troops, withdrew southwards to the town of Talavera de la Reina, where they awaited instructions from the Central Supreme Junta. But the mood among the soldiers was one of demoralization and indolence. Riots and desertions multiplied in the city of Toledo, close to Talavera de la Reina. In response, San Juan carried out a series of disciplinary measures that were very badly received by his men. On 7 January a mutiny broke out. Apparently, it was instigated by a friar, but the soldiers quickly backed it. Brigadier Heredia escaped at the last moment, but the luckless San Juan was lynched and his body dragged about the town. Later, some soldiers and officers of the Montesa Regiment were accused of his death. His colonel, Sardeñ, was imprisoned. Just a few weeks earlier San Juan had accused Sardeñ of being a traitor, leaving him behind in Somosierra.

Back in Somosierra Bonaparte was exultant. He proclaimed the Polish horsemen the bravest in his army, and included the regiment among his Imperial Guard units. Later, he would re-equip the unit, and they became Lancers. This unit remained faithful to Napoleon to the end, and he always liked to have it around. In 1812, during the Russian campaign, he was about to be captured by a regiment of Cossacks near the town of Horodnia, while making a reconnaissance of the land. Only the swift and forceful reaction of his Polish horsemen saved his life. At the head of them was none other than Jan Kozietulski.

Note

1. Although it is an extensively studied battle, unless specified otherwise this chapter is based on the exhaustive text available at: http://napoleonistyka.atspace.com/battle_somosierra.htm#_Napoleon_march_on_Madrid (accessed 10 December 2021).

Chapter Thirteen

The Fall of Madrid

Date: 2–4 December 1808, *Place*: Madrid. *Result*: Napoleonic victory.

Order of battle

Spanish Army: 300 men from different regiments, a couple of battalions of new conscripts and the Volunteers of Madrid under the command of the Marquis of Castelar.[1]

Napoleonic Army: I, IV and VI Army Corps under the command of Emperor Napoleon Bonaparte. I Corps, under Marshal Victor, comprised the 1st Division (Ruffin), 2nd Division (Lapisse), 3rd Division (Villatte) and the Cavalry Division (Carrière de Beaumont). IV Corps, under Marshal Lefebvre, had just the 1st Division (Sébastiani), but included most of the elite units of the Napoleonic Army, such as the Polish Lancers and the Westphalian Infantry. VI Corps, under Marshal Ney, comprised the 1st Division (Marchand), 2nd Division (Bisson) and 3rd Division (Dessoles). The Cavalry Division of General La Tour-Maubourg was an independent unit. In total, around 55,000–60,000 men.[2]

Background

The defeat at the battle of Somosierra *de facto* opened the gates of Madrid to Napoleon's armies. Clearly the capital was incapable of withstanding a siege like those that Zaragoza and Girona had suffered. It had no walls, nor could most of the buildings resist a bombardment; due to their construction materials, they would be quick to catch fire. The Governing Junta had entrusted the defence of the city to the Marquis of Castelar, assisted by Tomás de Morla, an extraordinary artillery general who would be in charge of organizing barricades and reinforcing what defences there were. His intention was not so much to prevent the entry of the French as to delay it as long as possible, waiting for reinforcements to arrive from the Reserve Army.[3] Furthermore, the city's militia was barely worthy of the name: 300 regular army troops and two levée battalions with very little military training. In the circumstances the military governor of the city, Fernando de Vera y Pantoja, decided to distribute some 8,000 rifles among the members of the militia and any new volunteers who wanted to defend themselves against the French. During the delivery of these rifles, riots broke out that ended with the lynching of the Marquis of Perales del Río; once again, accused of *afrancesado*, as it was rumoured that he was sabotaging the defence of the city by distributing adulterated gunpowder. Barricades were placed at the gates of Alcalá, Recoletos, Segovia, Santa Bárbara, Fuencarral, Conde-Duque and San Bernardino, as well as on various main streets, and as many walls and ramparts as possible were embanked. Then the citizens settled down to await the arrival of Napoleon and his Grand Armée.

The battle

On the morning of 2 December the dragoons of La Tour-Maubourg and La Houssaye appeared on the heights north of Madrid. Shortly afterwards, Napoleon himself arrived with the bulk of his army. He ordered an initial attack, which was repulsed, although not before the French had managed to gauge the quality of Madrid's defences. Napoleon sent a captured Spanish officer to the city with a letter ordering the Marquis of Castelar to surrender 'to avoid the disasters of a war';[4] the Spanish general, trying to gain time, responded ambiguously.

This was a useless trick that did not fool Napoleon. The next morning he ordered General Berthier, Prince of Neufchatel, one of his favourite commanders (and also at the time one of his best friends), to fire his cannon against the Retreat area. It did not take long to break through, and General Villatte's light infantry troops immediately began to take over the streets, buildings and palaces. However, the French suffered many casualties, notably General Maison, who was wounded, and General Bruyère, who died. Napoleon ordered a ceasefire and asked that a Spanish delegation come to confer with him to discuss an honourable surrender. General Morla and the writer Bernardo Iriarte duly appeared before the Emperor. It was an unpleasant meeting for the Spanish emissaries. Berthier introduced them to Napoleon, who angrily reproached them for the mistreatment of the Bailén prisoners, and berated Morla in particular for his actions in the surrender of the Cadiz squadron.[5] After presenting them with his terms for their surrender, he threatened that, if they were not accepted, Morla and the entire Madrid troop would be put to the sword.[6] After consulting with the Junta of

Madrid, it was decided to surrender the city. However, the Marquis of Castelar did not want to sign the act of surrender, so that same night he left the city with his troops (avoiding not only the French, but also the wrath of the people of Madrid, who were mostly opposed to the surrender) and headed to Extremadura.[7] The Viscount of Ghent, who had distinguished himself in the defence of the Segovia Gate, also marched away that night; his intention was to locate General Benito San Juan in Brunete and convince him to take his army to Madrid.

Morla, after signing the surrender document, did the same, and went to Cádiz. There, he had to endure a political campaign against him in which he was accused of cowardice for not defending Madrid and of being *afrancesado*. Saddened by this, he returned to Madrid, where he was warmly received by the French authorities, with whom he struck up a friendship, in a spirit of recognition and mutual admiration. Indeed, Joseph I, who held Morla in high esteem, awarded him the Grand Badge of the Royal Order of Spain. But his health was already beginning to fail, and in 1812 he retired to his residence in Seville, where he died shortly after.[8]

Some of those who stayed behind fared no better. Under the Chamartin Decrees, Napoleon ordered the imprisonment and expropriation of the assets of all those who, having sworn allegiance to Joseph I, subsequently betrayed him, going over to the Fernandino side. Several prominent personalities were arrested and deported. They included, among many others, Arias Mon, Dean of the Council, who died in captivity in Paris in 1811; Jerónimo Antonio Díez,[9] the prosecutor of the Council of Castile, who was responsible for the trial of various *afrancesados*; Paolo de Sangro y Merode, Prince of Castel-Franco,[10] whom Joseph I had confirmed in command of the Royal Walloon Guards Regiment, was deported to Italy, where he was imprisoned until the end of the war; and José Gabriel de Silva-Bazán y Waldstein, Marquis of Santa Cruz, who would spend the rest of the war in a French prison.[11] Another interesting example was the Count of Saint-Simon, an *émigré* from the French Revolution who had placed himself at the service of the Spanish Crown. Napoleon sentenced him to death, but was moved to relent by the pleas of Saint-Simon's daughter, and the sentence was commuted to life imprisonment in France, a fate that the daughter decided to share with her father.

After the surrender General Baillard's troops took possession of Madrid. On this occasion Napoleon's reprisals were limited to punishing the ruling elites and there were no reported cases of abuse by his troops during his stay in Madrid. But to Napoleon's surprise and anger, the fall of Madrid did not mean the surrender of Spain. The war continued.

Notes

1. Álvarez de Toledo (1809), pp. 5–6. The Duke del Infantado learned about the composition of this weak defence of Madrid through a report sent to him by the Marquis of Castelar himself.

2. Thiers (1849), p. 354.

3. Vega (1995), p. 203.

4. Thibaudeau (1835), p. 164.

5. See Chapter 5. Anyone interested in reading the transcript of the unpleasant reprimand can consult Thibaudeau (1835), pp. 165–6.

6. Vega (1995), p. 205.

7. Napier (1832), p. 405.

8. Vega (1995), pp. 208–9.

9. Díez was the promoter of the Treaty that declared the Abdications of Bayonne null and void. This Treaty can be consulted at: http://www.memoriademadrid.es/buscador.php?accion=VerFicha&id=8701&num_id=4&num_total=6.

10. Castel-Franco had arrived in Spain from his native Naples with the retinue of Charles III. He belonged to one of the most important Neapolitan families of the eighteenth century. In fact, his father Raymundo de Sangro, Prince of Sansevero and Castel-Franco, is a novelistic character (he starred in several stories), but a cultured and enigmatic man. He was the designer and owner of the Sansevero Chapel in Naples, perhaps one of the most overwhelmingly beautiful churches in Europe.

11. Upon his return to Spain he was appointed the first director of the Prado Museum, among other relevant positions.

Chapter Fourteen

The Battle of Uclés

Date: 13 January 1809. *Place*: Uclés, Castile La Mancha.
Result: Napoleonic victory.

Order of battle

Spanish Army: under the command of General Francisco Venegas, the following units: in Tribaldos, a column under the command of General Veremundo Ramírez de Arellano, with a battalion of Volunteers of Madrid, a battalion of the Chasseurs of Las Navas de Tolosa and the Regiment of Bailén. The column of the left, under the command of General Antonio Senra, with the Regiment of Cantabria, the Regiment of Light Infantry of Barbastro, the Regiment of Africa, the Provincial Regiment of Cuenca, the Regiment of the Military Orders and the 4th Regiment of Volunteers of Seville. The column of the right, under the command of General Augusto Laporte, with the Regiment of Light Infantry of Campo Mayor, the Regiment of Murcia, the Provincial Regiment of Toro, a battalion of Volunteers of Carmona, the 2nd Battalion of the Provincial Grenadiers of Andalucia, the Irish Regiment and the Royal Walloon Guards Regiment. In Uclés, Venegas, with the Provincial Regiment of Jaen, the Provincial Regiment of Chinchilla, the Regiment of Gerona, the Regiment of Burgos, the Regiment of the Queen, a battalion of Shooters of Castile, and the Provincial Regiment of Lorca. In the rearguard was a battalion of the Shooters of Spain, under the command of Major Copons. In the Division of Cavalry were troops from the Regiments of the Queen, Bourbon, the Prince, of Spain, the Mounted Chasseurs of Seville, Dragoons of Pavia, Dragoons of Lusitania, Dragoons of Castile and Royal Carabineers. In total, around 18,000 men.

Napoleonic Army: I Army Corps under the command of Marshal Victor, including the following units: 1st Division (General Ruffin), comprising the 9th Regiment of Line Infantry (3 bns), the 24th Regiment of Line Infantry (3 bns) and the 96th Regiment of Line Infantry (3 bns); 3rd Division (General Villatte), comprising the 27th Regiment of Light Infantry (3 bns), the 63rd Regiment of Line Infantry (3 bns), the 94th Regiment of Line Infantry (3 bns) and the 95th Regiment of Line Infantry (3 bns). The cavalry comprised the 1st Division of General La Tour-Maubourg, with the 1st, 2nd, 4th, 9th, 14th and 26th Regiments of Dragoons; General Carrière de Beaumont was in command of the 2nd Regiment of Hussars and the 5th Regiment of Mounted Chasseurs. The artillery, under the command of the General Sénarmont, had 48 cannon. In total, near 16,000 men.

Background[1]

Following the disaster at Tudela, it could be said that the Army of the Centre and the Reserve Army were practically dissolved. Many of the survivors withdrew to Zaragoza, following Palafox, while another group followed Castaños to Cuenca. The victor of Bailén was dismissed and the Duke of Infantado appointed in his place.[2] The Supreme Central Junta ordered him to retake Madrid, which had only a weak French garrison, although Marshal Victor's I Army Corps was located along the Tagus line. Instead, responding to a call for help from the mayor of Tarancón, the Duke of Infantado ordered his generals, Venegas and Serna, to attack the French squadron garrisoned in the town. However, this hasty action only served to put Victor on his guard and show him exactly where the troops of the new Centre Army were. Before the arrival of the French marshal, Venegas moved towards Uclés, where he hoped to receive reinforcements from the Duke of Infantado. In an effort to delay the Napoleonic advance, Venegas placed three infantry battalions and various detachments under Brigadier Ramírez de Arellano in the village of Tribaldos, a few miles northwest of Uclés. Meanwhile, he left four battalions in front of Uclés, and about eight battalions to the northeast of the town, on the Sierra del Pavo, under the command of Brigadier Girón; at the other end of the town, on the Spanish left wing, there were nine infantry battalions, leaving only the Spanish Rifle Battalion in the rear, commanded by Francisco Copons y Pavía. The bulk of the cavalry was located in front of the Sierra del Pavo.

The battle

The Napoleonic attack, as Venegas had planned, began at Tribaldos. Villatte's Division, as the vanguard, opened fire against Ramírez de Arellano's. When the Spanish could no longer contain the enemy, they retreated in good order towards Uclés.

Shortly afterwards, the second phase of the battle began. Victor sent Villate's infantry to attack the Spanish left flank, the weakest of the Spanish lines, which had neither cavalry nor artillery. Victor took advantage of this to envelop the Spanish with several squadrons of cavalry. Finding themselves overrun, the Spanish fled in disorder towards Uclés, taking with them the four battalions positioned in front of the town. Only Francisco Copons, commanding the Spanish Rifle Battalion, was capable of bringing some order and he managed to organize a minimum resistance (*see* Map 4).

Seeing how the front was crumbling, Brigadier Girón managed to organize his men into columns to try to bayonet their way out through the wall of men that formed Ruffin's Division before them. The Spanish ended up being surrounded on all sides and for the most part were taken prisoner.

As for the cavalry, some of the units that had formed up in front of the Sierra del Pavo managed to flee, including the Dragoons of Castile and the Lusitania and Texas Regiments. However, the Regiments of the Queen, the Prince and Bourbon, led by their brigadier, the Marquis of Albudeyte, found themselves overrun by Ruffin, although they tried to organize themselves to resist and protect the fleeing infantry. They were virtually annihilated in the process, most of those who survived the attack being imprisoned. Venegas, sick and wounded, escaped.

In Carrascosa the Duke of Infantado witnessed the defeat, but did little more than regroup those who were able to escape, before heading towards Murcia and then returning to La Mancha. The result of the battle was about 2,000 Spanish dead and wounded and some 5,600 prisoners.

Notes

1. Count of Toreno (1835); Gálvez (2016).
2. On this point, Aquillué's article, '*Castaños, el odiado*' ('Castaños, the hated'), is fundamental, in which it is explained how Palafox's entourage managed to make Castaños bear the weight of the defeat at Tudela, branding him a traitor. As a consequence, such a climate of animosity was created against the general that, on his way to Seville, in the La Mancha town of Miguelturra, he was almost lynched by a furious crowd. The Duke del Infantado, who replaced Castaños in command of the army, was related to the Palafox family.

Chapter Fifteen

The Second Siege of Zaragoza

Dates: 21 December 1808–3 March 1809. *Place*: Zaragoza.
Result: Napoleonic victory.

Order of battle

Spanish Army: the Army of the Centre under the command of General Palafox, comprising four divisions: Brigadier Butrón's division, with the Regiment of Extremadura, the Regiment of Palafox's Grenadiers, the Regiment of Fusiliers of the Kingdom, the Regiment of the Infante D. Carlos, the Light Battalion of Carmona, the Light Battalion of the Portillo, the Light Battalion of Torrero, the Light Battalion of Calatayud, the 1st and 2nd Light Battalions of Zaragoza, the Light Battalion of Cerezo, the Light Battalion of Catalan Chasseurs, the Battalion of Pioneers, and the 2nd Battalion of Volunteers of Aragon; Brigadier Fivaller y Bou's division, with the Battalion of the Royal Spanish Guards, the 1st Battalion of Volunteers of Aragon, the 2nd Regiment of Valencia, the Battalion of Volunteers of Doyle, and the 2nd Battalion of Chasseurs Fernando VII; Brigadier Manso's division, with the 1st Battalion of Volunteers of Huesca, the Battalion of Las Peñas de San Pedro, the Battalion of Shooters of Murcia, the Battalion of Floridablanca, the Battalion of Volunteers of Cartagena, the 1st, 2nd and 3rd Regiments of Volunteers of Murcia, and the Swiss Battalion of Aragon; and General Saint Marcq's division, with the 1st Battalion of Volunteers of Bourbon, the 1st Battalion of Volunteers of Castile, the 1st Regiment of Turia, the 1st Battalion of Chasseurs, the Regiment of Campo Segorbino, the Battalion of Volunteers of Chelva, the Regiment of Volunteers of Alicante, the Provincial Regiment of Soria, and the 5th Regiment of Murcia. In total, 32,421 men.[1]

Napoleonic Army: under the command of Marshal Mortier (from 15 December to 29 December 1808), General Junot (from 29 December 1808 to 22 January 1809) and Marshal Lannes (from 23 January 1809 to 3 March 1809), the following army corps:

III Army Corps (under the command of Marshal Moncey until 29 December 1808 and then General Junot until the end of the siege): the 1st Division (Grandjean), including the 70th Regiment of Line Infantry (1 bn) and the 2nd Regiment of Light Infantry (1 detachment), comprising the 1st Brigade (Habert), with the 14th Regiment of Line Infantry (4 bns) and the 2nd Regiment of Infantry of Vístula (2 bns), and the 2nd Brigade (Laval), with the 44th Regiment of Line Infantry (3 bns) and the 3rd Regiment of Infantry of Vístula (2 bns); the 2nd Division (Musnier), comprising the 1st Brigade (Brun), with the 114th Regiment of Line Infantry (4 bns) and the 1st Regiment of Infantry of Vístula (2 bns) and the 2nd Brigade (Razout), with the 115th Regiment of Line Infantry (4 bns); the 3rd Division (Morlot), comprising the 1st Brigade (Rostolland), with the 5th Regiment of Light Infantry (2 bns) and the 116th Regiment of Line Infantry (2 bns), the 2nd Brigade (Augereau), with the 117th Regiment of Line Infantry (4 bns), and the 3rd Brigade (Buget), with the 121st Regiment of Line Infantry (4 bns) and the 2nd Legion of Reserve (4 bns). The cavalry division of Brigade Wathier, comprising the 1st Provisional Regiment of Hussars (4 sqns), the 2nd, 4th (4 sqns) and 10th Regiments of Hussars (1 detachment), the 13th Regiment of Cuirassiers (4 sqns), the Regiment of Cavalry of Marche (4 sqns), the Regiment of Lancers of Vístula (1 detachment), and the Gendarmerie (1 detachment).

V Army Corps, under the command of Marshal Mortier, Duke of Treviso: the 1st Division (Suchet), comprising the 1st Brigade (Dumotier), with the 17th Regiment of Light Infantry (3 bns), the 34th Regiment of Line Infantry (4 bns) and the 40th Regiment of Line Infantry (3 bns), and the 2nd Brigade (Girard), with the 64th Regiment of Line Infantry (3 bns), the 88th Regiment of Line Infantry (2 bns); the 2nd Division (Gazan), comprising the 1st Brigade (Guérin), with the 21st Regiment of Light Infantry (3 bns), and the 2nd Brigade (Taupin), with the 100th Regiment of Line Infantry (3 bns), the 28th Regiment of Light Infantry (3 bns) and the 103rd Regiment of Line Infantry (3 bns). Cavalry from Brigade Delage, comprising the 10th Regiment of Hussars (3 sqns), the 21st Regiment of Mounted Chasseurs (3 sqns) and the Gendarmerie (1 detachment). Artillery under the command of General Dedon-Duclos. Engineers and sappers under the command of General Lacoste. In total, 49,956 men.[2]

Background[3]

After the blows received by the Napoleonic forces in the summer of 1808, the Emperor himself decided he would personally put an end to the 'Spanish problem'. Commanding his Grand Armée, he destroyed the Spanish armies that stood in his way, among them General Castaños's Army of the Centre and Palafox's Reserve Army, which had faced the French at Tudela. While Moncey pursued Castaños towards Castile la Mancha, the remains of the Reserve Army, chased by Mortier, took refuge in Zaragoza. Mortier's troops were joined by Mousnier's Army Corps to annihilate Palafox's army and, incidentally, to conquer the yet-untamed Zaragoza. On 20 December 1808 the second siege of the city began. Zaragoza had to fall, and this time the French generals had done their homework. On this occasion the Napoleonic troops numbered approximately 30,000 combatants, a figure that would eventually rise to 50,000. They also had a larger artillery force, with more than a hundred batteries, plus a colossal quantity of sapping tools.

The siege

The plan designed by Mortier and Moncey was relatively simple and forceful. It was based on their tremendous military superiority, allowing them to make a pincer attack on the city. One column, advancing from the southwest of the city would assault the heights of Torrero, Buenavista, La Bernardona and the right bank of the Huerva, while the other column, from the north, would attack the Arrabal district. Once these positions were taken, the artillery batteries could be set up to break the Zaragozans' iron will to defend themselves. The aim was to try to avoid the carnage that the first siege had become for General Lefebvre-Desnouettes' forces. But Mortier and Moncey had no idea what they faced.

At dawn on the 21st, the four French divisions on the right bank of the Ebro, commanded by Generals Morlot, Musnier, Suchet and Grandjean, prepared to attack the heights of Torrero, Buenavista, La Bernardona and the right bank of the Huerva. Altogether they numbered about 25,000 soldiers, far more than the 6,000 or so men available to General Saint Marcq for the defence of El Torrero. The French deployment was swift and forceful, especially the Laval and Habert brigades. Saint Marc, faced with the danger of being overrun, withdrew, abandoning the positions. But the people of Zaragoza, who were willing to die among the ruins of their houses, did not accept the retreat and tried to lynch Saint Marc when he crossed the Santa Engracia Gate. The firm intervention of José de Palafox saved his life at the most critical moment. For his part, Suchet had easily taken the Bernardona defended by O'Neill's men.

The pincer was to be closed by General Gazan's division, which was to take the Arrabal district. His attack started late. He had camped his troops some 15km (9 miles) from the city, and his advancing troops had to cross fields that had been flooded by the city's defenders, in anticipation of such an attack. The delays this caused were compounded by the fierce resistance they encountered at the Torre del Arzobispo, a fortified position defended by the Swiss Regiment of Aragon, who held on grimly for hours, despite calamitous losses (only 317 of the 666 Swiss troops commanded by Colonel Fleury were saved). In addition to inflicting a huge number of casualties on Gazan's troops, they gave General Villacampa's troops precious time to prepare to defend themselves in the Arrabal. The Spanish defences held, and after a bloody battle Gazan's men finally had to retreat. On that day, they had suffered 50 per cent casualties, dead and wounded. Losses on this scale were unheard of, unbearable. Once again, a French general had underestimated the fierce will of the Zaragozans to defend themselves. Moncey and Mortier had failed. The city could not be taken quickly. Colonel Lacoste's time had come.

Bruno Lacoste knew what he was up against. Without doubt, he was one of the best engineers in Napoleon's army and had already participated in the first siege. He designed a plan to dig trenches to attack the city, following the teachings of the great Vauban. That plan, which had the appearance of being definitive, was going to take time. But as the days went by, the morale of the French troops plummeted, an inevitable result of the cold and the lack of food. The situation inside the city was no better. Zaragoza lacked everything: food, clothing, ammunition. Despite this, some sorties were made against the French lines, with some success, especially that of Villacampa on 24 December and that of Gómez de Butrón and Palafox on the 31st of that same month. However, Lacoste's plan was still on course. The Spanish efforts delayed the digging, but could not stop it. The first trenches to reach their objective were those dug on the southeast front, along the Huerva river, which were intended to hit the city's two outer defensive redoubts: the convent of San José and the El Pilar redoubt. The fighting here was intense and the defenders heroic, but the convent fell into French hands on 10 January and the redoubt on the 15th. During the fighting a cannonball killed Colonel Antonio Sangenís, the head of the Spanish engineers, on the spot. Worse, the southern front of the city had been left exposed to the French, having lost all the outer defensive redoubts. Now the city depended on its weak walls. But the French did not attempt any assault, and limited themselves to digging new trenches from the areas they had conquered. The next few weeks were very hard for the combatants on both sides. Hunger, cold weather and the very high casualties in combat kept the situation at a stalemate. In addition, the French feared being attacked by a Spanish relieving force, but any such efforts by the Spanish were quickly neutralized by columns sent by the besieging army, so there was no real threat. But in mid-January one event would change everything: Marshal Lannes, the Duke of Montebello, arrived at Zaragoza to command the siege. Lannes was Napoleon's best marshal at the time, as well as being one of his best friends. Aquillué points out that, were it not for his arrival, the besieging troops would most likely have withdrawn. But the charismatic Lannes, and the tons of rations he brought with him, boosted the morale of the deeply demoralized French soldiers.

In the following days Lannes intensified the bombardment of the city, attacking not just military targets but civilian targets as well, with the aim of sapping the morale of the Zaragozans, thus making them the more ready to capitulate.

On 24 January the French presented the city with a last chance to surrender, but naturally the citizens rejected this with the utmost contempt. Therefore, after further intensifying the bombardment and achieving three practicable breaches, Lannes ordered a general assault for the morning of 27 January. The troops were divided into three columns for the attack. The only column that really achieved its objective was the one sent to capture the convent of Santa Engracia, or what was left of it. Even here, the French faced a fanatical defence for each inch of ground, fighting not only soldiers but friars, women and even children. By nightfall the entire convent was in French hands, but they were unable to advance further. But that day the nature of the siege changed: finally the French had a foothold in the city. In a few hours the battlefield was going to be the city's streets and buildings.

The next French target was the convents of Santa Mónica and San Agustín, which were fiercely defended and resisted until 30 January. By 2 February there was house to house fighting. On that day Bruno Lacoste, the chief of the imperial engineers, was killed in action, and the numbers of casualties on both sides were staggering. The French were horrified. They had never seen anything like it. Lannes wrote to Napoleon:

> I have never seen such fierceness as that shown by our enemies in the defence of this place ... It is necessary to organize an assault on every house. The siege of Zaragoza is nothing like our previous wars. It is a war that horrifies ... A siege in each street, a mine under each house. To be forced to kill so many brave men, or rather so many furious! This is terrible. Victory is pitiful.

Powerful words from a commander who had participated in the main battles in Central Europe.

The Aragonese, furthermore, were now suffering the onslaught of a new enemy: typhus, which decimated the defenders with more ferocity than the French themselves. But the French, despite the fact that nearly 9,000 of them were occupying different parts of the city, were totally defeated: even now the Zaragozans did not surrender. They had captured barely a fifth of the city but had suffered 25 per cent casualties. The numbers were unacceptable. Thus, Lannes decided to end the house-to-house assaults; from then on, any objective to be conquered would be first mined and reduced to rubble, and then attacked. He knew he must drastically reduce the number of casualties among his men, otherwise a retreat was unavoidable. Thus, successively, convents, churches, houses, palaces fell and the French conquered only their smoking ruins. But this process slowed the advance, and it took days just to cross a street. For example, on 10 February a 3,000lb gunpowder mine engulfed the San Francisco monastery, burying the grenadiers of the Valencia Regiment. Only one tower remained standing, but the Swiss defending it did not stop shooting. They would not surrender! The French had to dislodge them at bayonet point, killing them all except their commander, the heroic Colonel Fleury, who was taken prisoner. The French were becoming desperate. They could not understand the fanaticism with which the Zaragozans continued to defend themselves. They knew that there were hardly any combatants left, civilian or military, who had not been victims of war, famine or typhus, but even so, they fought savagely for every inch of ground.

Lannes was in a hurry to put an end to this madness. He fixed his objective, again, in the Arrabal, the last strong point of the defence of the city, in particular the convents of Santa Isabel and San Lázaro. Brigadier Manso stoutly defended the area until 18 February, when, after ten days of fighting without quarter, his original 2,000 defenders had all been killed or taken prisoner, including Manso himself, who died a few days later of typhus. On the 19th the Baron of Warsage, a nobleman of Belgian origin who, from the beginning of the conflict, had been a significant commander on the Spanish side, died leading a vain counterattack to reconquer the Arrabal. By the next day the French had already placed six mines under the Coso, the nerve centre of the city, where the Basilica of Pilar, the cathedral and the Seo and the Episcopal Palace were located. Everything was about to blow up. At this point a white flag was raised. Palafox, himself ill with typhus, had ceded his command to a commission that, in view of the situation, had no choice but to surrender. It is estimated that by that time there were about 14,000 inhabitants in the city, civilians and soldiers. This meant that during the second siege no fewer than 60,000 people had died. The city itself, known as the 'Florence of Spain' for its beauty and opulence, was nothing more than a jumble of rubble. The soldiers who had survived, including Palafox, were taken to France as prisoners. Others were less lucky, like the priests Boggiero and Sas, who were mercilessly executed. Lannes, depressed and exhausted, took the road back to France in March, leaving Suchet at the head of the government of Aragon. He never returned to Spain.[4]

Notes

1. Pérez Francés (2017), pp. 108–9.
2. Sorando (2010).
3. As in the case of the first siege, this chapter is based fundamentally on Aquillué (2021).
4. Aquillué (2021); Pérez Francés (2017); Sala Valdés (1908); Alcaide (1830); VVAA (1820), pp. 182–260.

Chapter Sixteen

The Battle of Valls

Date: 25 February 1809. *Place*: Valls, Catalonia.
Result: Napoleonic victory.

Order of battle

Spanish Army: Castro's Division, under the command of General Theodor von Reding, comprising the Regiment of Wimfpen, the Regiment of Reding, the Regiment of Granada, the Regiment of Santa Fe, the Regiment of Antequera, and the Regiment of Light Infantry de Tarragona. Marti's Division, comprising the Battalion of Royal Walloon Guards, the Battalion of Royal Spanish Guards, the Regiments of Baza, Almería, Soria, Saboya and Iliberia, the Battalion of Volunteers of Palma, the Battalion of Provincial Grenadiers of Old Castile, and the Battalion of Provincial Grenadiers of New Castile. Cavalry: the Regiment of Santiago, the Regiment of Hussars of Spain, and the Regiment of Hussars of Granada. Troops of *Miquetels*: Tercios of Igualada, Lleida and Tarragona. In total, around 15,000 men.[1]

Napoleonic Army: General Laurent Gouvion Saint-Cyr commanding the following units: Souham's division, comprising the 1st Regiment of Light Infantry and the 42th Regiment of Line Infantry; Pino's división, with the Brigade Mazzuchelli, including the 1st and 2nd Regiments of Light Infantry of the Reign of Italy, and the Brigade Fontane, with the 1st Regiment of Line Infantry of the

Reign of Italy (3 bns). Cavalry: the 24th Regiment of Dragoons, the 1st Regiment of Mounted Chasseurs 'Real Italiano' and the Regiment of Dragoons 'Dragoni Napoleone'. In total, near 13,000 men.[2]

Background

The Captain General of Catalonia, Domingo Traggia, was called to serve on the Supreme Central Junta, and was replaced by General Joan Miquel de Vives. However, the Spanish soon began to suffer serious defeats and some of the heroes of the first siege of Girona, such as Raymond de Caldagués and Narcís de la Valette, were captured and sent to France. But the Supreme Junta of Catalonia remained convinced that it was time to conquer Barcelona and strike a definitive blow in the war. As they did not have enough troops, they persuaded the Central Supreme Junta to send reinforcements. The new troops were sent under the command of Theodor von Reding, the victor of Bailén. He was a legend among the Spanish troops. The French responded by calling in General Laurent Gouvion Saint-Cyr, who managed to break the blockade. The French also hoped to eliminate all the military forces in Catalonia in order that they could conquer its main cities at a later date. Saint-Cyr therefore sought a confrontation with the Spanish, which he achieved at Cardedeu (16 December) and Molins de Rei (21 December), which resulted in two disasters for the army of General Vives, who was dismissed from his position as Captain General of Catalonia, being replaced by Theodor von Reding. Despite the desire to blockade Barcelona again, Reding was forced to retreat south towards Tarragona. Saint-Cyr guessed the Spanish intentions and placed his divisions astride two of the possible routes that Reding's men could use to return to Tarragona: Pino's division at Pla de Santa Maria and Southam's division at Valls.

The battle

On the night of 24/25 February Reding's troops, in the most sepulchral of silences, crossed the Francolí river over the so-called Goi bridge,[3] a few miles from Valls. About half of the Spanish forces had crossed the bridge when a French patrol discovered them and opened fire before riding away. Some Spaniards took off in pursuit and unwittingly ended up in the French camp, where they were taken prisoner. Saint-Cyr ordered Souham to send an advance guard of his light infantry to harass the Spanish and give Pino's division time to reach them. At last he had the chance to destroy the Army of Catalonia. Reding, unwilling to shy away from the battle, ordered the troops that had already crossed the bridge to fall back, placing Martí's division on the right of the bridge and Castro's on the left.

Noting the weakness of the French left flank, Reding ordered Martí to ford the river and try to outflank the enemy. But the French repulsed the initial attack and, with reinforcements already arriving from Pino's division, Martí feared that he would be outflanked, so Reding ordered the rest of the Spanish line to cross the river and concentrate their attack on the French centre. This diversionary manoeuvre worked. The Spanish attack was successful and the two lines stabilized, this time on the right bank of the Francolí. Reding and Martí talked again. With the arrival of the Pino's division, the Majorcan general was in favour of withdrawal. Reding, who refused to accept another defeat, was aware of his compromised situation. Furthermore, a retreat at such a time could easily become a rout, and even if the retreat was executed in an orderly manner, the baggage train would most likely be lost. So they agreed that Martí himself would ride to Tarragona and request reinforcements from the city's governor, Juan Smith, to enable him to protect the Spanish retreat. Martí rode to Tarragona, but would never return. Smith refused to commit his meagre garrison to an enterprise that he felt was unlikely to succeed. Martí was replaced in his role by General Jaime García Conde. Reding also sent the commander of his artillery, Juan de Ara, to the town of Constantí to look for a possible route of retreat.[4]

Meanwhile, Reding withdrew his troops back to the left bank of the Francolí. This operation was carried out in an orderly manner, partly thanks to French passivity. Without waiting for reinforcements from Tarragona (Reding did not suspect that they would never arrive), he slightly moved his line until his men occupied a steep hill. This was a solid defensive position. In fact, the hill was so steep that Reding decided to go onto the defensive, and instead of starting the retreat, he prepared to wait for the attack of Saint-Cyr's men. An offensive, in these circumstances, was little short of suicidal, but few generals could beat the Lorraine man in audacity. Once all of Pino's division had arrived, he arranged his army in four columns: the two on the wings commanded by the French brigadier generals Verges and Demoulin, and the ones in the centre by the Italian brigadier generals Mazzuchelli and Fontane. The cavalry was ordered to protect the flanks, except for the 24th Dragoons who were positioned near the Goi bridge. To the south the bridge known as Valls was easily taken by Demoulin's column and the Italian Chasseurs.

At 3.30pm the Franco-Italians began to advance. Contrary to Saint-Cyr's prediction, on this occasion the Spanish line held firm and did not flee in disarray as the enemy troops advanced inexorably towards them with fixed bayonets. There were a few minutes of intense fire, with a very high number of casualties among the attackers, but the advance continued. Seeing how difficult the situation was, Saint-Cyr decided to throw the 24th Dragoons into the centre of the Spanish infantry. This was a suicide attack: they had to cross the Goi bridge and climb the hill in the face of the Spanish fire. At the head of the dragoons was Colonel Jacques-Antoine-Adrien Delort, who had distinguished himself in numerous battles in Central Europe, notably at Austerlitz, where he had been badly wounded. Steel in hand, and calling to his men, he galloped across the bridge and rode to the top of the hill. Despite taking casualties, the dragoons managed to reach the Spanish centre lines and disrupt them. Gradually, the Spanish lines began to fall apart and the soldiers fled in disarray. The troops on Reding's flanks, seeing that they were likely to be overrun, also began to flee. For its part, the

Mazzuchelli Brigade hastily advanced towards the area where the Spanish artillery was stationed, and the guns were captured by the Dragoni Napoleone. By 4.00pm the vanguard line of the Army of Catalonia had crumbled. Initially, the rear line withstood the French onslaught. Reding himself and his staff, in a desperate attempt to defend themselves, launched themselves against the French, but found themselves surrounded by Imperial dragoons. A horseman named Bouzzon slashed at them, but shortly afterwards Second Lieutenant Bertinot recognized Reding and wanted to take him prisoner, but a member of the general's escort shot the French officer down and the Swiss general was miraculously saved.[5] The French set off in pursuit of the scattered Spanish troops, but as night fell, the darkness saved them.

Spanish casualties totalled 3,000 men, including dead, wounded and prisoners, in addition to the loss of the baggage train, with all the cannon and ammunition. General Theodor von Reding, hero of Bailén, would die in Tarragona a few days later from wounds suffered in the battle. In addition, Lieutenant Colonel Ramón Armenta of the Mounted Chasseurs of Catalonia and the Marquis of Sala, lieutenant of the Royal Walloon Guards, died in action. Colonel Carlos Briet de Saint-Ellier, in command of the García Conde Division, was wounded in the arm. Among those taken prisoner were the colonel of the Santiago Regiment, the Marquis of Castelldosrius (at the hands of the Dragoni squadron leader Napoleone Fortunato Schiazzetti[6]); Colonel Manuel Dumont, commander of the Royal Walloon Guards; Lieutenant Colonel Manuel Antúnez, commander of the Royal Spanish Guards; and three of Reding's aides-de-camp, Francisco Tobaldo Chichery, Carlos Osorno and British officer Charles Reed.[7] French casualties were 1,000 men. In the aftermath of the battle Saint-Cyr, with no army to contend with, roamed the Tarragona countryside. He left Pino's division at Valls and with Souham reached the walls of Tarragona. But the city, overcrowded with refugees, was suffering from a typhus epidemic and, without siege weapons, he decided to move on. Souham entered Reus and occupied it without opposition. Saint-Cyr retreated northwards and prepared for the capture of Girona.[8]

Notes

1. Esteban (2009), I, p. 79.
2. Esteban (2009), I, p. 81.
3. Also known as the Battle of Goi Bridge.
4. Cabanes (1815), p. 174. García Conde distinguished himself in the second siege of Girona and was later taken prisoner by Suchet near Lleida in 1810, spending the rest of the war in a French prison.
5. VVAA (1831), p. 325.
6. Blog *Los Viajes de Byron*. Saint-Cyr also mentions it in his memoirs, although in his case he is wrong in spelling the name of this Spanish officer, which he cites as 'Castel d'Orius' (p. 126). This nobleman, named Francisco Javier de Oms y de Santa Pau, spent the rest of the war as a prisoner in a French prison.
7. Iglesias (2013), p. 185. Spanish sources erroneously cite him as Reid, perhaps following Saint-Cyr (p. 423), who as a general was extraordinary, but his spelling was poor.
8. Esteban (2009), I and II; Murillo (2006); Rovira (2011); the memoirs of Saint-Cyr.

Chapter Seventeen

The Battle of Medellín

Date: 28 March 1809. *Place*: Medellín, Extremadura.
Result: Napoleonic victory.

Order of battle

Spanish Army: The Army of Extremadura under the command of Lieutenant General Gregorio García de la Cuesta: Vanguard Division, under the command of General Juan de Henestrosa, comprising the Battalion of General's Grenadiers, the Battalion of Provincial Grenadiers, the Regiment of Light Infantry of Antequera (2 bns), the Regiment of Light Infantry of La Serena (1 bn) and the Regiment of Light Infantry of Volunteers of Plasencia (1 bn); the 1st Division, under the Duke of Parque, comprising the Regiment of Royal Walloon Guards (2 bns), the Regiment of Royal Spanish Guards (1 bn), the Regiment of Jaen (2 bns), the Regiment of Volunteers of Osuna (2 bns), and the Regiments of the Provincial Militias of Burgos, Guadix and Salamanca; the 2nd Division, under General Francisco Trías, comprising the Regiment of Ireland (2 bns), the 2nd Regiment of Majorca (2 bns), the 2nd Regiment of Seville (1 bn), the 2nd Regiment of Catalan Volunteers (1 bn), the Regiment of Light Infantry Shooters of Mérida (1 bn), the Regiment of Light Infantry of Valencia-Albuquerque (1 bn), and the Regiments of the Provincial Militias of Badajoz and Toledo; the 3rd Division, under General Marquis of Portago, comprising the Regiment of Badajoz (2 bns), the 2nd Regiment of Madrid's Volunteers (2 bns),

77

the 3rd Regiment of Seville's Volunteers (1 bn), the Regiment of Murcia (1 bn), the 1st and 2nd Regiments of Córdoba (1 bn each), and the Battalion of the Provincial Militia of Cádiz. The Division of Andalucía under the Duke of Albuquerque, comprising the 2nd Regiment of Naval Infantry (1 bn), the Battalion Tercio Unido of Castilla, and the Regiments of Light Infantry of Cádiz and Campo Mayor (1 bn each). The Cavalry Division under General Ramón Villalba, comprising the Carabineers of Extremadura (1 coy), the Regiment of the King (2 sqns), the Regiment of the Infante (4 sqns), the Dragoons of the Queen (2 sqns), the Dragons of Almansa (4 sqns), the Spanish Hussars (4 sqns), the Hussars of Extremadura (4 sqns), and the Mounted Chasseurs of Alcántara (1 sqn), Andalucía (2 sqns), Córdoba (2 sqns), Sagrario de Toledo (2 sqns) and Granada de Llerena (2 sqns). Attached were 30 cannon and their artillerymen under the command of General Vicente Rosique. Engineers and sappers under the command of General Manuel Zappino. In total, 28,337 men.

Napoleonic Army: I Army Corps under the command of Marshal Victor, Duke of Belluno, including the 1st Division under General Ruffin, comprising the Chaudron-Rousseau Brigade, with the 9th Regiment of Light Infantry (3 bns) and the 24th Regiment of Line Infantry (3 bns); the Barrois Brigade, with the 96th Regiment of Line Infantry (3 bns); the 2nd Division under General Villatte, with the Cassagne Brigade, with the 27th Regiment of Light Infantry (3 bns) and the 94th Regiment of Line Infantry (3 bns); the Puthod Brigade, with the 63rd Regiment of Line Infantry (3 bns) and the 95th Regiment of Line Infantry (3 bns); the 3rd Division (in fact the 2nd Division of the IV Army Corps) of General Lasalle, with a battalion of *voltigeurs*; the Weler Brigade, with the 4th Regiment of Line Infantry of Baden (2 bns) and the 2nd Regiment of Line Infantry of Nassau (2 bns); the Schäffer Brigade, with the Regiment of Line Infantry of Frankfurt (1 coy) and the 4th Regiment of Line Infantry of Hesse (1 coy); and the Chassé Brigade, with the 2nd Regiment of Line Infantry of Holland (1 bn) and the 4th Regiment of Line Infantry of Holland (2 bns). Division of light cavalry under the command of the Count of Lasalle, with the 2nd Regiment of Hussars (1 sqn), the 4th Regiment of Hussars (1 sqn), the 5th Regiment of Mounted Chasseurs (3 sqns), the 10th Regiment of Mounted Chasseurs (3 sqns) and the 26th Regiment of Mounted Chasseurs (3 sqns). The 1st Division of Dragoons under General La Tour-Maubourg, with the Perreymond Brigade, with the 2nd Regiment of Dragoons (3 sqns); the Dullembourg Brigade, with the 14th Regiment of Dragoons (1 sqn); the Digeon Brigade, with the 20th Regiment of Dragoons (3 sqns) and the 26th Regiment of Dragoons (3 sqns). Artillery under the command of General Sénarmont, including 46 cannon and their artillerymen. In total, 17,995 men.

Background[1]

After the fall of Madrid, Napoleon Bonaparte considered the Spanish resistance quashed and he returned to France, to counter the Austrian invasion of the

Kingdom of Bavaria. The Fifth Coalition was looming. He believed that his generals in Spain would be capable of dealing with what he considered to be the last pockets of resistance, and he entrusted the invasion of Portugal to Marshal Soult, one of his best commanders. The plan, on paper, was simple. Soult's II Army Corps, helped by Ney's VI Corps, would invade Portugal through Porto, penetrating the country via Galicia. Meanwhile, Victor's I Army Corps would wait for Soult to reach Lisbon to attack either Andalusia or Portugal.

As for the Army of Extremadura, under the command of General José Galluzo, the situation was far from idyllic. He had not been able to help Madrid and could only gather and regroup the remnants of the Army of the Centre that took refuge in Talavera de la Reina. Faced with the advance of the French I Army Corps, at that time under the command of Lefebvre, Galluzo withdrew to defend the Tagus line, trying to prevent the French troops from crossing the five bridges he had to defend. But on 20 December the Archbishop's Bridge fell into Lefebvre's hands. On the 24th Galluzo lost the Conde bridge, and on the 25th the Almaraz bridge. After this, Galluzo retreated to Zalamea de la Serena in Badajoz. Near this town, in Mérida, he encountered the members of the Central Supreme Junta on their way to Seville. The atmosphere was tense as the people demanded solutions. Among the entourage was General García de la Cuesta, who had been arrested after his defeats with the Castilian Army and his bitter disagreements with the Central Supreme Junta. The old general was acclaimed by the people, who in turn demanded Galluzo's dismissal. The Junta, fearing an explosive popular reaction (by that point in the war there were already plenty of examples of lynchings between governors and generals), decided to depose Galluzo and proclaimed García de la Cuesta commander-in-chief of the Army of Extremadura.[2] His first action was to reorganize the soldiers who were widely dispersed, demoralized and seriously lacking in equipment and weapons. Many of these troops were either inexperienced or were the survivors of the serious defeats that had plagued the Army of the Centre, such as Tudela or Uclés. The good news was that the French troops halted their advance until mid-March. In addition, García de la Cuesta had received various units from the Division of the North, with which he trusted that his army would enjoy a notable qualitative leap forward. By mid-March his troops were distributed as follows: Henestrosa's Vanguard Division was in Almaraz; about 15km (9 miles) to the south, in Mesas de Íbor, was the 1st Division under the Duke of Parque; about 10km (6 miles) further south, in Fresnedoso, was the 2nd Division under Trías; while in the rear were quartered the Cavalry Division and the 3rd Division under the Marquis of Portago, as a reserve, together with the General Headquarters.

On 15 March Marshal Victor, who had not heard from Soult for weeks, took his I Army Corps across the Tagus. The Napoleonic offensive had begun. The first clash took place in Mesas de Íbor on 17 March. The Duke of Parque had troops as strong as the Royal Walloon Guards, the Royal Spanish Guards and the Jaén Regiment, as well as the Infante Cavalry Regiment and the Hussars of

Extremadura, not to mention a very steep terrain that was favourable for defence. In front of them Leval's Division was sent to attack with its German battalions. The action lasted all day and, despite the fierce resistance of the Spaniards, the Germans' drive and numerical superiority finally tipped the balance in their favour. At the end of the day the Duke of Parque had no choice but to order a retreat, which was carried out in good order, largely thanks to the efficient work of the cavalry. Both forces met again the next day in Valdecañas, causing the Duke of Parque to withdraw one more time. Seeing the risk of his divisions being overrun, García de la Cuesta decided to withdraw 90km (60 miles) south to Trujillo, where he arrived on the 19th. Pursued by Victor's forces, he didn't stop in the town but continued on his way south. The next day Victor entered Trujillo. That day the so-called Combat of the Berrocales took place, in which a part of the Henestrosa Division managed to ambush 450 horsemen of the French 5th Chasseurs, who were pursuing a detachment of Royal Carabinieri. The French suffered a setback that cost them between 80 and 100 casualties.

On 21 March the Spanish troops crossed the Miajadas. Henestrosa realized that the 10th Chasseurs had approached the main body of the Napoleonic army and, with the help of the Infante and Almansa cavalry regiments, ambushed them once again. The general had ordered no quarter. The French suffered 126 casualties, including 63 dead. The survivors recounted how many of their comrades had been killed in cold blood. A wave of indignant rage swept through the French ranks. The next day the Army of Extremadura arrived in Medellín. Cuesta and Victor spent a few days playing cat and mouse. The Cantabrian general knew that he could not retire indefinitely. Meanwhile, the French marshal was clear that his objective was to conquer Badajoz and he could not entertain himself by pursuing the Army of Extremadura southwards. The time had come for a decisive battle. Victor, learning that Cuesta had divided his troops, finally decided to cross the Guadiana river on the 28th. This was an extremely reckless manoeuvre, since Cuesta was very close and all the French troops had to cross over the Austrias bridge, built in 1630. The Army of Extremadura was located in the town of Don Benito, barely 10km (6 miles) from the bridge. It was the opportunity that Cuesta had been waiting for.

The battle

The first French units to cross the Austrias bridge were Lasalle's light cavalry followed by La Tour-Mabourg's dragoons and Leval's German infantry division. The marshal had also crossed, occupying the castle of Medellín. A critical moment had now arrived for the French. The Spanish troops had marched up and, to Victor's surprise, were already deploying for battle. General Lasalle urgently met with the colonels of his cavalry regiments and they decided to march against the enemy. La Tour-Maubourg's dragoons were not going to be left behind. Cuesta had risked a deployment in a long line, with no more reserves than Zayas' battalions. Moreover, forming up such a long line had to be a slow process so that it remained organized. When the first shots were fired, Leval's German division, badly punished in the actions of the previous days, had to hold its ground to allow the rest of the French infantry to pass over the bridge. The arrival of the Senarmont artillery gave Victor a break. The artillerymen quickly deployed their batteries and the Spanish lines were contained (*see* Map 5).

Towards midday there took place what was probably the biggest duel of *voltigeurs* of the Peninsular War. Both sides were also bombarded by enemy artillery. La Tour-Maubourg seemed to see a gap between the Duke of Parque's lines and charged towards it. However, a timely response from the Spanish infantry and artillerymen forced him to retreat. But Victor was still buying precious time to move all his troops to the south bank of the Guadiana and balance the forces on the battlefield.

By 4.00pm García de la Cuesta saw that the key to the battle lay in beating the extreme right of the French line, where ten cannon were located, defended by the 9th Light Infantry. Various squadrons of Spanish cavalry charged. Brigadier General Meusnier ordered his men to form a square, repelling the attack. But it seems that luck was with the Army of Extremadura. The French *voltigeurs* pulled back on all fronts as the Spanish lines advanced steadily. Everything seemed to indicate that the battle was going the way of the Spanish. The French were forced to launch the dragoons in a desperate charge. In reply, Cuesta launched his squadrons of Almansa, Infante and the Imperial Chasseurs of Toledo, but they faltered and retreated in disorder into the Spanish infantry line. In an instant, the Spanish front became chaotic. Cuesta and his general staff tried in vain to allow their cavalry to pass through, but in the midst of the confusion La Tour-Maubourg's dragoons attacked the Spanish left wing. Some of the battalions there fell apart, while others surrendered *en masse*. The Royal Walloon Guards tried to hold on, but they were unsupported and were slaughtered. Villatte moved his men forward, who had just destroyed the entire left wing. The Trias Division, seeing itself also overrun, broke up. Only the right wing, under the command of General Eguía, remained firm, but he did not react in time to the events on the field and his men became infected by the general panic. General Lassalle saw an opportunity to launch his hussars against the Andalusian Chasseurs, who fled. Only the Albuquerque Division kept its composure, at least until the Lassalle Hussars arrived. The infantry troops who had not fled in terror were surrounded and mercilessly annihilated. Some cavalry squadrons, such as the Spanish Voluntary Chasseurs and the Hussars of Extremadura, tried to break through the encirclement. In the French lines they began to shout that no prisoners would be taken, and all the Spanish troops who fell into their hands were killed. Entire battalions begged to surrender, but no quarter was given. It was carnage. Those who managed to flee were cut down by hussars and dragoons. There seemed to be no escape from this slaughter, until in the afternoon torrential rain fell on the battlefield.

By nightfall the Army of Extremadura had suffered 10,000 casualties, of which only 1,850 were prisoners. Some regiments, such as the 2nd Majorca or Campo Mayor, were totally annihilated. Of the 750 men of the Provincial Militia of Toledo who started the battle, only 55 survived. Of the 650 men of the Tiradores de Cádiz, 150 escaped. Among the dead and prisoners were a multitude of officers, most notably General Francisco Trías, who had been wounded seven times and was left for dead on the battlefield. The French picked him up and healed him, letting him go on his word of honour never to take up arms against them again. He retired to Cádiz, where he spent the rest of the war. The French also suffered a high number of casualties, estimated at 4,000. The units that suffered the most were the German cavalry and infantry units, which had repeatedly suffered heavy losses and would cease to be operational in a few months. Among the illustrious wounded were Colonel Louis Huguet-Chataux, Marshal Victor's aide-de-camp and son-in-law, since he was married to his eldest daughter Victorine,[3] and the colonel of the 2nd Nassau Regiment, August Heinrich Ernst von Kruse, who would continue to fight tirelessly in Spain until the battle of Vitoria but who, in 1813, when Nassau changed sides, became Napoleon's enemy, forming part of Wellington's general staff at Waterloo.

The next day the battlefield was a scene of desolation, with thousands of abandoned corpses, most of them still with their rifles. The French razed Medellín to the ground, destroying some 290 houses (representing more than half the population), as well as many of its most emblematic buildings, such as two convents, the town hall, the Ecclesiastical Council building, the Orphans' Asylum and even the birth house of the famous *conquistador* Hernán Cortés.[4]

Yet, for Victor, Medellín was a Pyrrhic victory. He had had no news of Sebastiani, Ney or Soult. Guerrillas massacred his couriers and raided his overstretched supply lines, and in addition he had to face the threat of the renewed Army of Extremadura and the British troops in Portugal. So, a few weeks later, Victor withdrew again towards Castile la Mancha. Fighting in Spain was madness. Meanwhile, in the revitalized Army of Extremadura García de la Cuesta was recognized for the great work of his infantry; he was confirmed in office and sent new reinforcements. And while it is true that some cavalry officers were punished, a shield of distinction was created to reward troops for their remarkable performance on the battlefield.[5] In addition, numerous promotions were granted to their officers, along with a number of life pensions, and the Duke of Parque was awarded the Grand Cross of the Order of Charles III.[6]

Notes

1. Unless otherwise indicated, this chapter is based on the report of General García de la Cuesta published in the *Extraordinary Government Gazette* dated 11 April 1809 and on the work of Sañudo Bayón (2009).
2. Sarmiento Pérez (2010).
3. Here is a story that deserves to be told. Chataux was an excellent officer. In 1814 he was already a general, when he took part in the battle of Montereau in France after the Central European armies

Episode du siège de Saragosse: assaut du monastère de Santa Engracia, le 8 février 1809, by Louis-François, Baron Lejeune. (*Musée National du Château de Versailles*)

Portrait of Ferdinand VII, by Vicente López Portaña. (*Museo del Prado*)

Portrait of Joseph Bonaparte, by François Gérard. (*Musée National du Château de Fontainebleau*)

Portrait of Juan Martín Díaz, known as El Empecinado ('The Undaunted'), by Francisco de Goya.
(National Museum of Western Art of Tokyo)

Juan Malasaña avenging his daughter Manuela Malasaña on the streets of Madrid during the Dos de Mayo uprising, by Eugenio Álvarez Dumont. (*Museo del Prado*)

Battle of Tudela, by January Suchodolski. (*National Museum in Warsaw*)

Monument to the Constitution of 1812 (1912), by Modesto López Otero and Aniceto Marinas. A tribute to the first Spanish constitution, drawn up and signed during the siege of Cádiz.

Bronze statue dedicated to the Drummer of Bruc by Frederic Marès (1956) in Corinto Street in Barcelona. Numerous Spanish towns and cities commemorate the heroes of the Peninsular War with statues. Oddly, there are three statues dedicated to the Drummer of Bruc in Barcelona. (*Author's collection*)

The great day of Girona, by César Álvarez Dumont. (*San Fernando Castle, Figueres, Spain*)

The promulgation of the Constitution of 1812, by Salvador Viniegra. (*Museo de las Cortes de Cádiz*)

Heroic combat in the pulpit of the Church of San Agustín in Zaragoza during the Second Siege of 1809, by César Álvarez Dumont. (*Museum of Zaragoza*)

The Third of May 1808,
by Francisco de Goya.
(*Museo del Prado*)

*Le maréchal Suchet, duc
d'Albufera*, by Adèle Gault.
(*Musée de l'Armée, Paris*)

Portrait of the ancient general Castaños, by Vicente López Portaña. (*Museo del Prado*)

Battle of Somosierra, by January Suchodolski. (*National Museum in Warsaw*)

The surrender of Bailén, by José Casado de Alisal. (*Museo del Prado*)

Spanish medals of the Peninsular War: two medals of Bailen, Medal of the Escape of the Division of the North; Medal of Nalda; Medal of Pontesampaio; and Medal of the Siege of Girona. (*Collection Jaume Boguñà*)

The Disasters of War: with or without reason, by Francisco de Goya. (*Museo del Prado*)

The Disasters of War: the same, by Francisco de Goya. (*Museo del Prado*)

The Disasters of War: and they are fierce (or *And they fight like wild beasts*), by Francisco de Goya. (*Museo del Prado*)

Barcelona, *Monument to the Heroes of 1809* (1929), by Josep Llimona, Vicenç Navarro Romero and Pere Benavent. A tribute to the Barcelonians who were executed following an uprising against the French troops occupying Barcelona.

Madrid is full of references to the May uprising. In the centre of the city is the Plaza de la Lealtad, where we find the Monument to the Fallen for Spain, which until 1985 was called the Monument to the Fallen in the May Uprising. It houses the remains of the officers Daoiz and Velarde, who have another monument in the Plaza de España.

cornered Napoleon. At the most delicate moment of the battle, Chataux led a charge at the head of his men, which would ultimately bring victory – but the general was seriously wounded. Victor ran to the side of his son-in-law, who died in his arms. He was 35 years old. Stunned by the loss, Victor was no longer able to continue giving orders. After the battle, Napoleon was furious with him. Victor, confessing the death of his beloved son-in-law, burst into tears. The emperor, moved, consoled him and Victor replied: 'I will not leave the army, I will take up a weapon. I have not forgotten my old job. Victor will be placed in the ranks of the guard …' In 1811 Chataux had married Victorine, with whom he had two children. The misfortune would not end for this family with his death, since Victorine passed away two years later, aged only 24.

4. Stampa (2011), p. 513.
5. *Gaceta de Madrid* dated 2 April 1809.
6. *Gaceta Extraordinaria del Gobierno* dated 11 April 1809. The Order of Charles III was at that time the second most important order in Spain.

Chapter Eighteen

The Battle of Alcañiz

Date: 23 May 1809. *Place*: Alcañiz, Aragon. *Result*: Spanish victory.

Order of battle

Spanish Army: The Army of the Right under the command of Blake: General Areizaga's Division with the following battalions: Daroca, Reserve of Aragón, Shooters of Murcia and 2nd of the Aragon's Volunteers; General Tejada Division with the Battalion of Volunteers of Valencia, the Regiment of America (2 grenadier coys), the 5th Swiss Regiment (*aka* Taxler Regiment, 2 grenadier coys); General Roca's Division; the Marquis of Lazan's Division, with the 2nd Regiment of Valencia and artillery under Brigadier García Loygorri. Cavalry, under the command of Brigadier Ibarrola, included the Regiment of Santiago (2 sqns), the Hussars of Aragon (2 sqns) and the Hussars of Olivencia (1 sqn). In total, around 9,000 men.

Napoleonic Army: III Army Corps under the command of General Suchet, including its own guards and the 1st Division of General Laval, with the 14th Regiment of Line Infantry (2 bns) and the 3rd Legion of the Vístula (2 bns); the 2nd Division, under General Musnier, with the 64th (1 bn), 115th (3 bns) and 121th (2 bns) Regiments of Line Infantry, and General Fabre's Brigade with the 114th Regiment of Line Infantry (3 bns) and the 1st Legion of the Vístula (2 bns). Cavalry: the 4th Regiment of Hussars and the 13th Regiment of Cuirassiers. Artillery: 18 cannon and their artillerymen. In total, near 7,500 men.

Background

While the second siege of Zaragoza was taking place, Suchet knew that he had to crush the surrounding towns to prevent the organization of relief columns that could counterattack them. Thus, his forces successively occupied Tarazona, Daroca, Calatayud, Huesca and Jaca, among other towns. At the end of January 1809 General Wathier arrived in Alcañiz, a town of great strategic importance. Its imposing castle was used as a prison for French soldiers during the last siege of Zaragoza. Before Wathier approached, the prisoners were transferred to Tortosa. The French general tried to avoid combat by sending an emissary with a reasonable surrender agreement, but the local Junta responded by imprisoning the man. Alcañiz was in a state of alarm and ready for battle. Some 1,500 local residents of the town had armed themselves, while in support a company of volunteers called the 'Serranos de Albarracín' arrived from Albarracín. From the castle of Mequinenza they sent cannon and ammunition.[1] On 26 January approximately 700 Alcañizans went to look for Wathier's men on the outskirts of the town, but they were easily defeated. The defenders retreated into the town, which became the scene, for about 7 hours, of bloody street-by-street fighting. Both sides had suffered tremendous numbers of casualties, but French victory was inevitable and their revenge implacable.

The fall of Zaragoza did not mean the pacification of Aragon. In a few weeks towns like Barbastro and Monzón rose up against the invaders. On 20 May the 'Action of Cinca', also known as the battle of Fonz, took place in the east of the province of Huesca, next to the border with Catalonia. This battle occurred when General Habert prepared a punitive expedition against Monzón. Near the town of Fonz he tried to cross the Cinca river, despite weather conditions that made such a move inadvisable. When about 600 of his men had already crossed, the river level rose so much that it was impossible to continue and those men on the right bank were cut off. As they searched for a crossing point, they encountered some Spanish troops from the 2nd Battalion of Huesca Volunteers, the Cariñena Volunteers and the 1st Tercio of *Miquelets* of Lleida. The French, disorganized, engaged in a brief battle, but soon surrendered. In chains, they were forced to parade through the town of Fonz and pass in front of the house of the Countess of Bureta, a heroine of the sieges of Zaragoza.[2] Afterwards, the prisoners were sent to the sinister island of Cabrera.

The battle

A few miles further south, on 20 May Blake appeared near Alcañiz with the Army of the Right, almost 9,000 troops. The French garrison, unable to take on such a huge force, withdrew towards Zaragoza. Suchet, determined to stand up to Blake, presented himself at Alcañiz with an army of some 7,500 men. The Spanish general prepared for the battle by placing his divisions on the different promontories close to Alcañiz: to the right, on the Los Pueyos hill, he placed Areizaga's men; in the Tiro de Cañón, those of Pedro de Tejada; to the left of this, those of Pedro Roca; in Perdiguer hill, closing the rear, were two batteries and the troops of González de Menchaca; on the left flank, Ibarrola's cavalry; and in the centre the Marquis of Lazán with the batteries of García Loygorri. Blake's actions were not without controversy. Behind him was the Guadalupe river and in the event of a disaster, it would have been a deathtrap.

Suchet arrived with his men along the Zaragoza road at 6.00am. He attacked with everything he had, leaving only a part of his cavalry in reserve. In the centre General Fabre tried to make his way to the gates of Alcañiz. On the right General Laval tried to encircle Los Pueyos hill, leading a frontal attack with the rest of his men. This was a key position, since its conquest would enable him to overrun the Spanish army and perhaps reach Alcañiz. But Areizaga's troops held on grimly, and there was carnage around the hill, in which the Polish units were the most affected. However, the French push did cause some disorder in the Spanish line, so Blake ordered Menchaca to leave the rear to support Los Pueyos hill with his men. Suchet then decided to concentrate his offensive in the centre, sending forward Fabre's division, with the 114th Line Infantry Regiment and the Poles from the Vistula; the French advanced, excited and confident. In their path were the 2nd Regiment of Valencia and the artillery of García Loygorri, who ordered his men not to open fire until the last moment. The barrage, when it came, caused huge losses among the attackers. The survivors of Fabre's column had no choice but to retreat. The battle lasted 7 hours. The French had barely been able to hold the ground they had conquered after their impetuous start. Suchet chose to regroup. In the afternoon his troops took up positions on the Hambre hill, but no attack was ordered. Most activity took place in the field hospitals, where the surgeons treating the wounded could not keep up with the sheer numbers of casualties. Taking advantage of the night, the French general ordered a withdrawal towards Samper de Calanda. As at El Bruc, a local legend claims that a young drummer banged his drum, causing panic among the French soldiers who thought the Spanish were attacking. However, Blake's men, battered in the heavy fighting, did not set off in pursuit of their enemy and instead remained in Alcañiz for several days. The French had suffered some 500 killed and some 2,000 wounded, while in the Spanish camp casualties numbered about 300 men.

The double epilogue of this battle left a sour taste in Spanish mouths. While Blake rested his men in Alcañiz, Suchet took advantage of the time to reorganize his troops. Eventually Blake's troops resumed their march towards Zaragoza. The fate of the capital on the next day would be decided in the town of María de Huerva. It was a battle that could also decide the outcome of the war: in the event of victory, the Napoleonic forces would be forced to withdraw from Zaragoza and all of Aragon, which would compromise the rest of the French troops on the Peninsula. The battle took place on 15 June. Suchet's men attacked the Spanish troops fiercely, but once again Blake's men stood firm, enjoying a clear numerical superiority. But just as everything seemed to indicate that the Spanish success at

Alcañiz could be repeated, a terrible hailstorm interrupted the battle; in the nick of time reinforcements reached Suchet, balancing the numbers more evenly. When fighting resumed, Wathier's cavalry destroyed the Spanish cavalry commanded by O'Donojú, and surrounded the right flank of the Spanish infantry. Areizaga, the future 'hero' of Ocaña, remained motionless in the rear, so that the rest of the Spanish troops were forced to withdraw. The Spanish left on the battlefield more than 1,000 dead and most of their artillery, stranded in the mud. Some 400 were taken prisoner. Blake retreated eastward, paralleling the Huerva river, to regroup what was left of his army; in addition to the casualties, there had been an enormous number of desertions. Suchet did not wait to hunt down his enemy and on the 18th the two armies met at Belchite. With no chance to flee, Blake decided to fight. Suchet chose to attack on the flanks, with Musnier's men on the left and Habert's men on the right. When the latter advanced, a lucky shot from one of their cannon hit the Spanish ammunition train, causing a shocking chain of explosions. Blake's troops, fearing they were surrounded, fled in terror, throwing away packs and muskets. The French showed no mercy to their enemies, who suffered more than 2,000 casualties in dead, wounded and prisoners. Blake's army had been destroyed, and with it went the Spanish dream of retaking Zaragoza.

Notes

1. Pellicer Marco, Luis Antonio: 'Alcañiz con el gobierno francés. 1808–1814'. Available at: https://www.asociacionlossitios.com/batallaalcaniz.htm (accessed 14 October 2020).
2. The Countess of Bureta was one of the great heroines of the sieges, turning her palace into a hospital for wounded fighters, a canteen for soldiers and a refuge for families who were left homeless. She also participated in the rescue of the wounded, putting her life in serious danger; she organized the militiamen on the front lines and acquired medical supplies, food and clothing for those who had lost everything.

Chapter Nineteen

The Reconquest of Galicia: from Vigo to Pontesampaio

Date: 28 March–8 June 1809. *Place*: Galicia. *Result*: Spanish victory.

Order of battle

Spanish Army: Miño Division, under the command of General Gaspar María de la Nava y Álvarez, Count of Noroña, comprising the Regiment of Lobeira, the Regiment of La Unión, the Regiment Victory or Death, the Battalion of Mourentán, the Battalion of Morrazo, the Battalion of Monforte de Lemos, the Battalion of Shooters of Miño, the 1st Battalion of Catalan Volunteers, the General's Regiment, the Battalion of Benavente, the Battalion of Shooters of the Army, and the Literary Battalion of Santiago. The Spanish fleet included the frigates *Ifigenia* and *Tigre* and three gunboats, while the Anglo-Portuguese fleet included the frigates HMS *Lively*, HMS *Venus*, HMS *Cadmus*, HMS *Curiosa* and one gunboat. In total, around 10,000 men.[1]

Napoleonic Army: VI Army Corps under Marshal Michel Ney, Duke of Elchingen and Prince of the Moskva, with the following units: 1st Division, under the command of General Jean Gabriel Marchand, comprising the Maucune Brigade, with the 6th Regiment of Light Infantry and the 69th Regiment of Line Infantry, and the Marcognet Brigade, with the 39th Regiment of Line Infantry; the

2nd Division of General Lagrange, comprising the Bardet Brigade, with the 25th Regiment of Light Infantry and the 27th Regiment of Line Infantry, and the Labassé Brigade, with the 50th and 59th Regiments of Line Infantry; the 4th Division of General Dessolles, comprising the Godinot Brigade, including the 12th Regiment of Light Infantry and the 51st Regiment of Line Infantry, and the Rey Brigade, with the 43rd and 55th Regiments of Line Infantry. Cavalry Division, with the 3rd, 4th and 13th Provisional Regiments of Dragoons. Division of Light Cavalry of General Colbert, with the 3rd Regiment of Hussars and the 15th Regiment of Mounted Chasseurs. Gendarmerie. Detachment of Artillery. The garrisons of Vigo, Lugo and Tuy. In total, near 11,000 men.[2]

Background

At the beginning of the nineteenth century Galicia was one of the most populated areas in Spain. Its almost 1.5 million inhabitants accounted for 13 per cent of the Spanish population,[3] this being predominantly rural (93 per cent of the population). At the beginning of the French occupation the Galician authorities were complacent about the new status quo. The new governor general of the region was Antonio Filangieri, a Neapolitan closely linked to Murat. But the widespread institutional collaborationism was soon overwhelmed by popular rebellion. The first uprising took place in Corunna on 30 May, and was replicated in other nearby towns in the following weeks. In Corunna the Superior Junta of the Kingdom of Galicia was instituted on 5 June, which both Filangieri and other *afrancesados* welcomed. In the same month was created the Army of the Left, commanded by Joaquín Blake. Filangieri moved to Villafranca del Bierzo with the Navarra Regiment and sailors from Corunna. In a dark episode, on the night of 24 June, he was killed by a group of Spanish soldiers.[4] For his part, Blake, who favoured a defensive strategy, was forced to move to Castile to participate in General Castaños's offensive. There, his troops suffered a disastrous defeat at the battle of Rioseco (14 July). Subsequently Blake went to the Cantabrian mountains, where he continued fighting the French until the battle of Espinosa de los Monteros (10–11 November), during which Marshal Victor virtually annihilated the Army of the Left.[5] Command of the army then passed to the Marquis de la Romana, who had landed with his intrepid troops from the Division of the North on 20 October. By this time the British Army, commanded by General John Moore, had landed in Portugal, about 250km (155 miles) from the Galician border. Once in Spain, events obliged Moore to retreat towards Corunna, where he was forced into battle with Soult's army. Although the bulk of the British expeditionary army managed to embark on naval ships and escape, Moore himself was killed during the battle. After this the Galician Junta was dissolved and its leaders fled to Portugal. Galicia was left at the mercy of the Napoleonic troops.

Meanwhile, in Asturias the Marquis de la Romana was reorganizing his forces. There was a political-military conflict between the Junta de Asturias and the Marquis de la Romana. He demanded more troops to face Ney in Galicia, but the

Asturians refused, being more concerned about the possibility of French troops arriving from Cantabria led by General Kellerman. In addition, de la Romana was openly liberal, but the Asturian Junta had a clearly absolutist agenda. The conflict led to the first *coup d'état* in the history of Spain, when de la Romana entered Oviedo at the beginning of March and dismissed the members of the Junta of Asturias.[6] While de la Romana tried to stabilize the political situation, he trained his troops with methods that did not require large resources. But his problems were not only political: the bulk of Ney's VI Army Corps was on his trail. Meanwhile, Soult's II Army Corps invaded Portugal after winning the battle of Porto. The Galician powder keg was ready to explode.

With a large proportion of Soult's troops now in Portugal, the revolts in Galicia became more widespread, showing the French that they were very far from controlling the territory. In addition, two officers, Manuel García del Barrio and Pablo Morillo, arrived from Seville; sent by the Central Junta, they had been tasked with provoking insurrection in Galicia. To their surprise, this was already under way. Soon, there were successes against the French and several Galician towns were liberated. About this time was created the Junta de Lobeira, chaired by the charismatic Bishop of Ourense, Pedro Quevedo de Quintano. At the same time, following the instructions of the Marquis de la Romana, the Galician volunteers began to receive military training. Thus the Lobeira Regiment was created, comprising three battalions, with a total of 2,147 troops.[7] Bernardo González del Valle, known as Cachamuiña, was sent to Ourense by the Marquis de la Romana to organize the different guerrilla groups, joining them into the Provincial Grenadier Battalion. The Lobeira Regiment was the basis of the future Miño Division. In Portugal Marshal Soult, busy with his campaign, had left detachments of troops in the most important cities in Galicia, without suspecting that the Spanish would defy the conquest. Vigo had been occupied by the French at the end of January, although it was not until a month later that its new military governor, Colonel of Dragoons Jacques Antonie Chalot, arrived.

The reconquest of Vigo
Date: 28 March 1809.

Nothing foreshadowed the future that awaited Chalot in Vigo.[8] Despite his youth, he was an experienced officer. Born in Paris, to a family of the lower nobility, he sympathized with revolutionary ideas, and at the age of 18 he took part in the assault on the Bastille.[9] A veteran of Eylau and Austerlitz, he had arrived in Galicia with Soult's troops in pursuit of Moore's expeditionary army. He had previously served as the governor of other towns, including Amstetten in Austria and Fürstenfeldbruck in Bavaria,[10] so he was the perfect candidate to deal with Vigo. But if Chalot expected the people of Vigo to emulate the peaceful character of the inhabitants of central and northern Europe, he was sorely disappointed. The people of Vigo were far from resigned to accepting the Napoleonic invasion, and from the first moment Chalot had to deal with the awkward and sarcastic attitude of the local authorities, especially Vigo's mayor, Francisco Javier Vázquez Varela, who was dedicated to hiding supplies from the French, causing starvation among the enemy soldiers. By mid-March citizen militias had begun to gather around Vigo and were preparing to attack the town.

These militias were headed by Joaquín Terneiro, a Galician lawyer, who had recruited a large group of volunteers. They were joined by the Abbot of Valladares and João Baptista Almeida, a Portuguese officer, who brought about fifty Portuguese soldiers. Faced with this situation, Chalot requested and received reinforcements from Santiago,[11] and the next day he ordered the town gates to be closed. This only aggravated the shortages for his hungry troops, a situation only exacerbated by the arrival of the British frigate HMS *Venus*, commanded by Captain James Coutts Crawford, which began a sea blockade. On 22 March Chalot sent an emissary to negotiate terms of surrender with Crawford, but the captain refused. Sensing the weakness of the French, he called his immediate superior, McKinley, who arrived the following day with the frigate HMS *Lively*, to reinforce the blockade. It should be noted that during all this time the delivery of weapons and ammunition from the British to the Spanish troops continued.

On the 25th Colonels Morillo and Colombo arrived on the outskirts of Vigo at the head of the volunteer troops they were training and the Provincial Grenadiers of Cachamuiña. From the outset, however, the relationship between these two detachments was strained. Colonel Morillo demanded to be the sole commander in the attack on Vigo, but Terneiro flatly refused, claiming that Almeida should be in command since his contingent had arrived earlier. The tension reached such a point that, according to Terneiro's account, Morillo sent a detachment of soldiers to enforce his demand or they would be arrested and shot. Apparently, McKinley, who was present, was able to mediate and managed to keep matters under control.

On the 27th Chalot sent a new delegate to negotiate the surrender. He met with Morillo and McKinley, but again the terms were refused. That same day, at 8.00pm, the French artillery began firing on the British frigates and the Spanish troops, who responded immediately. On the 28th the attack was begun by the Spanish, who prepared to take the city by assault, smashing the gates of A Falperra and A Gamboa with axes; the latter was opened by Cachamuiña himself. Inside the town, Vázquez Varela's 300 volunteers took an active part in their own liberation. The French, staring defeat in the face and greatly fearing the actions of the vengeful Galicians, began to flee towards the sea, where they were taken prisoner by the English.

The Spanish casualties amounted to some 200, almost all of them wounded. The French suffered an undetermined number of deaths, but HMS *Lively* and HMS *Venus* received between them some 1,300 prisoners, about 100 of whom died before they could be sent to British prisons. Chalot spent the rest of the war as a captive in England. A group of French prisoners left in the city were killed a few days later. The loot obtained was substantial. Apart from everything that the French had stolen and looted across the region, Soult's vast wealth was also captured in Vigo. Southey indicates that the Spanish came across a chest full of jewels that General de La Houssaye had been stealing since he entered Spain and that Chalot had been keeping safe for him. Cachamuíña, despite being wounded in the combat, was appointed the military governor of Vigo.

The siege of Tuy

Date: 15 March–11 April 1809.

Aware of the events in Vigo, a group of local leaders from Tuy managed to gather a contingent of some 8,000 militiamen; most of them were unarmed, and they had more impetus than discipline. Tuy, a strategic city on the border of Portugal and watered by the Miño river, was better defended than Vigo; it had a larger garrison with more artillery, and was under the command of General Thomas Mignot, Baron de Lamartinière,[12] another veteran of the battles of the Fourth Coalition, who had arrived in Galicia with Soult. The state of the besieging Spanish troops at Tuy was so pitiful that Mignot managed to send a contingent of about 450 men to help defend Vigo.[13] By the time they arrived, however, Vigo had already fallen. Their return journey saw them massacred and only about 150 reached Tuy alive. The rest were killed or taken prisoner.

On 30 March, after the fall of Vigo, Colonels García del Barrio and Morillo came to Tuy, along with a newly created militia, the Volunteers Shooters of Vigo. The command of all the besieging troops fell, although not without the usual discussions, to García del Barrio, another of the soldiers sent by the Central Junta. His first mission was to try to bring some order to the chaos outside the city walls.[14] Soon news came of the arrival of two imperial columns to help defend the city: one from the north, under the command of General Maucune, who had taken advantage of the trip to raze Porriño, and the other from Oporto, under the command of General Heudelet de Bierre, who was returning to Spain. García del Barrio organized two assaults, but both were complete disasters, with the loss of dozens of lives and all the artillery. On 11 April Heudelet de Bierre's column arrived in Valença do Minho, on the Portuguese side of the Miño river. With more than a third of the garrison in Tuy hospitalized and food already rationed,[15] the two French generals decided that it was not worth trying to hold the city, which was evacuated to Valença do Minho. Tuy was liberated. Maucune turned back and returned to Santiago, leaving a trail of destruction and death along the way. His forces were relentlessly harassed by the guerrillas throughout their journey.

The siege of Lugo

Date: from 17–22 May 1809.

On 17 May General Mahy's troops began to concentrate near Lugo. The town's governor was General Fournier-Sarlovèze – if Mahy had known him, he would surely have withdrawn immediately. Fournier-Sarlovèze was a typical light cavalry officer: hard drinking, quarrelsome, usually insubordinate, tremendously arrogant, brave to the point of recklessness and obsessed with duelling.[16] He was fluent in Latin and insisted on practising it with any bishop or clergyman he came across. The writer Joseph Conrad used him as the protagonist of one of his most famous novels, *The Duellists*, based on the true story of two French cavalry officers, Fournier-Sarlovèze and Dupont de l'Étang[17] (renamed in the novel as Feraud and D'Hupert, respectively), who over the course of nineteen years duelled thirty times, taking turns to exact revenge and cultivating a deep and cloudy mutual hatred that they gave vent to with all kinds of duels, whether on foot or on horseback, and using all kinds of weapons.

The next day Fournier-Sarlovèze, who, as we might imagine, would not wait to be attacked, had his men lined up outside ready to do battle. Before him, General Mahy placed his men in two columns, one under the command of Brigadier Mendizábal and the other under the command of Brigadier Taboada, together with cavalryman Juan Caro, while he left a column in reserve under the command of Brigadier Losada. The fight was fierce, but the Imperial cavalry unexpectedly retreated, dragging the stunned infantrymen back with them. Such was the enthusiasm of the Spanish vanguard that they began to chase after the French, and a large part of the Battalion of Catalan Volunteers entered the city. But when the gates closed behind them, they had to flee, helped by the residents whose houses adjoined the walls, from which they hurriedly climbed down to escape the trap. Mahy, lacking weapons for a siege, sent an emissary with a proposal for the garrison to surrender. Fournier-Sarlovèze's response was to report that the next emissary sent would be hanged.[18] The resulting impasse lasted until Mahy was informed that Soult, coming from Portugal, was approaching Lugo. Hearing this news, he lifted the siege and went to meet Romana's army.

The Battle of Pontesampaio

Date: 7–8 June 1809.

The French response to the unrest was to increase repression and violence. Among many others, the towns of Cee, Corcubión, Porriño, Redondela, Porto-marín and Monforte de Lemos[19] and the regions of Terra de Montes and Trasdeza were looted. For his part, Ney returned from Asturias, tired of chasing the elusive Marquis de la Romana, and met up with Soult, whom Wellesley had just kicked out of Portugal. The two marshals, both so dear to Bonaparte, hated each other with a deep and irreconcilable hatred. Such was their enmity that during a heated meeting in Lugo, they even unsheathed their sabres and began to fight, copied by the members of their respective staffs.[20] When the situation had calmed down, they agreed to carry out a pincer movement (Ney from the north and Soult from the south through Ourense) to destroy the Miño Division, reconquer Vigo and pacify Galicia. Soult, however, instead of executing his part in the plan of battle, decided to abandon Ney and instead went to Castile. In this way, Ney had approached Pontesampaio with his army, unaware that he was unsupported. On 25 July the two marshals left the city, which was also evacuated by the eminent Fournier-Sarlovèze garrison.

In mid-May a ship arrived from Cadiz with a group of officers and a shipment of supplies. Among the officers were Gaspar María de la Nava y Álvarez, Count of Noroña, who took command of the Miño Division, and Martín de la Carrera, who was appointed his divisional lieutenant. With his troops, Noroña set out for Santiago de Compostela, where he faced a column of combined infantry and cavalry forces under the command of General Popon de Maucune. The French were defeated and those who escaped joined Ney's army, which began to pursue the Miño Division.[21] On 6 June Noroña arrived at Pontesampaio, to find that Morillo had destroyed two of the bridges, so his troops had to cross the Verdugo river in barges. With Ney hot on his heels, he decided that if they had to face the Duke of Elchingen, this would be a good place.

On 7 June Ney appeared on the battlefield. An intense artillery and rifle fire began between the forces on the opposite banks of the Verdugo river, without major damage on either side. Ney sent part of his light infantry to explore upriver looking for a ford or a bridge that would allow them to outflank Noroña's troops. They discovered the Caldelas bridge, about 10km (6 miles) upstream, and Ney hastened to send part of his army to cross there. But the bridge was defended by the Lobeira Regiment,[22] reinforced with a detachment of the Catalonian Volunteers led by the tireless Ambrosio de la Cuadra.[23] Suffering huge casualties, the French withdrew.

That same day also saw the arrival of the Spanish and Anglo-Portuguese fleets on the river. The Spanish fleet, under the command of Captain Juan José de Carranza, aboard the frigate *Ifigenia*, was made up of three gunboats and a schooner called *Tigre*, under the command of Lieutenant Toledo. The Anglo-Portuguese fleet was under the command of the experienced naval captain George McKinley,[24] in the frigate HMS *Lively*; his fleet was completed by the frigate HMS *Venus*, commanded by James Coutts Crawford; the corvette HMS *Cadmus*, commanded by Delamore Wynter; the Portuguese schooner *Curiosa*, commanded by Lieutenant Alves; and a gunboat under the command of Lieutenant Jefferson, who was very active all day.

At 5.00am on the 8th the gunboats opened fire on the French, who in mid-morning tried to cross the river. Ney ordered each cavalryman to carry an infantryman behind his saddle and cross the river at a ford. But between the gunboats and intense enemy rifle fire, the cavalry squadrons were forced to withdraw. In another attack on the Caldelas bridge, it was the turn of the Morillo Regiment of Unión, the Morrazo Battalion and the Literary Battalion to cover themselves with glory.[25] Meanwhile, on the river the English ships HMS *Lively* and HMS *Cadmus* resupplied the Spanish with weapons and ammunition. In fact, the Spanish situation in terms of equipment was so precarious that the *Ifigenia*, in the heat of battle, distributed 4,000 pairs of boots and a batch of cartridge belts.[26]

Ney, seeing that he had not inflicted any damage on Noroña's troops, and that crossing the Verdugo river was an impossible mission, and now aware that Soult had already begun his retreat towards Castile, on the morning of the 9th ordered his VI Army Corps to retreat. The French had lost some 400 casualties, the Spanish around 100. When Spanish forces crossed the Verdugo river on the 9th, they found the French camp littered with unburied bodies and the wounded abandoned to their fate, as well as weapons, equipment and provisions. Ney's withdrawal was cruel and bloody, his men burning houses and crops, killing defenceless civilians, and looting the towns and villages along their path. The Spanish response was up to the task. Guerrillas pursued the Duke of Elchingen's rearguard, torturing and murdering any soldiers who were lost or left behind. Their harassment was violent and furious. Finally, on 26 June, the last Frenchman left Galicia. They would never come back.

Notes

1. Robertson (2020), p. 298.
2. Vaquero (2012). Of which: 9,000 infantrymen and 2,000 cavalrymen.
3. As a reference, today its 2.7 million inhabitants represent 6.13 per cent of the total population. Source: Galician Institute of Statistics, Government of Galicia.
4. González Lopo (2010) says they were soldiers of the Regiment of Navarra, while García Luengo (1908) explains that they were sailors from Corunna incited by a sergeant whom Filangieri had publicly humiliated in the past.
5. One of the most affected units was the Literary Battalion, made up of students from the University of Santiago, which was practically exterminated: see Gonzáles (2010). Of its 1,600 troops, only 200 returned alive.
6. Calpena y Junqueras (2003), p. 133.
7. González Lopo (2010), p. 43.
8. Troncoso (2011), pp. 223–40.
9. One of the Parisian prison assailants on 14 July 1789, kicking off the French Revolution.
10. To contextualize, at the beginning of the nineteenth century, Vigo had about 10,725 inhabitants; Ghent, 58,000; Amstetten, about 4,000; and Fürstenfeldbruck, about 6,000.
11. Troncoso (2018), p. 280.
12. VVAA (1829).
13. Oman (1903).
14. Santiago (1896), p. 528.
15. Troncoso (2018), p. 305.
16. Burnham (2011).
17. See Chapter 7.
18. Marcel (1814).
19. Monforte de Lemos suffered three lootings during the French occupation, the one on 20–21 April being the worst of all. On those days 3,000 Napoleonic soldiers assaulted a population of barely had 460 souls. Their desperate resistance could not stop the invaders, who entered the town with blood and fire. In two days they razed all the churches, stole everything that had any value, no matter how small, and burned all the religious symbols they could find. But the worst part was that many local people could not take refuge in the nearby mountains and were massacred. In two days more than 100 people were murdered. Rico (2009), p. 6.

20. Ancely (2015).
21. Artaza (1888), pp. 435–6; Osuna & Osuna (1999), pp. 86–7; Napier (1832), p. 7; Quintero (2005); Martínez (2009), pp. 75–6.
22. Osuna & Osuna (1999), p. 87.
23. Martínez (2009), p. 76.
24. Curious, McKinley had already boarded the frigate *Ifigenia* under different circumstances, thirty years before. In 1778, aged 12, he was sailing on the frigate HMS *Ceres* on his first mission when a French frigate named *Iphigenie* captured the British ship, taking the young sailor prisoner. In 1795 the French frigate was captured by the Spanish and was renamed *Ifigenia*. Troncoso (2018), p. 315.
25. Pena (2007), p. 56.
26. Troncoso (2018), p. 322.

Chapter Twenty

The Battle of Aranjuez

Date: 5 August 1809. *Place*: Aranjuez, Madrid. *Result*: Spanish victory.

Order of battle

Spanish Army: Three divisions from the Army of La Mancha, under the command of Brigadier Pedro Agustín Girón: the 1st Division under Brigadier Luis Lacy, with the Regiment of Alcalá la Real, the 1st Regiment of Burgos, the Regiment of Spain, the 1st Regiment of Loja, the 1st Regiment of Volunteers of Seville, the Regiment of the Provincial Militia of Cuenca, the Regiment of La Unión, plus a detachment of artillery, engineers and sappers; the 2nd Division, under Brigadier Gaspar Vigodet, with the Regiment of the Crown, the 1st Regiment of Guadix, the Regiment of the Military Orders, the Regiments of the Provincial Militias of Alcázar de San Juan, Córdoba, Ciudad Real and Ronda, plus a detachment of artillery, engineers and sappers; the 3rd Division, under Brigadier Pedro Agustín Girón, with the Battalion of the Royal Spanish Guards, the Regiment of Bailén, the Regiment of Alpujarras, the Regiment of Light Infantry of Vélez-Málaga, the Regiments of the Provincial Militias of Écija and Jaén, and a detachment of artillery, engineers and sappers. In total, 15,701 men.[1]

Napoleonic Army: IV Army Corps under the command of General Sebastiani de la Porta; the 1st Division under General Rey, comprising Rey's Brigade with

97

the 28th and 32nd Regiments of Line Infantry, and Liger-Belair's Brigade with the 58th and 75th Regiments of Line Infantry; the 2nd Division (*aka* the Polish Division), under the command of the Count of Valence, with the Infantry Brigade of the Grand Duchy of Warsaw, with their 4th, 7th and 9th Regiments of Line Infantry; the 3rd Division (*aka* the German Division), under the command of Barón Leval, with the Regiment of Nassau (2 bns), the Regiment of Baden (2 bns), the Regiment of Hesse-Darnstadt (2 bns), the Regiment of Holland (2 bns), the Battalion of Frankfurt and a detachment of artillery. Cavalry Brigade under Count Merlín with the 10th and 26th Regiments of Mounted Chasseurs, Polish Lancers, Westphalian Light Cavalry and a detachment of Mounted Artillery. The 2nd Division of Dragoons under General Milhaud, including the 3rd Regiment of Dutch Hussars and the 5th, 12th, 16th, 20th and 21st Regiments of Dragoons. In total, around 15,000 men.[2]

Background

After the battle of Talavera, Joseph I and Sebastiani withdrew with their forces towards Toledo, while Victor stayed in Cazalegas, to later occupy Talavera and pursue García de la Cuesta's forces to the Arzobispos Bridge, where he defeated them. Defending the way to southern Spain there was now only the weak Army of La Mancha commanded by General Venegas. He had orders to harass Sebastiani's rearguard, and could advance to Madrid, now free of French troops. But Venegas, always hesitant and excessively cautious, did not move and thus lost a great chance to occupy the capital. On 3 August he received a letter from García de la Cuesta informing him of the Allied victory at Talavera and the subsequent withdrawal of the Allies. This was the right time for Venegas to retreat, but surprisingly, he decided to attack the enemy. He himself explained the reasons:

> Your Excellency knows perfectly well that this army is left to my own forces, inferior in number to those of the enemy; and when the Captain General recognizes that these are more manoeuvrable, he leaves me no other recourse than to make a shameful retreat, since it is already a second, and hateful for the towns that we have occupied and have left behind, a retreat that would consequently discourage the soldiers by diminishing their moral strength, and would cause national enthusiasm to decline to the highest degree, especially in all these towns. These truths, which I feel at once, make me decide to stop and fight if I am attacked, preferring to be torn to pieces, to the disgraceful game of escape. Venegas.[3]

There was a time during the Peninsular War when it seemed that everyone had written a manifesto complaining about the ineptitude of Francisco Xavier Venegas. The Duke of Infantado wrote the *Manifiesto de las operaciones del Exército del Centro desde el día 3 de diciembre de 1808 hasta el 17 de febrero de 1809* ('Manifesto of the operations of the Army of the Centre from 3 December 1808 to

17 February 1809'), in which he complained about Venegas's disastrous command during the action of Tarancón, a pyrrhic victory that almost ended in disaster owing to poor instructions from Venegas, among other calamities. Likewise, General García de la Cuesta wrote his *Manifiesto que presenta a la Europa el Capitán General de los Reales Egércitos don Gregorio García de la Cuesta sobre sus Operaciones Militares y Políticas desde el mes de junio de 1808 al 12 de agosto de 1809 en que dejó el mando del Egército de Extremadura* ('Manifesto presented to Europe by the Captain General of the Royal Armies, Don Gregorio García de la Cuesta, on his Military and Political Operations from June 1808 to 12 August 1809 in which he left the command of the Army of Extremadura'), complaining about Venegas's passivity during the fighting at Talavera and his subsequent absurd offensive. And while it is true that Venegas responded to them,[4] the fact is that nobody believed Venegas. Even the decision to give him command of the Army of La Mancha caused some astonishment among his colleagues. On the battlefield (for example at Tudela or Uclés) he did not prove to be a particularly brilliant general; quite the opposite, in fact. Some even remembered how, during the battle of Bailén, when he was commanding the right wing, he made a mistake that led to the French cavalry decimating his best unit, the Regiment of Military Orders.[5] But his uncle, Francisco de Saavedra, was the president of the Central Junta, so it seems that, once again, political connections were more important than military skills when army commands were being distributed.

The battle

One good decision made by Venegas was to give command of three divisions to the resolute Pedro Agustín Girón to prevent Sebastiani's Division from crossing the Tagus at Aranjuez, after first disabling the bridges at Reina, Barcas and Verde. Venegas himself, in a report signed on 8 August 1809, described the disposition of the troops and the development of the battle.[6] General Girón distributed his forces in the following way: on the heights overlooking the Reina bridge were the troops of Lacy Division. Brigadier Luis Riquelme's battalions of Military Orders, under the command of Colonel Alejandro de Ojea, and the 2nd of Córdoba, under the command of Colonel Andrés Creagh and Bailén, defended the Reina bridge alongside four pieces of artillery under the command of Riquelme himself. The Battalion of Alpujarras, under the command of Lieutenant Colonel José del Castillo, was positioned in the Plaza de San Antonio. Two 8-pounder guns, under the command of Captain Miguel Antonio Panes, were placed on the Barcas bridge with a second line of defence led by Commander Juan Carmona. The Battalion of Vélez-Málaga, commanded by Colonel José Antonio Sanz, was assigned to defend the ford in the esplanade known as the Garden of the Infante Don Antonio. The Regiment of Écija, led by Colonel Marquis de las Cuevas del Becerro, defended the Verde bridge. The Regiment of Ciudad Real, led by Colonel Ángel Pedrero, with two 4-pounder guns, under the command of Lieutenant Juan Guiral, established a position at the Largo ford. In reserve were the Regiments of Ronda and the 1st of Guadix, in another esplanade called Calle de la Reina; the Regiment of the Crown, commanded by Josep Ruiz de Lihory,[7] and the Regiment of Jaén, commanded by José María de Andrade, were stationed on the Ocaña road; while the battalions of the Royal Spanish Guards, temporarily commanded by Colonel Vicente Ferrer, and the Cavalry Brigade of Diego Ballesteros were placed in the vicinity of the Royal Palace.

At 2.00pm Sebastiani's men arrived. Without wasting any time, an attack was launched at the ford in the Garden of the Infante Don Antonio. Despite the sturdy defence of the Battalion of Vélez-Málaga, the situation was compromised, so Girón sent in the battalions of the Royal Spanish Guards, who managed to repel the French. The attack then continued along the entire front line, but was repulsed. Sebastiani, not discouraged, launched a second attack, concentrating his forces again at the ford in the Garden of the Infante Don Antonio. Brigadier Lacy, seeing that the situation was worsening at the Reina bridge, led a counter-attack, which forced the French to flee. The Regiment of Guadix courageously reinforced the Largo ford. At the Barcas bridge Captain Panes was seriously wounded, but he refused to be evacuated and continued fighting alongside his men, inspiring and encouraging them with his determination. Meanwhile, the Regiment of Ronda, which was waiting in reserve, was called to help in the defence of the ford in the Garden of the Infante Don Antonio. Ballesteros's cavalry was deployed along the entire line of combat, proving courageous at the points of greatest danger. At sunset, after a third attack had failed, Sebastiani decided to withdraw. The advance had proved much tougher than expected, and his forces had already suffered some 500 casualties. But it was not long before he was able to take his revenge on the Army of La Mancha. Among the Spanish, casualties were approximately 200 men. The euphoric victors of the battle of Aranjuez seemed more eager than ever to crush Sebastiani's army. Soon they would have a new opportunity to do so, but this time they would not be under the command of General Girón. Venegas also wanted his share of glory.

Notes

1. Sañudo Bayon (2011), p. 216.
2. Ibid., pp. 218–19.
3. Calvo Alvero (2014).
4. To the first in *Contestación al Manifiesto del Excelentísimo Duque del Infantado, dada por Francisco Xavier Venegas* ('Response to the Manifesto of the Most Excellent Duke del Infantado, given by Francisco Xavier Venegas'). And to García de la Cuesta in *Vindicación de los agravios infundados, injustos y groseros con que el Capitán General d. Gregorio de la Cuesta ha intentado manchar la reputación del Teniente General y Virrei de Nueva-España d. Francisco Xavier Venegas* ('Vindication of the unfounded, unfair and rude offences with which the Captain General d. Gregorio de la Cuesta has tried to tarnish the reputation of the Lieutenant General and Viceroy of Nueva España d. Francisco Xavier Venegas'), in his manifesto printed in Palma, Mallorca, in 1811.
5. Stampa (2012), p. 7.
6. *Gazeta de Madrid* dated 15 August 1808, pp. 45–51.

7. From an aristocratic family of Valencian origin, his son became mayor of Valencia and an important promoter of Valencian culture. One of his granddaughters, Margarita Ruiz de Lihory y de la Bastida, was a spy, and lover of a diverse list of characters from Abd el Krim to Henry Ford. Her second husband was the Catalan politician Josep María Bassols; both were strongly interested in occultism and rose to notoriety in Spain around 1950 when they were accused of mutilating the corpse of Margarita's daughter, in what was known at the time as 'the Case of the Severed Hand'. The marriage ended in a psychiatric hospital, from which they left shortly after.

Chapter Twenty-One

The Battle of Almonacid

Date: 11 August 1809. *Place*: Almonacid, Castile La Mancha.
Result: Napoleonic victory.

Order of battle

Spanish Army: The Army of La Mancha, under the command of General Francisco Javier Venegas, comprising the 1st Division under Brigadier Luis Lacy, with the Regiment of Alcalá la Real, the 1st Regiment of Burgos, the Regiment of Spain, the 1st Regiment of Loja, the 1st Regiment of Volunteers of Seville, the Regiment of the Provincial Militia of Cuenca, the Regiment of La Unión, and a detachment of artillery, engineers and sappers; the 2nd Division, under Brigadier Gaspar Vigodet, with the Regiment of the Crown, the 1st Regiment of Guadix, the Regiment of the Military Orders, the Regiments of the Provincial Militias of Alcázar de San Juan, Córdoba, Ciudad Real and Ronda, and a detachment of artillery, engineers and sappers; the 3rd Division, under Brigadier Pedro Agustín Girón, with the Battalion of the Royal Spanish Guards, the Regiment of Bailén, the Regiment of Alpujarras, the Regiment of Light Infantry of Vélez-Málaga, the Regiments of the Provincial Militias of Écija and Jaén, and a detachment of artillery, engineers and sappers; the 4th Division, under General Francisco González Castejón, with the Royal Spanish Guards (1 bn), the 1st Regiment of Loja, the Regiment of Málaga, the 5th Regiment of Volunteers of Seville, the

Battalions of Provincial Militias of Córdoba, Bujalance and Jerez, and a detachment of artillery, engineers and sappers; the 5th Division under the command of General Courten, with the Regiment of Córdoba, the 2nd Regiment of Spain, the Regiment of Light Infantry of Chasseurs of Carmona, the Battalion of the Provincial Militia of Seville, and a detachment of artillery, engineers and sappers. The Cavalry Brigade under the command of General Zeraín, with the 1st Regiments of Alcántara, Spain, Farnesio, Montesa and the Prince, and the *guerrillas* of Zea y Osorio. Cavalry Brigade under the command of Viscount Zolina, with the Regiments of Fernando VII, the Queen, the 2nd of Santiago, and the Dragoons of the Queen, Granada and Madrid, and the Mountain Chasseurs of Córdoba. In total, 28,107 men and 27 cannon.[1]

Napoleonic Army: The Imperial Army under the command of King Joseph Bonaparte (although the battle was actually commanded by General Sebastiani), including the Division of the Royal Reserve, under General Desolles, with the Royal Guard, comprising the 1st Regiment of Grenadiers, the 1st Regiment of Shooters, the 1st Regiment of Mounted Chasseurs, the Regiment of Line Infantry of Toledo and the Mounted Artillery. The Royal Army, with the 1st Regiment of Madrid and the 2nd Regiment of Toledo. Madrid's Garrison, under the command of General Godinot, with the 51st Regiment of Line Infantry, the 12th Regiment of Light Infantry, the 27th Regiment of Mounted Chasseurs, and artillery. IV Army Corps, under the command of General Sebastiani de la Porta: the 1st Division of General Rey, including Rey's Brigade, with the 28th and 32nd Regiments of Line Infantry; Liger-Belair's Brigade, with the 58th and 75th Regiments of Line Infantry; the 2nd Division (*aka* the Polish Division), under the command of the Count of Valence, with the Infantry Brigade of the Grand Duchy of Warsaw, with their 4th, 7th and 9th Regiments of Line Infantry; the 3rd Division (*aka* the German Division), under the command of Barón Leval, with the Regiment of Nassau (2 bns), the Regiment of Baden (2 bns), the Regiment of Hesse-Darnstadt (2 bns), the Regiment of Holland (2 bns), the Battalion of Frankfurt and a detachment of artillery. The Cavalry Brigade under Count Merlín, with the 10th and 26th Regiments of Mounted Chasseurs, Polish Lancers, the Westphalian Light Cavalry and a detachment of Mounted Artillery. The 2nd Division of Dragoons under General Milhaud, including the 3rd Regiment of Dutch Hussars, and the 5th, 12th, 16th, 20th and 21st Regiments of Dragoons. In total, 28,797 men and 50 cannon.[2]

Background

At the end of June Venegas had not obeyed the order to harass Sebastiani's army that was on its way to fight the battle of Talavera. Nor did he take the opportunity to occupy unarmed Madrid. After the withdrawal of the allied forces of Wellington and García de la Cuesta towards Extremadura, Venegas was left alone in Castile La Mancha. The Supreme Central Junta ordered him to return to

Andalusia, since any defeat of the Army of La Mancha would leave Andalusia defenceless. However, Venegas did not withdraw. He decided to stay, and justified the decision in the manifestos that he would write months later: he considered it dishonourable to continue withdrawing, and preferred to be destroyed rather than go through the ignominy of such a withdrawal. It may be that Venegas was jealous of the successes of some of his colleagues, such as Castaños or García de la Cuesta, or perhaps he was tired of suffering bitter defeats such as those at Tudela and Uclés. Be that as it may, this time he was determined to confront Sebastiani.

At the beginning of August Venegas sent General Girón with three divisions to prevent Sebastiani's men from crossing the Tagus through Aranjuez. It was a minor battle, but the Spanish troops behaved worthily, under an efficient and resourceful general. It was probably a bittersweet victory for Venegas, since General Girón was also the nephew of General Castaños, whom Venegas hated.

On 6 August, the day after the battle at Aranjuez, he placed the 1st Division in Aranjuez, the 2nd and 3rd in Guardia, the 4th in Tembleque and the 5th Division on the outskirts of Toledo to keep watch on French movements. At dawn on 8 August the troops of King Joseph I and Sebastiani crossed the Tagus near Toledo, putting Zeraín's 5th Division in a tight spot. To reinforce this position, Venegas sent González de Castejón's 4th Division, which reached Almonacid. These movements must be considered imprudent at the very least, given that he was spreading out all his divisions over a distance of some 40km (25 miles). On the 9th Sebastiani launched two attacks on Zeraín's 5th Division and Lacy's 1st Division at the Añover fords, near Aranjuez. Zeraín held off the French as long as he could but, seeing that he was going to be overrun, he managed to retreat in good order and save his division. Things went badly for Lacy, however; at the height of the battle eighty lancers from the Regiment of Spain fled in terror before the French cavalry, leaving their infantry in a very weak situation. Only resolute action by the colonel of the Regiment of Ferdinand VII and the Lancers of Utrera (the new name of the legendary *garrochistas*) avoided a disaster. But Lacy's casualties had been significant. Among the dead was a nephew of General Girón himself.

On the 10th Sebastiani concentrated south of the Tagus, while Venegas gathered his troops in Almonacid, believing that the Corsican general had only 14,000 troops. Relying on this information, he met with his General Staff and they decided to attack the French army. The atmosphere was exultant: this was their big chance. However, in the afternoon two informants told Venegas that the French in fact had almost 30,000 troops. The commander of engineers Juan de Bouligny recommended a withdrawal, but Venegas replied that 'I am willing to attack because I do not want to be called General Withdrawal.'[3] Despite knowing that the French were within striking distance, Venegas went to sleep without taking any protective measures for his troops, even though he should have been aware of the Napoleonic habit of attacking at dawn.

The battle

As expected, the French attacked early in the morning of the 11th. A patrol was able to warn the Spanish of their arrival in time, and hastily Venegas arranged his divisions, from right to left: the 2nd Division, a little behind the rest; followed by the 4th Division; then the 5th Division; next to it, the 1st Division; and finally, in the rear, as a reserve, the 3rd Division, on the Cerrojones hills. On the two wings were the cavalry brigades. At the last minute Venegas made two decisions that would prove disastrous. First, he placed General Viscount Zolina in command of one of his cavalry brigades. Zolina was a brave cavalry officer, but he habitually charged the enemy with his sabre sheathed and reciting the rosary;[4] also he was extremely superstitious. The second decision, worse if possible, was to assign four of Girón's seven battalions to other points along the battle line, thus beginning the battle with practically no reserve infantry. There are those who suspect that Venegas was jealous of Girón's success in the battle of Aranjuez and wanted to give him only a secondary role in the new battle, as he feared the popularity that Girón might gain if the troops under his command were again to decide the fate of the combat (*see* Map 6).

The battle began with a very intense artillery fire, which caused many casualties among the infantry, particularly in the Spanish camp, as the French had twice as many cannon as the Spanish. Sebastiani knew that victory would be in his hand if he managed to surround the left wing and take over the Cerrojones hills, and so that was where his main effort was directed. But the Corsican general, unaware of the forces defending those hills, deployed the Polish Division of General Valence and the German Division of General Leval on the right. This meant that Girón, whom Venegas had abandoned to his fate with just three battalions, had to face fifteen Napoleonic battalions. General Lacy, seeing the Polish Division advancing on his left, sent his elite units, the Grenadiers and Chasseurs, to face them, led by Colonel Olazával. The fury of Lacy's men repulsed the Polish advance, and the Colonel of the 7th Infantry Regiment, Count Sobolewski, died in the combat. But Valence attacked Girón's men again, supported by Olazával's men, on two more occasions. And while on the first occasion they had to retreat, on the second, with the support of the German Division, they managed to overcome the Spanish defenders, who retreated in order but with a large number of casualties. As the left wing of the Spanish line was sinking, Venegas offered one of his more embarrassing displays of unfitness to command, sending an order to Girón that read briefly: 'Centralize.' In addition, the remaining reserve battalions had already been engaged in other points of the battle, and just to make matters worse still, the mounted artillery was missing. Bouligny, next to Venegas, was desperate.[5] At this point Venegas ordered the Regiment of Dragoons of Granada and the Lancers of Utrera, commanded by the eccentric Viscount Zolina, to charge against the infantry battalions of General Valence. But when the charge was at its height, Zolina's horse was killed and, superstitious as he was, he ordered the charge halted, to the surprise of some and the horror of many more, abandoning his horsemen at the worst possible moment. His men were annihilated and the squadrons were left practically without officers. Francisco Javier Idiáquez, Viscount Zolina, Grandee of Spain and related to the cream of the Spanish aristocracy, was not reproached for this inconceivable conduct.

For their part, Girón, Olazával and the rest of Lacy's Division had retreated towards the second peak of the Cerrojones hills, but they continued to be pressured by the Valence and Leval Divisions. The Spanish, without reinforcements or clear orders, and suffering heavy casualties, finally gave way when the Royal Spanish Guards weakened. At that moment, the Germans charged, but suddenly General Zerain appeared with a large detachment of cavalry. Hurriedly the Germans organized themselves into a square and repulsed Zerain's cavalry. General Merlin's cavalry counterattacked and defeated the Spanish, again causing heavy casualties. But the Spanish horsemen did not give up and Zeraín charged with new units, although in the end the Imperial forces won and held the two peaks of the Cerrojones, putting their defenders to flight towards the Cruz hill.

In the centre of the Spanish line was the 5th Division under the command of General Courten. Before them stood the Desolles Division and Godinot's Garrison of Madrid. Courten was an inexperienced general, and this, taken together with Venegas's passive attitude, left the 5th Division stoically awaiting orders under a constant cannonade from the French artillery. Finally Courten realized that he had no other choice but to retreat towards the Santo hill. On his right was González de Castejón's 4th Division, positioned between the 5th Division and an olive grove. After withstanding the French artillery, they endured the attack of the infantry, which pressed them until they were forced to retreat towards the town of Almonacid. Vigodet's 2nd Division, which had been somewhat delayed in the deployment of its troops, had also no choice but to retreat.

Meanwhile, Venegas watched everything without taking any action; observing while his divisions were being bled dry and each general was left to act as best he could, without support and trying to maintain order among ranks that had lost a large proportion of their officers, and while the cavalry tried to protect the retreating infantry, but always paying a very high price in each charge. And yet, the withdrawal took place in relative order until the first infantry units reached the Guazalete stream. Thirsty, they broke formation and rushed into the water. At that point Merlin and Milhaud's cavalry appeared and the carnage began. The Spanish divisions fled in disarray towards the village of Mora. Sebastiani had defeated Venegas, who remained unperturbed by the flight of his men, to which he responded with shameless haughtiness, rejecting all blame for the defeat.

Casualties among the French were about 2,000 men,[6] and twice that number on the Spanish side. Perhaps the worst blow to the Spanish was the large number of brave and experienced officers who fell on the battlefield or were captured by the enemy. For example, the colonel of the cavalry Regiment of Spain, Vicente Martínez, was killed in action; while Joaquín Clarebont and José Valdivia, colonels of the 1st Regiments of Volunteers of Seville and the Alcalá la Real, respectively, were seriously injured. Amon those taken prisoner were Diego Ballesteros and Juan Terán, colonels of the Dragoons of Granada and the Dragoons of the Queen. It was an absolute disaster. Surprisingly, the Army of La Mancha managed to regroup, although the Supreme Central Junta decided to transfer its command to General Eguía, relegating Venegas to be his lieutenant. Venegas did not accept the demotion and left his post to be appointed as Military Governor of Cádiz. There he succeeded only in increasing the number of his enemies, and was subsequently sent to be Viceroy of Mexico. There, his arrogant attitude served to spread the notion of independence among the Mexicans, which would culminate in the loss of one of the pearls of the Spanish Empire.

The battle of Almonacid reached a gruesome epilogue in the hermitage of the Virgen de la Oliva, where the imperial troops had sheltered several hundred wounded men.[7] The guerrillas commanded by Isidro Mir, Ventura Giménez and the priest León Yacer slipped into the hermitage and, after driving off the small escort left to protect the wounded, they slaughtered all the soldiers who had been beaten in combat. It was a shameful end to an infamous battle.

Notes

1. Sañudo Bayon (2011), pp. 216–17.
2. Ibid., pp. 218–19.
3. Ibid., p. 173.
4. Ibid., p. 178.
5. It may not be surprising that after living through this kind of experience, shortly afterwards he joined the Napoleonic army.
6. In his report of the battle, published in the *Gazeta del Gobierno* dated 31 August 1809, General Venegas increased the number of French casualties to 8,000, a figure that was clearly a fantasy.
7. French reports indicate between 200 and 500 wounded.

Chapter Twenty-Two

The Battle of Tamames

Date: 19 October 1809. *Place*: Tamames, Castile-Leon.
Result: Spanish victory.

Order of battle

Spanish Army: Army of the Left under the command of Lieutenant General Vicente Diego de Cañas y Portocarrero, Duke of Parque, comprising the Vanguard Division under General Martin de la Carrera, with the Regiment of Aragón (1 bn), the 1st Battalion of Barbastro, the Battalion of Monforte de Lemos, the Battalion of Morrazo, the Regiment Victory or Death (1 bn), the Regiment of the Prince (1 bn), the Regiment of Zaragoza (1 bn), the 1st and 2nd Regiments of Light Infantry of Catalonia, the Regiment of Light Infantry of Volunteers of Ciudad Rodrigo, the 1st Regiment of Light Infantry of Girona, the Battalion of Escolares de León, the Battalion of Monforte de Lemos, the Battalion of Victory Volunteers, the Dragoons of Lusitania and the Lancers of Ciudad Rodrigo; the 1st Division under General Losada, with the Regiment of Aragón (1 bn), the 4th Battalion of Provincial Grenadiers of La Unión, the 1st Regiment of Light Infantry of Barcelona, the Regiment of Light Infantry Volunteers of the Crown, the Regiment of Light Infantry of Galicia and the Battalion of the General, the Regiments of the Provincial Militias of Betanzos and Ourense; the 2nd Division under the command of General Ramón Patiño, Marquis of Castelar, with the

Regiment of Hibernia (1 bn), the Regiment of Lobera (1 bn), the 1st Regiment of Majorca (1 bn), the Regiment Inmemorial del Rey (1 bn), the 1st Regiment of Seville (1 bn) and the 1st Regiment of Toledo, the Regiments of Light Infantry Volunteers of Benavente, Navarra and Santiago, the Guides of the General, the Battalion of the General, and the Regiment of the Provincial Militia of Salamanca; the 5th Division, under the Marquis of Castrofuerte, with the Regiment of the Provincial Militia of Valladolid. The Cavalry Division under the command of General Pedro de Alcántara, with the squadrons of Bourbon, the 2nd of Algarve, of the Infante, of Montesa, the 2nd of the Queen and the 1st of the King; the Dragoons of Villaviciosa, Pavía, Sagunto and the Queen's, the Mounted Chasseurs of Granada and the Mounted Chasseurs of the General. A detachment of artillery, engineers and sappers. In total, near 23,600 men.[1]

Napoleonic Army: VI Army Corps under General Jean Gabriel Marchand, comprising the 1st Division, under its own command, with the Maucune Brigade, with the 6th Regiment of Light Infantry and the 69th Regiment of Line Infantry, and the Marcognet Brigade with the 39th and 76th Regiments of Line Infantry; the 2nd Division of General Maurice Mathieu, with the Labasse Brigade, with the 27th and 59th Regiments of Line Infantry and the 25th Regiment of Light Infantry. The Cavalry Division under the command of General Jean Lorcet, with the 10th, 15th and 25th Regiments of Dragoons, the 1st and 3rd Regiments of Hussars, and the 15th Regiment of Mounted Chasseurs. A detachment of artillery, engineers and sappers. In total, around 16,000 men.[2]

Background

In the spring of 1809 the Army of the Left, under the command of the always energetic Marquis de la Romana, succeeded in expelling the French from Galicia and Asturias. The Marquis left some of his units to defend those territories and, following the orders of the Central Junta, moved his army to Ciudad Rodrigo. There he was appointed to join the Supreme Central Junta as a representative of the military establishment, leaving the direction of his army to the Duke of Parque. His troops included some veterans of his expedition to Denmark, together with the Galician units that had served so well in the spring campaign, after the defeats of 1808.

The Duke of Parque's career before he was given command of the Army of the Left had had its ups and downs. It is true that he was part of Ferdinand VII's inner circle, but his ambiguous stance on the abdication of Bourbon and the appointment of Joseph Bonaparte as King had earned him the distrust of much of the Supreme Central Junta, which did not approve of his being given command of any military unit. García de la Cuesta gave him the opportunity to command one of his divisions, with which he fought in the calamitous battle of Medellín. However, his behaviour on that fateful day was admirable, and as a result he was granted command of the Army of the Left. Moreover, it should not be forgotten that some of the best generals had been dismissed or imprisoned by the Supreme Central Junta, largely thanks to the manoeuvres of Francisco de Saavedra and the Palafox clan,[3] while others, including Solano, Filangieri, the Count of Torre del Fresno[4] and Benito San Juan,[5] were accused of being cowards or *afrancesados* and killed by the mobs. Therefore, the Spanish Army was not overflowing with capable senior commanders. As had happened before, the command of the troops ended up being granted to generals with better political contacts than military skills, such as Venegas and Aréizaga.

As for the British allies, after the signing of the Armistice of Znaim in July 1809, which put an end to the hostilities between France and Austria as a result of the wars of the Fifth Coalition, Spain remained the only battlefield where they could take on the French emperor. Wellington reacted by retreating to Portugal, believing that it was wiser to defend the Portuguese country than to remain in Spain, faced with an enemy that clearly outnumbered his forces and an ally he did not trust.

As for the French side, Marshal Ney's VI Corps had become lord and master of the western part of Castile and León, at least on paper: the reality was very different. As in the areas occupied by the French in the rest of the peninsula, they were only masters of the terrain on which they stood. Everywhere they moved, they were harassed by relentless guerrilla attacks, which kept their forces exhausted and suffering a constant trickle of casualties. In addition, their informants warned them of the activity of the Army of the Left[6] in Ciudad Rodrigo, and they feared that at any moment the Spanish might attempt to capture Salamanca. Ney, who had defeated General Wilson's army in the battle of Puerto de Baños (Extremadura), was recalled by Napoleon, leaving interim command of his Army Corps to General Marchand. Moreover, the numerous requirements for units in other parts of Spain meant that by October the VI Corps retained only around half of its total strength. Thus the 3rd Division of the Army of the Left, under the command of General López Ballesteros, harassed Marchand's forces in the north, forcing the French to leave significant detachments behind to protect the provincial capitals and various communication hubs.

Meanwhile, the Supreme Central Junta had drawn up a new plan to conquer Madrid. With the Army of the Left he would pressure the French from Old Castile, while the Army of the Centre, under the recently appointed General Aréizaga, marched from Despeñaperros towards Madrid.

The battle

In early October the two armies set out to engage in battle. Neither of the two generals knew the precise details of the enemy's forces, but the Duke of Parque, recognizing the greater capacity for manoeuvre of the French, endeavoured to find a location that was favourable for combat. He found it in Tamames, to which he skilfully lured Marchand's divisions, making them believe that he was retreating. On 17 October he occupied the town and positioned his forces for combat: in front of the town was the Vanguard Division, with Martín de la Carrera's Division on the left and Losada's 1st Division on the right; behind was the Reserve Division of Ramón Patiño, Marquis of Castelar.[7]

On the 18th the French arrived. Marchand, still convinced that he was pursuing a retreating army, and convinced that the divisions now in front of him were its rearguard, divided his army into three columns with the intention of overrunning the Spanish left wing and exterminating it.

The Duke of Parque, who had hidden a large part of his force behind some hills, understood the French strategy and reinforced the left wing with units from the Reserve Division. Marchand launched his attack with Maucune's Brigade and Lorcet's light cavalry. Martín de la Carrera's infantry held up well against the enemy infantry, but weakened with the arrival of the French cavalry. The Duke of Parque sent a cavalry brigade to their aid, but Marchand's men, proud of their discipline and strength, easily repulsed them. The Spanish front line was overwhelmed and six artillery pieces were lost.

The Maucune Brigade pursued the disbanded Spanish forces to the top of the hill, only to encounter there the tight ranks of the infantry battalions of the Marquis of Castelar and those men of Martín de la Carrera's division who had managed to recover order and courage. Among them, Generals Mendizabal and de la Carrera were on their feet, sabres drawn, and exhorting their troops to battle; with fixed bayonets, after a rifle charge, the Spanish troops charged towards the French. With their cavalry too far behind to support them, Maucune's men fled in disarray, abandoning their rifles and backpacks on the way. It was a most unedifying scene for any admirer of the Napoleonic armies, albeit an unusual one. The Spanish managed to recover their lost artillery and even gained one more cannon.

On the right wing and in the centre things were no better for Marchand. Marcognet's Brigade, despite their clear numerical inferiority, were trying to ascend a steep slope in the face of relentless fire from the Spanish *voltigeurs* who were wreaking terrible damage on the advancing troops. A retreat seemed inevitable, but the French rallied and returned to the advance; but Losada's Division, supported by some Patiño battalions, held firm and even launched a counterattack with bayonets drawn, putting the French to flight. The 76th Regiment of Line Infantry suffered a true disaster, leaving behind on the battlefield not only a multitude of men but even its flag and its eagle.[8]

At 3.00pm Marchand realized that his troops could continue no longer and ordered them to retreat, a move that was covered by the Reserve Division. The Duke of Parque decided to stay in Tamames and not pursue the French, although Sir William Parker Carroll, Colonel of the Regiment of Hibernia, tells us that some 200 soldiers of the Barbastro Battalion could not restrain themselves from going out after the French to avenge past troubles.[9] As for casualties, the French losses totalled about 3,000, although some sources give a lower figure. Spanish casualties were 672 men, 112 of them dead. Apart from the aforementioned flag and eagle, the loot seized by the Spanish forces was substantial, not least in terms of rifles, ammunition and the backpacks that the French forces had abandoned in their hasty flight. There is no evidence that prisoners were taken.

The next day Ballesteros's 3rd Division joined the Spanish contingent, while the French troops reached Salamanca; Marchand, knowing he would not be able to defend the city, prepared a further retreat, which took place on 24 October. In the city were abandoned 3,000 prisoners and a large quantity of supplies, not least because Marchand needed space in his transports for all the silver, jewellery and works of art that he had stolen from all over the region. The next day the Duke of Parque entered Salamanca, obtaining large quantities of clothes and shoes for his dishevelled soldiery. He also took the opportunity to reinforce the 5th Division of José María Jalón, Marquis of Castrofuerte, with the new Provincial Battalions of León, Toro, Valladolid and Logroño.

In conclusion, it is worth noting that the action at Tamames was one of the few Spanish victories in a pitched battle against a Napoleonic Army. Typically, Spanish generals concluded their battle reports with a list of men deemed worthy to be rewarded for their actions on the battlefield. This list usually included only officers, and it is less common to read about the deeds of individual soldiers. But here, the Duke of Parque presented a list of recommendations to reward some of the common soldiers who carried out actions of merit in Tamames. We remember three of them: Francesc Planes, of the 1st Light Infantry of Barcelona, who killed six Frenchmen with his bayonet; the *voltigeur* José Ayer, of the Regiment of Aragón, who captured the flag with the eagle of the 76th French Regiment, killing its standard-bearer; and finally José Calvo, from the Regiment of the General, a 13-year-old drummer, who while drumming for the attack encouraged the soldiers by shouting: 'Long live Ferdinand VII!'[10]

Notes

1. Sañudo Bayon (2013), pp. 248–51; Vela (2016), p. 23.
2. Sañudo Bayon (2013), pp. 252–3.
3. Generals Castaños and García de la Cuesta suffered this fate.
4. Military governor of Extremadura. Lynched by a mob in 1808 falsely accused of being *afrancesado*.
5. Assassinated by his own troops after the defeat in the battle of Somosierra. In the mutiny, Castaños himself was about to be assassinated.
6. These two armies had already faced each other in the battle of Puentesampaio.
7. Ramón Patiño has already been quoted in this book. Specifically, he was involved in the Escorial Conspiracy and was in command of the defence of Madrid in the fall of 1808. Godoy's gaoler was named in the official report of the Duke of Parque (Supplement of the *Gazeta del Gobierno* of 16 November 1809), but also in other consulted works (Sañudo Bayon, 2013; Vela, 2016), as the Count of Belveder, another of his titles. In order to avoid confusion, he is referred to in this book as the Marquis of Castelar.
8. Pitollet (1933), p. 245; Napier (1834), p. 80. The Eagle is now missing.
9. Vela (2016), p. 42.
10. *Gazeta*, p. 440.

Chapter Twenty-Three

The Battle of Ocaña

Date: 19 November 1809. *Place*: Ocaña, Castile La Mancha.
Result: Napoleonic victory.

Order of battle

Spanish Army: the Army of the Centre under the command of General Juan Carlos de Areizaga, comprising the Vanguard Division under Brigadier José Pascual de Zayas y Chacón; the 1st Division under Brigadier Luis Lacy; the 2nd Division, under Brigadier Gaspar de Vigodet; the 3rd Division, under Brigadier Pedro Agustín Girón; the 4th Division, under General Francisco González Castejón; the 5th Division under General Tomás de Zeraín; the 6th Division under General Pelegrin Jácome; and the 7th Division under Brigadier Francisco Copons. Cavalry Corps under General Manuel Alberto Freire, with the 1st Division under General Juan Bernuy; the 2nd Division under Brigadier José Rivas; the 3rd Division under Brigadier Miguel March; and the 4th Division under Colonel Vicente Osorios. A detachment of 60 cannon and their artillerymen. In total 59,723 men.

Napoleonic Army: the command of King Joseph Bonaparte (although the battle was actually commanded by Marshal Soult, Duke of Dalmatia), with the following units: IV Army Corps under the command of General Horace Sébastiani, with the 2nd Division (Leval) and the 3rd Division (Werlé). Cavalry: the

113

3rd Division of Dragoons (Milhaud); V Army Corps under the command of Marshal Édouard Mortier, with the 1st Division (Girard) and 2nd Division (Gazan de la Peyrière). Cavalry Corps: Division of Light Cavalry of Paris, Division of Cavalry of Woirgard (or Beauregard), and the Division of Cavalry of the Royal Guards. Detachment of artillery under the command of General Alexandre-Antoine de Sénarmont, including 45 cannon and their artillerymen. A Reserve Division under the command of General Dessolles. In total, near 43,000 men.

Background[1]

Since the end of July, when the battle of Talavera took place, the situation on the La Mancha front had settled into a sort of deadlock. Although the allies might be considered to have won on the battlefield, the French managed to keep hold of Madrid and were able to consolidate their position in the northern area of La Mancha. However, they could not go further south. This does not mean that there were no clashes in the province of Toledo, but such actions as did take place, such as at Almonacid in August, which ended with a clear victory for the Napoleonic Army, did nothing to affect the territorial status quo.

The Supreme Central Junta was determined to put an end to this impasse. They wanted to strike a blow against Joseph Bonaparte's troops and clear the way to Madrid. In an unprecedented financial effort, the Supreme Central Junta managed to assemble the largest Spanish army in decades, indeed one of the largest in its history, with no fewer than almost 60,000 men (twice as many as at Almonacid, for example) and to equip them reasonably well (at least by the standards the Spanish troops were accustomed to). One of the principal problems was the usual lack of experienced officers; worst of all, though, command of the troops was given to one of the least competent generals in the Spanish Army: Juan Carlos de Areizaga. No one could deny his bravery, but he had neither the experience nor the ability to command an army like that of La Mancha. For the planned offensive, the Supreme Central Junta counted on the participation of both the Army of Extremadura under the command of the Duke of Albuquerque, which was to carry out diversionary manoeuvres, and Wellington's Anglo-Portuguese troops, but Wellington, who was in Seville during the preparations for the offensive, advised against it. The Junta turned a deaf ear to his arguments.

Areizaga assembled the new Army of the Centre in La Carolina on 1 November and set out to cross Despeñaperros. On the 6th he set up his headquarters in Daimiel (already in La Mancha), while his vanguard encountered some Napoleonic outposts. In these first clashes the Spanish forces usually came off best, so Areizaga confidently headed for Madrid. On the 10th they spent the night in Dosbarrios, in the province of Toledo, after a march of just over 100km (62 miles). Three days later Areizaga ordered part of his army to cover the main fords across the Tagus, but unexpected torrential rains caused the river to rise and, consequently, the Spanish forces did not cross it. Marshal Soult's forces, by contrast, managed to cross the river using various boat bridges. The French had manoeuvred skilfully and were now heading towards Ocaña. Faced with this threat to his route of retreat, Areizaga ordered his troops to withdraw to positions between Ocaña and Dosbarrios.

On 18 November Sebastiani, with the squadrons of Generals Milhaud and Paris, crossed the Tagus through Aranjuez and in Ontígola, just 4km (2.5 miles) to the south, encountered some of Areizaga's horsemen. The Spanish enjoyed numerical superiority, with some 4,000 Spanish horsemen facing near 3,000 French. This was the greatest number of cavalrymen engaged in combat in the entire Peninsular War. At first, the charges by the Spanish cavalry seemed to give them the advantage, but a counter-charge led by General Paris himself caused the Spanish to withdraw and disband. The Spanish cavalry suffered an undetermined number of casualties, although it is assumed that there were hundreds of dead, wounded and missing, among the latter being the distinguished writer and future politician, Ángel de Saavedra,[2] younger brother of the Duke of Rivas, who would later turn up wounded. The French troops lost some 100 casualties, the most regrettable being General Paris himself, who died during the charge that turned the battle. The survivors took refuge in Ocaña; upset by the disaster on the battlefield, they ruthlessly sacked the town.

The battle

The next morning General Areizaga, who had spent the night in Dosbarrios, arrived in Ocaña despite the seriousness of the situation. He arranged his troops in two lines, flanking the town of Ocaña, which he defended with parapets. In the first line, from left to right, he placed the Vanguard Division (Zayas), the 2nd Division (Vigodet), the 3rd Division (Girón), the 4th Division (Castejón) and the 1st Division (Lacy). In the second line were the 7th Division (Copons), behind Girón; the 5th Division (Zerain), behind Castejon; and the 6th Division (Jácome), behind Lacy. On the left wing were Rivas's cavalry units and on the extreme flank Freire's cavalry. The artillery was in the centre. The left and central edge of Areizaga's defensive line was protected by an uneven plateau, which became smoother as it lengthened towards his right flank. Soult, who was accompanied by King Joseph, was convinced that now was the time to attack, even though he had 17,000 fewer infantry as Victor's troops had not yet arrived. But he resolved that if he focused his attack on the Spanish centre and right flank, using Sebastiani and Mortier's divisions, he would have a chance of victory; he placed Joseph Bonaparte's men against the Spanish left flank, which was protected by the ravine of the Mesa de Ocaña. On the extreme left of his front he placed the cavalry units of Beauregard, Milhaud and General Paris, who had died the day before. It was probably at this point that the famous scene occurred when General Areizaga, spyglass in hand to observe the French deployment, exclaimed from the bell-tower of the church of Ocaña, 'What a mess, what a mess!' (*see* Map 7).

Once again, the first stages of the battle seemed to favour the Spanish. Their artillery began to hit the French positions hard, while the divisions of Lacy, Castejón and Girón managed to disrupt the offensive undertaken by Sebastiani's divisions, with Mortier's divisions to their rear. In fact, this movement was taken on the initiative of the aforementioned generals, as they did not receive any orders from Areizaga throughout the day; from his vantage point, he was a mere spectator to the disaster that was approaching, except for giving contradictory orders to Zayas first to attack and then to retreat. With General Leval's division in serious trouble and Dessolles' Reserve Division compromised, Sebastiani launched his cavalry against Freire's; unable to withstand the thrust, especially from the Polish lancers, the Spanish horsemen ended up disbanding and leaving the infantry on the flank, precisely where Lacy was distinguishing himself, in a seriously compromised situation. The French cavalry now began to run wild, overpowering the Spanish regiments fighting in the front line, which began to flee in disarray.

Some of the second-line regiments panicked and disbanded, while others managed to contain themselves and retreat in good order. A few, such as the 1st Marine Infantry of the Jácome Division or the 2nd Marine Infantry of Copons, tried to cover the retreat of the Vanguard units but were practically annihilated by Sebastiani's cavalry. Girard managed to enter Ocaña, where Spanish troops were trying to save what they could of their artillery; in the event, only twenty of the sixty guns were rescued. Seeing the scale of the disaster the Spanish left flank also gave way, and Zayas's men fled. Areizaga, on seeing that Girard's men were taking the town of Ocaña, climbed down from the bell-tower and fled in the direction of Daimiel, without bothering to give any instructions regarding the retreat.

Between 4,000 and 5,000 Spanish troops were killed or wounded, while the French took between 13,000 and 15,000 men prisoner. Yet after the battle Areizaga and his generals were only able to muster around 20,000 men to defend the Andalusian border. In other words, some 20,000 men had deserted. This was a scandalous figure. In addition, Soult's forces seized enormous quantities of Spanish arms and military supplies, and no fewer than thirty flags of Spanish regiments.

Areizaga tried to quit his post but his resignation was not accepted, and he had to defend the Andalusian passes with his meagre remaining forces. Unsurprisingly, he did not succeed, and Napoleon's troops penetrated Andalusia on 20 January 1810. With the troops that remained, Areizaga withdrew to Granada, where he handed over his command to General Blake. When the Supreme Central Junta fell, the Regency granted him various postings, usually as governor of places far from the front and where there was no need to move contingents of troops, and in September 1811 a trial was opened against him for the defeat at Ocaña. He was acquitted in July 1814. By then Ferdinand VII was already in Spain, and Areizaga was promoted to Captain General of Guipúzcoa and decorated with some of the most important Spanish orders. He died in Tolosa (Basque Country) in 1820.

Notes

1. Count of Toreno (1838), Vol. II; Guzmán, *La Batalla de Ocaña*.
2. (Cordoba, 1791–Madrid, 1865). Writer, ambassador, senator, in mid-century he became minister and president of the government (although only for two days). He would inherit the title Duke of Rivas from his older brother, after the latter's death without issue. His most outstanding work is *Don Álvaro o la fuerza del sino* (used by Verdi for his opera *La forza del destino*).

Chapter Twenty-Four

The Battle of Alba de Tormes

Date: 28 November 1809. *Place*: Alba de Tormes, Castile-Leon.
Result: Napoleonic victory.

Order of battle

Spanish Army: the Army of the Left, under the command of Lieutenant General Vicente Mª Diego de Cañas y Portocarrero, Duke of Parque, comprising the Vanguard Division under General Martin de la Carrera, with the Regiment of Aragón (1 bn), the 1st Battalion of Light Infantry of Barbastro, the Battalion of Monforte de Lemos, the Battalion of Morrazo, the Regiment Victory or Death (1 bn), the Regiment of the Princess (3 bns), the Regiment of Zaragoza (3 bns), the 1st Regiment of Light Infantry of Catalonia (1 bn), the 2nd Regiment of Light Infantry of Catalonia (1 bn), the Regiment of Light Infantry Volunteers of Ciudad Rodrigo, the 1st Regiment of Light Infantry of Girona, the Battalion of Escolares de León, the Battalion of Victory Volunteers, the Dragoons of Lusitania and the Lancers of Ciudad Rodrigo; the 1st Division, under General Losada, with the Regiment of Leon (2 bns), the 1st Regiment of Light Infantry of Aragón (2 bns), the 2nd Regiment of Light Infantry of Aragón (1 bn), the Regiment of Light Infantry Volunteers of the Crown (2 bns), the Regiment of Grenadiers of the Provincial Militia of Galicia and the Battalion of the General, the Regiments of the Provincial Militias of Ourense and Betanzos, and the 1st and 2nd Battalions of La Unión; the 2nd Division, under the command of

118

General Ramón Patiño, Marquis of Castelar,[1] with the Regiment Inmemorial del Rey (2 bns), the Regiment of Seville (1 bn), the Regiment of Toledo (1 bn), the Regiment of Zamora (1 bn), the Regiment of Hibernia (1 bn), the Regiment of Lobera (1 bn), the Battalion of Light Infantry Volunteers of Navarra and the Battalion of Light Infantry Volunteers of Santiago; the 3rd Division, under the command of General Francisco Ballesteros, with the Regiment of Navarra (2 bns) and the Regiment of the Princess (2 bns), together with the Battalions of the Provincial Militias of Oviedo, Covadonga, Villaviciosa, Candás, Castropol, Pravia, Cangas de Tineo, Grado, Infiesto and Lena (from the previous Asturian Army); the 5th Division, under the command of José María Jalón, Marquis of Castrofuerte, including the 1st Battalion of the Provincial Militia of Ciudad Rodrigo, the 2nd Battalion of the Provincial Militias of Ciudad Rodrigo Fernando VII, León, Toro, Valladolid and Logroño. Cavalry Division under the command of General Pedro de Alcántara, Prince of Anglona, with the Squadrons: Bourbon, 2nd of Algarve, of Infante, of Montesa, 2nd of the Queen and 1st of the King; Dragoons of Villaviciosa, of Pavía, of the Reina and of Sagunto; Mounted Chasseurs of Granada and Mounted Chasseurs of the General. A detachment of artillery, engineers and sappers. In total, around 36,000 men.[2]

Napoleonic Army: VI Army Corps under General Jean Gabriel Marchand, comprising the 1st Division, under his own command, with the Maucune Brigade, with the 6th Regiment of Light Infantry and the 69th Regiment of Line Infantry, and the Marcognet Brigade, with the 39th and 76th Regiments of Line Infantry; the 2nd Division, under General Maurice Mathieu, with the Labasse Brigade, with the 27th and 59th Regiments of Line Infantry and the 25th Regiment of Light Infantry. Cavalry Division under the command of General François Ettiene Kellerman, with the 10th, 15th and 25th Regiments of Dragoons; and, under the command of General Jean Lorcet, the 1st and 3rd Regiments of Hussars and the 15th Regiment of Mounted Chasseurs. A detachment of artillery, engineers and sappers. In total, around 16,000 men.[3]

Background

On 25 October, a few days after the victory over Marchand's army at Tamames, the Duke of Parque entered Salamanca with the Army of the Left. He needed to take a few days of rest for his men and to reinforce them with General Ballesteros's 3rd Division. New provincial regiments were also to join the weak 5th Division of General José María Jalón, Marquis of Castrofuerte; these new levy units (from León, Toro, Valladolid and Logroño) needed to receive at least basic instruction, as well as the necessary equipment. The Duke of Parque also took the opportunity to move some of the commanders. For instance, the experienced Ambrosio de la Cuadra[4] was assigned to serve as Castrofuerte's lieutenant.

On the French side, the interim command of VI Corps had passed into the hands of the energetic Françoise Etienne Kellerman, Duke of Valmy. He was the descendant of a noble family of Saxony settled in Alsace for two centuries; his father, Françoise Christophe Kellerman, was also a general during the French Revolution and the Napoleonic Wars. The Duke of Valmy had won Napoleon's esteem since he charged at the head of the cavalry at the battle of Marengo, which led to a radical turn of the battle in favour of the French. He also shone in the battle of Austerlitz, proving to be one of the most skilled cavalry officers in the Napoleonic armies. He accompanied Junot in the invasion of Portugal and, after the defeat at Vimeira, he used his diplomatic skills (during the French Revolution he was appointed ambassador to the United States) to obtain the advantageous conditions of the Treaty of Cintra. He was then sent to Spain to take part in the invasion led by Napoleon in the second half of 1808. Kellerman was neither a newcomer nor inexperienced. In November he ordered Marchand to move his troops to Tordesillas and from there to Medina del Campo, where he waited for the arrival of the Godinot Brigade that Joseph I had sent as reinforcements from Madrid.

The Duke of Parque, informed that the French were accumulating a large number of troops in Medina del Campo, decided to advance towards the town of Carpío, a few miles away, where a French detachment was camped. His plan was to attack them before reinforcements arrived. The battle of Medina del Campo took place on 23 November. After a day of intense fighting, in which artillery caused a large number of casualties on both sides, Kellerman threw his cavalry against the Spanish lines, which managed to repulse them. At the end of the day, when it began to get dark, the Duke of Parque decided to give his men a well-deserved rest, retreating towards Carpio. The next morning he was informed that the French had abandoned Medina del Campo, and he decided to stay in the town and wait to see how events would unfold. When he received the news of the catastrophe of the Army of the Centre in the battle of Ocaña, he decided to retreat. General Marchand, who had come back to command the VI Army Corps, began his pursuit.

The battle[5]

After a few days of marching, on 27 November the Duke of Parque halted his Army of the Left at Alba de Tormes, a town about 25km (15 miles) southeast of Salamanca. He found it a favourable place for his troops to rest and, trusting that the French Army was still a great distance behind, he made the crucial mistake of dividing his troops between the two banks of the Tormes river, leaving the 3rd and 5th Divisions on the right bank and the Vanguard, 1st and 2nd Divisions, together with the cavalry and the baggage train, on the left. According to García Fuertes (2006), he ordered the Prince of Anglona to send his horsemen out on patrol to watch for any indication of a French advance, but either through negligence or passivity the cavalry units did not deploy (*see* Map 8).

On the morning of 28 November, the troops of the Army of the Left were scattered around Alba de Tormes, resting after their long march. Suddenly, to their horror, they saw 4,000 French horsemen bearing down on them. The cavalry of Generals Lorcet and Kellerman were on the attack. With their formations broken, they had no time to organize their defence. Panic-stricken, they tried to cross the only bridge across the Tormes river, and the most desperate of them threw themselves into the cold water, while the French horsemen slaughtered the Galician and Asturian recruits without difficulty. Losada and Castelar's divisions, the 1st and 2nd respectively, suffered the most. The Duke of Parque, from the opposite bank of the river, could do little more than be a desperate spectator of the slaughter. The bridge, blocked by the baggage train, hardly allowed any traffic across. The Prince of Anglona tried to throw in his cavalry to repel the French, but his troops were outnumbered 4 to 1 and were quickly routed.

General Kellerman had been very skilful. His cavalry division, along with Lorcet's Hussars, had advanced ahead of the bulk of Marchand's infantry. Arriving in the vicinity of Alba de Tormes, he saw that the Spanish troops were unprepared for an attack. Without hesitating, he organized his horsemen into lines, with Lorcet's Hussars in the front, followed by two lines of his Dragoons, and then the rest of his cavalry. He had it in his hands to annihilate the Army of the Left.

However, the slaughter had given the rest of Castelar's men and Martín de la Carrera's Vanguard Division precious time to prepare themselves. The energetic General Mendizábal, the Duke of Parque's lieutenant, who was on the riverbank under attack, managed to organize infantry squares on the slopes of the Tejares hill. Now the second phase of the battle began. Kellerman and Lorcet regrouped their horsemen and threw themselves on the Spanish squares. For the first time in the entire war the Spanish infantry squares were able to repel French cavalry charges without dispersing or fleeing in panic. Kellerman launched three cavalry charges and all three hit the Spanish wall. However, the clever French general was not concerned with breaking the squares; he was simply buying time for Marchand's infantry to arrive. Once their forces were combined, surely they could destroy what was left of the Spanish Army.

Two hours later Marchand arrived at full speed on the battlefield. It was mid-afternoon but already beginning to get dark. Maucune's Brigade was in the van, and its troops threw themselves against the Spanish troops. Marchand offered Mendizábal the chance to surrender. There was no real choice but to surrender or die. But Generals Mendizábal and Carrera decided to continue resisting and to try to organize an orderly retreat towards the bridge, which had already been cleared of the baggage train. The Vanguard Division was the last to cross. Despite withdrawing in orderly fashion, repeated enemy cavalry charges and infantry fire caused heavy casualties among the Spanish. Those who fell wounded could not be picked up as it was forbidden to stop.

After dark the French artillery was engaged in shelling the town of Alba de Tormes, while the French infantry and cavalry massacred the Spanish soldiers who had straggled behind and finished off the wounded. Rumour had it that the Spanish had executed French prisoners after the battle of Medina del Campo, and on this occasion the French took their revenge by murdering dozens of Spanish soldiers who had surrendered. Among those executed were some 200 brave men who had stayed behind to defend the bridge so that their comrades could escape.

In the final balance of the battle, the Spanish troops had to add some 3,000 dead and some 2,000 prisoners. During the night and the following morning the Duke of Parque tried to reorganize his troops, but rumours that French cavalry were already crossing the river caused a rout, with large numbers of soldiers deserting, fleeing to Portugal, joining the guerrillas or simply returning home. Weeks later, when the general finally managed to rally his troops, only about 17,000 soldiers remained out of the nearly 30,000 in the Army of the Left. Shortly afterwards, the Duke of Parque was dismissed and sent to the distant Canary Islands as governor. Command of the army passed to General Mendizábal, who was also given the title Count of the Cuadro de Alba de Tormes (literally, Count of the Square of Alba de Tormes). The French suffered just under 500 casualties. Subsequently, the new organization of the armies by the Council of Regency divided the surviving troops into new armies that were cantoned in Asturias, northern Extremadura and on the border between Portugal and Andalusia. Marchand left Alba de Tormes occupied and retreated towards Valladolid.

Notes

1. As previously mentioned, in the sources he is commonly quoted as the Count of Belveder.
2. García García (2016). The Army of the Left had also the 4th Division under the command of General Mahy, but since the beginning of 1809 he had been in the north, specifically in Asturias, defending the border with Cantabria from the advance of Napoleon's forces.
3. Sañudo Bayon (2013), pp. 252–3.
4. Veteran from the Division of the North, and the battles of Puentesampaio or Tamames, among others.
5. Kellerman's statement can be found in *The Journal de l'Empire* (Tuesday, 19 December 1809), García Fuertes (2006) and García García (2016).

Chapter Twenty-Five

The Sieges of Girona

Date: 9 May–10 December 1809. *Place*: Girona, Catalonia.
Result: Napoleonic victory.

Order of battle

Spanish Army: The military governor of the city was General Mariano Álvarez de Castro, with Julián de Bolívar as his second-in-command, Enrique O'Reilly as his major general, and Blas de Fournàs in command of the *Miquelets*.[1] At their disposal were the following units: the Ultonia Regiment (3 bns), the Bourbon Regiment (3 bns), the 2nd Barcelona Volunteer Battalion, the 1st Girona *Miquelets* Battalion and 1st Vic *Miquelets* Battalion, plus the Sant Narcís Squadron, the Royal Artillery Corps, the Mariners of the Coast, the Corps of Engineers and Mining Sappers (Guillermo Minali). In addition, throughout the siege, fresh troops managed to enter the city, including the *Miquelets* of the 2nd Girona Tercio, the Santa Fe Infantry Regiment, the Cervera Battalion of *Miquelets*, the Tarragona Volunteer Battalion, the Regiment of Infantry of Baza (1 bn), the Grenadiers of the Iberia Regiment, the 1st and 2nd Battalions of *Miquelets* of Talarn, and the 2nd Battalion of *Miquelets* de Vic. In total, 5,723 men.[2]

Napoleonic Army: the Generals-in-Chief were Marshal Saint-Cyr from May to August, and Marshal Augereau from August to December, with Jean Antoine Verdier as the second-in-command. Their forces comprised General Joseph

123

Souham's Division, with 1st Light Infantry Regiment (3 bns), the Provisional Regiment (4 bns), the 42nd Line Infantry Regiment (3 bns) and the 24th Dragoon Regiment (3 sqns); General Chabot's division, with the 2nd Neapolitan Line Infantry Regiment (2 bns) and the Chasseurs des Pyrénées-Orientales (1 bn); General Verdier's Division, with the French Brigade, with the 32nd Light Infantry Regiment (1 bn), the 2nd Line Infantry Regiment (1 bn), the 16th Line Infantry Regiment (1 bn), the 56th Line Infantry Regiment (1 bn); the German Brigade, with the Würzburg Regiment (2 bns), and the 1st and 2nd Berg Regiments (2 bns each; General Domenico Pino's Italian Division, with the 4th Line Infantry Regiment (3 bns), the 6th Line Infantry Regiment (3 bns), the 7th Line Infantry Regiment (3 bns), the 1st Light Infantry Regiment (3 bns), the 2nd Light Infantry Regiment (1 bn), the Royal Dragoons Regiment (3 sns), and the Royal Horse Hunters Regiment (3 sqns); General Morio de L'Isle's Division, with the 2nd Westphalian Regiment (2 bns), the 3rd Westphalian Regiment (2 bns), the 4th Westphalian Regiment (2 bns), and the 1st Light Infantry Battalion; the Lechi Division, with the Velites Reales (1 bn), the 5th Line Infantry Regiment (2 bns), the 1st Neapolitan Regiment (1 bn) and the 1st Italian Regiment (2 bns). In addition, Engineer and Sapper Regiments (Sanson) and an Artillery Regiment (Tassel). In total, more than 30,000 men.[3]

Background[4]

After Reding's death, Spain lost one of its best generals. Catalonia also lost its Captain General. The command was temporarily assumed by Antoine Malet, Marquis de Coupigny, until May, when he was replaced by Joaquín Blake, who tried to develop a real army in Catalonia. But despite his efforts, he was unable to impose order on the undisciplined Catalan troops. They were not good soldiers, but without doubt they were the most effective and cruel guerrilla fighters in Spain. For the Italian historian Gabriele Pepe, the Catalan insurrection was not about gaining a military victory, but rather about exterminating the enemy. Clarós and Milans del Bosch were compared to Attila and Nero. Their prisoners were not only killed: they were tortured and their bodies dismembered. This plunged the young Napoleonic soldiers into the deepest terror.

Saint-Cyr, the French Captain General of Catalonia, without any army to face, roamed freely through Tarragona's countryside. Leaving Pino's Division in Valls, and with Souham in support, he reached the walls of Tarragona. But with the city was overcrowded with refugees and suffering from a typhus epidemic; lacking siege weapons, he decided to leave. Souham entered Reus, which was occupied without opposition. Saint-Cyr withdrew to the north and decided to prepare for the capture of Girona. However, the Napoleonic Army had its own problems. To begin with, it was a heterogeneous, multinational army; its troops were made up of French, Polish, Saxon, Westphalian, Lombard and Neapolitan soldiers. In his memoirs Commander Baron Desvernois complained bitterly about the indiscipline and constant drunkenness of the Germans and Italians.

One Westphalian division, for example, arrived with 5,000 soldiers, but after six months only had a few hundred troops left. And in the case of the Italians, of the almost 25,000 who arrived in Catalonia throughout the war, only about 9,000 returned, and most of them were wounded. These soldiers were fighting for a foreign country in a foreign country, in an extremely hostile environment, factors which led to widespread demotivation and indiscipline.

This attitude was greatly exacerbated by the attitude of their commanders, especially Duhesme and Lechi, who were concerned with enriching themselves at any price and indulging in a licentious life far removed from a strict military spirit. Giuseppe Lechi, for example, as commander of the Barcelona garrison surrounded himself with a motley crew of characters, each one more sinister and corrupt than the next, who dedicated themselves to extortion, theft and murder. On one occasion they stabbed a Milanese moneylender, known as Canton. The case so scandalized the French authorities that they imprisoned Lechi's entire court; they were subsequently tried and imprisoned in Paris until 1813. After his release, Lechi returned to Italy to serve his friend and mentor, the King of Naples, Murat. However, for some Barcelonians, Lechi's departure meant the loss of one of the finest experiences to be had in the city: a stroll in front of Madame de Ruga's balcony. It is said that the impudent and brazen Ruga was one of the most beautiful women in Milan. Her husband, Sigismundo Ruga, was a careerist lawyer who had become rich with the arrival of the French in the Kingdom of Italy. His wife soon became the mistress of several French generals. Indeed, Lechi took her to Barcelona and installed her in the Larrard palace, where Madame de Ruga liked to show off her generous cleavage to the passers-by who, with that excuse, walked up and down the street for hours. In her memoirs, the always caustic Duchess d'Abrantes describes Madame de Ruga as a woman of extraordinary beauty, but with a moustache like a drum major which spoilt her otherwise perfect features. Needless to say, it would not be bushy enough for the people of Barcelona not to be able to enjoy her other charms.

The First Siege: 22 July–20 August 1808

Confident that the situation in Barcelona was stable, Duhesme planned the siege of Girona, knowing that it would require more than a mere assault by his elite troops. Thus, on 22 June he arrived at the gates of Girona with the two brigades from the Chabran Division, a brigade from the Lechi Division, three cavalry regiments and a siege train. On the 24th Reille's Division arrived from Figueres. At the same time, the 1,400 men of the 2nd Barcelona Volunteer Battalion also managed to enter the city, since the French had not managed to close off the entire perimeter of the city.

Duhesme began a bombardment of the city with the aim of wrecking its defences and sapping the morale of the citizens, but he did not dare to launch the first assault until the night of 13/14 August, on the castle of Montjuïc.[5] But by then, the new Spanish Captain General of Catalonia, the Marquis of Palacio, had already been able to gather various troops to attack Duhesme from the outside. Colonel Raymond de Caldagués of the Regiment of Bourbon, a French émigré in the service of the Spanish crown, arrived from Majorca with his own regiment and the grenadiers of the Regiment of Soria. On his arrival, Caldagués managed to contact the defenders of Girona and organize a counterattack, in which offensives from the inside and the outside would be mounted simultaneously. Thus, on the 16th two columns set out from inside the city, the first under the command of Narcís de la Valette, and the second under the command of Enrique O'Donnell. On the outside, Caldagués's forces were joined by the *Miquelets* of Milans del Bosch and Clarós. The Spanish forces totalled some 5,000 men.

Duhesme's men managed to hold out for a few hours, but ended up giving up the ground they had gained for so much blood during the previous days, and retreated to the Ter river line. That night Duhesme, fearing that the Catalan forces might be more numerous than he knew, and that he would be overrun from the rear, ordered fires to be lit and ordered his troops to withdraw stealthily towards Barcelona. Girona had successfully resisted the siege. However, some of the heroes of the first siege would never return to Girona, at least until after the war. A few months later both Caldagués and Valette were captured and sent to France, where they were held until the end of the war.

The Second Siege: 2 May–10 December 1809

At the beginning of 1809 the enthusiastic General Mariano Álvarez de Castro took over as Governor of Girona and Julián de Bolívar returned to his former position as *teniente de rey*.[6] Preparations quickly began to defend the city from a possible new siege, a task in which Engineer Colonel Guillermo Minali, a Milanese in the service of the Spanish crown, excelled. There had also been changes in the Napoleonic leadership of Catalonia. Now the command was under General Laurent de Gouvion Saint-Cyr, who in April began to accumulate troops to subdue, once and for all, the unruly city of Girona. On 2 May 1809 Saint-Cyr began to position his artillery and to distribute the best regiments at his disposal.

In Girona Álvarez de Castro, supported by his enraged citizens, rejected any possibility of surrender, although their chances of beating off the French a second time were practically nil: with an insufficient garrison and walls that had hardly been updated since medieval times, they could hardly withstand a modern siege. But the watchword was clear: resist until death. The entire city prepared to fight, to resist and to die. A group of women even organized themselves into the so-called Santa Bárbara Company; they asked for permission to fight, but when this was denied, they took charge of collecting the wounded and carrying water and weapons to the front. Organized into four squads, all of them were wives, mothers or daughters of men fighting for the city. Thus, for example, the commander of one of the squads was Lucía Jonama de Fitzgerald, wife of a captain in the Regiment of Ultonia. Their performance was crucial for the defence of the city; indeed, when Ferdinand VII returned to Spain he met them personally and they were decorated and received a pension.

On the French side the main aim of the plan of attack designed by Verdier was, just as had happened in the first siege, to conquer the castle of Montjuïc, a key strongpoint in the defences of Girona. If Montjuïc fell, the city would fall with it. The governor of the castle was another émigré of the French Revolution, Colonel Blas de Fournas de Labrosse from Narbonne. On 19 June the French conquered the bastion of Sant Lluís, the most advanced point of the castle. Afterwards, its other bastions would fall successively: Sant Narcís, Sant Daniel and Sant Joan, the latter representing a serious blow for the defenders, since it was the bastion that connected the castle with the city. On 8 July French infantry entered the castle, but it was not until 10 August that its last defenders withdrew. The sapper commander Hubert Rohault de Fleury was the first to storm Montjuïc castle, for which he received a Legion of Honour. This officer would go on to become a major general under Napoleon III.

On the outside, the Captain General of Catalonia, Joaquín Blake, did not have enough forces to break the French encirclement of the city, but far from maintaining a passive attitude, he was able to locate the weak points of the Napoleonic forces, allowing the entry into the city of fresh troops and supplies no fewer than four times: on 1 July, 3 and 17 August, and 1 September. The latter was especially humiliating for Angereau, who had just replaced Saint-Cyr, since Blake managed to bring in a convoy under the command of Colonel Enrique O'Donnell with 1,500 oxen loaded with weapons and food, as well as the entire Regiment of Baza. The French general prepared his final assault for 19 September. That day, taking advantage of a breach that the artillery had opened in the area known as the German Barracks, the French finally penetrated the city. But they had not counted on the furious response of the defenders who, despite their obvious inferiority, managed to drive them out. Since then, 19 September has been celebrated as 'the Great Day of Girona'.

The success of that day encouraged the defenders to carry out a surprise sortie to disable part of the French artillery and try to finish off the besiegers, whose morale must already have been at rock bottom. Some families in the city, concerned for their safety, asked to be escorted to Santa Coloma de Farners, where Blake was positioned. For this reason, Enrique O'Donnell planned an attack for the night of 14/15 October with a column of some 1,200 men. Taking advantage of the darkness, O'Donnell's force attacked various French camps, among them that of General Souham himself, who had to flee in a hurry on horseback wearing his nightgown. The Spanish troops seized large amounts of money, ammunition, horses, food and even Souham's decorations.[7] Despite being pursued by a detachment of dragoons, O'Donnell's column managed to reach Santa Coloma de Farners with their booty and the civilians who had wanted to keep safe. For this action, O'Donnell was promoted to general.

In view of subsequent events, it can be concluded that, without detracting from its merit, this sortie was still a Pyrrhic victory. O'Donnell, from the outside, could hardly counter the French troops, although he tried, with more courage than effectiveness. After this event, Augereau reinforced the siege of the city, making it increasingly difficult for the Spanish to bring in food and ammunition. The forces inside the city were dwindling and there were Dantesque scenes of hunger, death and destruction. Álvarez de Castro refused to surrender, although some dissenting voices began to be heard among the city's patricians. But the citizens and soldiers were with Alvarez de Castro to the death. He fell seriously ill with fever on 8 December and was replaced by Julián de Bolívar. Two days later Girona surrendered. Casualties were staggering on both sides. The French had lost about 4,000. Their dead included Colonel Pietro Foresti,[8] the man who had thrown Álvarez de Castro out of the castle of Montjuïc in Barcelona, when the Napoleonic troops occupied the city; and the sapper captain Hyacinthe Hullin de Boischevalier, Brigitte Bardot's great-great-grandfather![9] The city lost more than a third of its population, with just over 6,000 casualties. The Spanish forces suffered 5,122 deaths, including Joaquín de Mendoza,[10] and 4,248 taken prisoner, including Bolívar, Fournas de Labrosse and Minali. All of them were taken to France, where they spent the rest of the war. General Alvarez de Castro, who was already seriously ill, could not be transferred to France and died in prison in the castle of Figueres on 10 January 1810. A man died, but a legend was born.

Notes

1. In the traditional organization of the armies of Catalonia, the name given to the volunteer corps who presented themselves to fight outside their municipalities and under a certain military discipline. They were unlike the *Somatenes*, who never left their place of origin and, although they obeyed a certain hierarchy, had much laxer discipline.
2. Minali (1840).
3. Ibid.
4. Ibid.; Fuster Vilaplana (1959); Noulans (1990).
5. Not to be confused with the castle of the same name in Barcelona. In addition, the city had three forts: Condestable, Santa Ana and Capuchinos; as well as various bastions, the most important being Sant Lluís, Sant Narcís, Sant Daniel and Sant Joan.
6. The lieutenant of the governor.
7. Grahit i Grau (1959), p. 289; Longman et al. (1811), pp. 789–90; VVAA (1813), pp. 647–8; VVAA (1815), pp. 334–5.
8. Lombroso (1843), pp. 264–5.
9. https://www.alsace-genealogie.com/spip.php?article162 (accessed 14 February 2022).
10. The deposed governor of the city, imprisoned in May 1808 for allegedly being *afrancessado*, asked Álvarez de Castro to release him so that he could participate in the defence of the city. He died on 24 August in the Sarracines at the head of the troops he commanded.

Chapter Twenty-Six

The Retreat of the Army of Extremadura

Date: 10 January–5 February 1810. *Place*: from Don Benito (Extremadura) to Isla de León (Andalusia). *Result*: Spanish victory.

Order of battle

Spanish Army: under the command of General José María de la Cueva y de la Cerda, Duke of Albuquerque, with the Regiment of the Royal Spanish Guards (2 bns), the Battalions of the Provincial Militias of Sigüenza, Guadix, Córdoba, Ciudad Rodrigo, Trujillo and Ronda, the 2nd Battalion of Volunteers of Madrid, the Battalion Imperiales de Toledo, the Battalion Volunteers of the Fatherland, the Battalion Loyals of Fernando VII, the 2nd Battalion Light Infantry of Catalonia, the Battalion of Light Infantry of Campo Mayor, the Battalion of Light Infantry of Valencia de Albuquerque, the Battalion of Grenadiers of the Canary Islands, the Battalion of the Canary Islands, the Battalion of Ayamonte (1 coy), the Infantry Company of Marbella, the 2nd and 4th Battalions of Volunteers of Seville, the Battalion of Distinguished Volunteers of Jerez, the Battalion of Shooters of Spain, and the Regiment of Loja (1 bn). Cavalry Division: the Regiment of Royal Carabineers, the Regiment of the King, the Regiment of Dragoons of Granada, the Regiment of Calatrava, the Regiment of Dragoons of

129

Villaviciosa, the Regiment of Mounted Chasseurs of Spain (*aka* the 4th Regiment of Hussars), and the Regiment of Perseguidores de Andalucia. In total, 11,000–14,000 men.[1]

Background[2]

Following the retreat of the allied army after the battle of Talavera in July 1809, the French forces had relentlessly pushed the Spanish troops westwards. Thus, while Wellington entered Portugal, the Army of Extremadura remained in the region from which it took its name. At its head was General Gregorio García de la Cuesta. No one can deny that he was a fine military man, certainly among the best of Spain's high command. However, he had a great facility for making powerful enemies. Neither Wellington nor many members of the Supreme Central Junta could stand him, so much so that in early December 1809 he was dismissed. In his place they appointed someone radically opposed to Cuesta: General José María de la Cueva y de la Cerda, Duke of Albuquerque. A talented young military man (García de la Cuesta was almost twice his age), he also had a very good relationship with Wellington, not least because the units under his command at Talavera attracted the attention of the British general for their brilliance.

During the second half of November Spain suffered two defeats that wiped out its two largest armies. On the 19th General Areizaga lost the largest and best-equipped Spanish Army in decades at the battle of Ocaña, where the Army of the Centre was destroyed. On the 29th the Army of the Left, under the command of the Duke of Parque, suffered a terrible defeat at Alba de Tormes, in which it lost almost half of its forces. With these victories, the French had opened the door for their conquest of Andalusia.

The retreat[3]

Since the end of December 1809 the Army of Extremadura, under the command of the Duke of Albuquerque, had been quartered near Don Benito, a town 110km (68 miles) east of Badajoz, 85km (52 miles) southeast of Cáceres and 210km (130 miles) north of Seville.

In mid-January 1810 the Central Supreme Junta ordered Albuquerque to move to Almadén to reinforce the troops of Brigadier Zeraín, part of the remnants of the Army of the Centre. On arriving at Campanario, about 25km (15 miles) away in the province of Badajoz, Albuquerque received the news that Zeraín had been defeated. So he decided to change his route and head towards Seville, as he rightly considered that Almadén was already in French hands. For its part, the Junta of Extremadura ordered him to send troops to defend Badajoz. Thus, on 16 January Albuquerque divided his troops: the artillery, escorted by half his cavalry, would take the route of the Camino Real through the towns of Santos, Monasterio, Santa Olalla and Ronquillo. Under the command of General Menacho,[4] he sent the Regiment of Osuna, a battalion of the Regiment of Light

Infantry of Seville and a battalion of the Chasseurs of Zafra towards Badajoz.[5] Meanwhile, he sent the division of General Senén de Contreras, composed of the battalion of the Tiradores de Mérida, the Chasseurs of Serena and the Regiment of Light Infantry of the Loyalists of Ferdinand VII, towards the Aracena Mountains, in the north of the province of Huelva.[6] As for Albuquerque, he continued with the bulk of his troops towards Seville, along the way picking up scattered elements from the Zeraín and Copons divisions,[7] although the bulk of the men from these divisions, with their generals, took an alternative path towards the southwest and could not be contacted by the Army of Extremadura.

On 23 January the Central Supreme Junta ordered Albuquerque to go to Córdoba. Prudently, he sent one of his aides, General Álava, to Seville. There, on 24 January, Álava witnessed the Dantesque spectacle of a rioting city. The members of the Supreme Central Junta, with the French at the gates, had granted General Castaños command of their armies and the rank of Captain General of Andalusia; this was the man they had unjustly defenestrated after the defeat at the battle of Tudela and whose malicious propaganda had brought him to the brink of being lynched in the Castilian town of Miguelturra. The veteran general from Madrid only escaped with his life thanks to the energetic actions of his bodyguard, who pulled him out of the arms of the crowd.[8] Now, the members of the Central Supreme Junta decided to withdraw towards Cádiz, a move that was seen as a betrayal by the citizens of Seville. The selfless Castaños escorted them on their way, saving them from being lynched in some towns, as was the case in Jerez de la Frontera.[9] No one can say that Castaños was spiteful. On 29 January the members of the Supreme Central Junta arrived in Cádiz, but on the way they had lost what little prestige they had left. Once in Cadiz, they all resigned *en bloc* and the creation of a Regency Council was proclaimed, which was presided over by General Castaños. That same day a momentous meeting of the French high command took place in Carmona, during which they decided to occupy Seville instead of pursuing the Junta to Cadiz, mistakenly believing that the fall of Seville would cause the surrender of the Spanish throughout Spain.

Meanwhile, the Seville uprising had led to the release of Francisco de Palafox and the Count of Montijo from prison, where they had been confined for their conspicuous conspiracies against the Junta. They, along with the Marquis de la Romana, now formed a new Supreme Governing Junta, and their fiery patriotism led them to call upon the people of Seville to resist the French. The people armed themselves as best they could. Montijo himself, with a flimsy excuse, abandoned the city the next day.[10] In fact, when the French troops approached, most of the members of all the Juntas (the two Supreme and the one from Seville) fled towards Cádiz. On 30 January Joseph Bonaparte's army arrived in Torreblanca de los Caños[11] and Eusebio de Herrera, one of the few members of the Seville Junta who had decided to stay, went there to negotiate with the invaders and agree the terms of the occupation. And while it is true that the occupation of Seville was peaceful, it is no less true that the cultural and artistic despoilment suffered by the city was unparalleled in history. On 1 February Joseph Bonaparte entered Seville and appointed Eusebio de Herrera as mayor. Córdoba and Jaén had already fallen into French hands on 23 January. On the 28th Granada fell, and Malaga on 5 February. Almería was not reached until 15 March.

Meanwhile, the Duke of Albuquerque, in view of the wider situation, and finding himself surrounded by Napoleonic armies, decided to disobey the orders of the Supreme Central Junta and retreated south, instead of heading towards Cordoba. It was a crucial decision, as it would save not only Cadiz, but perhaps the fate of the patriot cause in the whole of Spain. On the 27th he reached Écija (halfway between Seville and Córdoba), where he met his old enemy, General Digeon,[12] whose 16th and 24th Regiments of Dragoons managed to take several prisoners from among the cavalry squadrons of the Dragoons of Granada and Calatrava, although the bulk of Albuquerque's troops managed to continue their way south. On the 28th they arrived in Carmona, where Albuquerque decided to divide his troops and establish Jerez de la Frontera as a meeting point. From then on, there were constant encounters with French outposts. In these battles Albuquerque's cavalry, under the command of Colonel José Escudero Lisón, showed extraordinary bravery in the face of superior and better armed forces.

Finally, on 30 January Albuquerque reached Jerez de la Frontera, some 30km (18 miles) from Cádiz. On 2 February the vanguard of the Army of Extremadura crossed the Zuazo bridge, the only bridge leading to the island of León.[13] The Regiment of Calatrava was still in the rear, fighting the French dragoons, desperately buying time for the bulk of the army to reach safety on the island. General Victor was not aware of the size of the force commanded by Albuquerque until it was too late. He began a pursuit, but when he reached the Zuazo bridge on 5 February the last Spanish units were already crossing it, escorted by the squadrons of the Regiment of Calatrava, which was still fending off Victor's advance guard. Between 6 and 11 February the Portazgo battle took place. General Victor offered terms for the surrender of the city of Cádiz and the troops of Albuquerque on the island of León, but this was utterly rejected. For five consecutive days the French launched attacks on the Zuazo bridgehead, the only land route giving access to the city. But all the efforts of General Victor were in vain, due to the tenacious resistance of Albuquerque's exhausted troops and the effective artillery commanded by Diego de Alvear. On the 11th the landing of Anglo-Portuguese troops convinced Victor of the impossibility of taking the city by assault, and instead he began work on the siege of the city. The imperial eagles would not nest in Cadiz.

What followed was a regrettable act of ingratitude and disloyalty. At first the people and the Junta of Cádiz welcomed their saviours with open arms, and even offered the post of governor of the city to Albuquerque himself, which he refused.[14] But soon there were disagreements between the Junta and the general, which began with the Junta's refusal to allow his soldiers, even the many wounded, to enter the city of Cádiz, forcing them to remain on the island of León. This decision was perhaps understandable, given that the city was already full of refugees. What was more difficult to accept was the delay in supplying food and medical help to the wounded. Meanwhile, Albuquerque's troops were busy fortifying the island to defend it against Victor's troops, who were already preparing the siege.

Political power in Cádiz at that time was divided between the Regency Council, presided over by General Castaños, in charge of governing free Spain, and the Junta of Cádiz, in charge of local government, controlled by General Venegas.[15] The Duke of Albuquerque received only empty promises from the Junta of Cádiz, and fed up with waiting for his requests to be satisfied, he lodged a complaint with the Regency Council; this provoked a furious backlash from the Junta of Cádiz, which accused him of disloyalty. Then the Regency Council decided to send the Duke of Albuquerque to London as ambassador and Venegas to Mexico as viceroy. Cadiz and the island of León would endure a siege that lasted until 24 August 1812, when the troops commanded by Marshal Soult, then in charge of the siege, decided to withdraw, following Wellington's entry into Madrid on 6 August of the same year.

For his part, José María de la Cueva, Duke of Albuquerque, was received in London as a hero, being feted by the British authorities. However, the new destination was bittersweet for the Spanish general, since he considered his honour to have been outraged. In London he would write his famous *Manifesto of the Duke of Albuquerque*, in which he bitterly exposed the injustice that had been committed against him and his men. Barely eleven months after his arrival in England he became seriously ill as a result of the tuberculosis he had suffered in 1809. He died on 18 February 1811 at 47 Portman Square,[16] just 35 years old.

Notes

1. Not all of these troops were part of the Army of Extremadura. Some of them were scattered units that Albuquerque absorbed into his army along his march. In addition, part of his troops stayed in Extremadura defending towns and castles like Badajoz.
2. The most detailed work on the withdrawal of the Duke of Albuquerque with the Army of Extremadura to León Island was written by José Manuel Guerrero Acosta (2011), whose narration is followed in this chapter.
3. Guerrero Acosta (2011).
4. Marabel Matos (2016), p. 170. This author indicates that the march of Menacho and Senén de Contreras took place a few days before Guerrero Acosta suggests.
5. General Rafael Menacho would later be appointed military governor of Badajoz, where he would resist the onslaught of various French attacks. The last attack began on 26 January and the city surrendered on 10 March. On 4 March Menacho died from the impact of a cannon shot while defending one of his bastions.
6. For their part, the troops of Senén de Contreras, after a series of unfortunate encounters against the French vanguard, suffered a bitter defeat on 9 April in the town of Constantina, next to Seville, against the division of General Gazan, who perpetrated a criminal massacre among the surrendered residents of the town, which was looted. After this defeat Senén de Contreras was removed from his command and ordered to report to Cádiz. But his loss only resulted in his being

promoted to general. Later, he reappears in the defence of the city of Tarragona, where he served as military governor during the siege.

7. These generals, with the rest of their troops, had headed towards Tarifa and Lepe.
8. Moreno Alonso (2012), p. 357.
9. Ibid., p. 377.
10. It is not the object of this study to narrate the continuous disputes and conspiracies which the Central Supreme Junta in Seville lived through (and fomented) and its talent in forging enemies. Anyone interested should read Moreno Alonso (2012).
11. At that time a small village on the outskirts of Seville. Today it is the Seville neighbourhood of Torreblanca.
12. Napier (1836), p. 325.
13. A small island between the city of Cádiz and the Iberian Peninsula. After the war it was renamed San Fernando in honour of King Ferdinand VII.
14. Alburquerque himself tells it in his *Manifesto* (p. 10). For the duke it was not possible to combine the position of governor with the command of his army, so he handed over the position to his deputy, Andrés López de Sagastizabal.
15. Venegas was not the most brilliant of the Spanish generals during the Peninsular War. Under his command, for example, his armies were defeated in the battles of Uclés and Almonacid. However, this aristocrat was very well connected politically, as his uncle was the intriguing Francisco de Saavedra, a former minister of Charles IV who later became president of the Supreme Central Junta and the Regency Council.
16. Fernández Fernández (2010) describes the journey of the duke's corpse. A few days before his death, de la Cueva had received notification that his mission in London had ended and he was given command of the Army of Galicia. His unexpected death occurred while he was preparing his return trip. Due to the economic difficulties of the Regency Council, the body could not be repatriated until the end of July, on board a merchant ship transporting coal to Cádiz. The ship, *Asia*, arrived in Cádiz on 18 August, the date on which the duke was buried in the church of Carmen, next to Gravina, the hero of Trafalgar. And there they lay together until 1883, when the admiral was transferred to the Pantheon of Illustrious Sailors. When they exhumed Gravina, they discovered to their astonishment that the corpse was just as it was when he died, since his afflicted fellow sailors had not only embalmed it but, for better preservation, submerged it in pomace brandy from Chiclana.

Chapter Twenty-Seven

The Siege of Astorga

Date: 21 March–22 April 1810. *Place*: Astorga, Castile-León.
Result: Napoleonic victory.

Order of battle

Spanish Army: the Military Governor of Astorga, Brigadier José María Santo-cildes, with the town garrison comprising the Regiment of Santiago (942 men), the Regiment of Lugo (687 men), the Battalion of Volunteers of León (680 men), the Battalion of Chasseurs of León (290 men), the Battalion of Shooters of El Bierzo (154 men), the Battalion of Buenos Aires (66 men), plus 13 cavalrymen from the Hussars of León and 43 artillerymen. In total, 2,875 men, together with a number of volunteers from Astorga itself.[1]

Napoleonic Army: the VIII Army Corps, under the command of General Jean-Andoche Junot, comprising the 1st Division under General Clauzel, with the Ménard Brigade, with the 19th Regiment of Line Infantry, the 25th Regiment of Line Infantry, the 28th Regiment of Line Infantry, and the 34th Regiment of Line Infantry; the Taupin Brigade, with the 15th Regiment of Light Infantry, the 46th Regiment of Line Infantry and the 75th Regiment of Line Infantry; the Godard Brigade, with the 22nd Regiment of Line Infantry; the 2nd División under General Solignac, with the Gratien Brigade, with the 15th Regiment of Line Infantry and the 86th Regiment of Line Infantry; de Thomières Brigade,

135

with the 65th Regiment of Line Infantry, and the Regiment of Prussia (1 bn). Cavalry Brigade under the command of General Escorches de Saint-Croix, with two squadrons from each of the 1st, 2nd, 4th, 14th and 26th Regiments of Dragoons. Detachment of artillery under the command of General Jean Noël. Detachment of engineers and sappers under the command of Lieutenant Colonel Valazé. In total, around 5,500 men.

Background

The first occupation of Astorga by French troops occurred during the withdrawal of Moore's army in 1809. The British refused to fight the French in that town, despite its magnificent fortifications, and abandoned the place when the French arrived. Coming from Madrid, Napoleon himself slept in the episcopal palace before embarking on his journey back to France. He left Brigadier General Pierre-Guillaume Chaudron-Rousseau,[2] of Kellerman's Division, as commander of the city, with a garrison of almost a thousand men. However, the failures of Ney and Soult in Galicia and Portugal, respectively, caused their troops to withdraw, and the French abandoned Astorga on 27 July 1809. General Francisco Ballesteros came to take possession of the city, and appointed Cayetano Izquierdo as mayor. In October of that same year Astorga was attacked by French forces under General Carrier, but the attack failed. Afterwards it was decided to appoint José María Santocildes as military governor, and he also assumed civilian power in the town.[3]

In 1810 Napoleon ordered Marshal Masséna to invade Portugal. To secure their rear, the French first had to take two Spanish fortified cities: Astorga and Ciudad Rodrigo. On 11 February General Louis Henri Loison, commanding the 3rd Division of Ney's VI Army Corps, arrived on the outskirts of Astorga. Although he had an impressive attack force of more than 12,000 men, he did not have enough materiel for the siege, so he limited himself to blockading the town. On 21 March Junot's VIII Corps arrived.

The siege[4]

During the first days of the siege General Noël supervised the placement of artillery pieces and the sappers carried out entrenchment work under the supervision of Lieutenant Colonel Valazé.[5] For their part the defenders made various sorties to hinder them and destroyed various buildings in the suburbs so that they could not be used by the Napoleonic forces. On 1 April the French seized the convent of San Dictino; the defenders withdrew in order, with only two wounded and two men taken prisoner. More seriously, that same day the defenders also lost the only source of drinking water that supplied the town. On 2 April Santocildes, seeing that they could not defend the convent of Santa Clara, also outside the city walls, ordered it to be burned so that it could not be used by the French. The nuns who inhabited the convent refused to abandon it, but the Spanish general was determined to defend the city at any cost. The nuns were rehoused in a house within the city walls.[6] Later, some scouts arrived in Astorga who informed the authorities both of the disposition of the besieging forces and of the impossibility of General Mahy rendering any assistance from Villafranca del Bierzo.

The following days continued with a kind of routine in which attackers and defenders fought to occupy the outskirts of the city, while their respective artillery pounded the enemy. Finally, events accelerated in mid-April when the enemy batteries began to shell the walls of Astorga and the French infantry captured the suburb of Reitivia. On 21 April Noël's artillerymen finally managed to open a huge breach in one of the city walls. At this point Junot sent a Spanish prisoner with a surrender proposal; this was rejected, even though the city was already short of both food and gunpowder and there was no hope of help from outside. Many of the city's patricians and their soldiers advocated a stubborn defence to the last. Thus, as the Irish troops of Solignac's Division rushed into the breach, they were quickly repulsed by a volley of rifle fire from the Battalion of the Volunteers of Leon.

The French did not stop fighting until night fell (which at that time of year would have been around 7.00pm), and they took cover in the best positions to launch a new attack the following morning. The Spaniards, with no hand grenades and almost no gunpowder, could do nothing to drive them off. That same night the besieged officers met to decide whether a general sortie was possible, since there were no means available to resist a second attack. But there was not enough time to organize it, nor was it known in which direction Spanish troops could be found to support them. So, with a view to protecting the lives of the Astorgans, it was decided to send the second-in-command of the Regiment of Lugo, Lieutenant Colonel Pedro Guerrero, to Junot's camp to negotiate an honourable surrender. At 2.00pm on 22 April Astorga capitulated. It is believed that the number of Spanish casualties was around 50 dead and 110 wounded, while the French had 160 dead and about 400 wounded. The surviving Spanish troops were taken prisoner and taken to France. However, some of them managed to escape, as in the case of General Santocildes. But not all Astorgas's defenders were prepared to surrender. One of them, a hussar named Tiburcio Álvarez, refusing to be taken prisoner, rushed at a French aide-de-camp with his sabre in his hand. He was captured and brought before Junot, who ordered him to be shot immediately and buried under the tree where he was executed. His remains now lie in the Cathedral of Astorga, next to the tomb of General Santocildes.

With Astorga defeated, Ney's troops headed for Ciudad Rodrigo, which had been under siege since the end of April. It was defended by some 5,000 men under the command of General Andrés Pérez de Herrasti, an experienced military man who had participated in the battles of Tudela, Tarancón and Tamames. Herrasti, aged 60 in 1810, came from an old Andalusian aristocratic family, and during his defence of Ciudad Rodrigo he adopted their motto: 'the thumb breaks, but it does not bend'.[7] The city endured a 76-day siege, being razed to the ground by French bombs. On 9 July, with a breach made in its walls, Herrasti accepted that he had no choice but to surrender. The sieges of Astorga and Ciudad Rodrigo, although they ended in Spanish defeats, managed to delay until the autumn the French invasion of Portugal, and furthermore depleted many of the French units that would take part.

Notes

1. The story of the Spanish troops can be found in the statement written by Brigadier Santocildes. However, he seems to forget the sixty-six soldiers of the Battalion of Buenos Aires, previously known as the *Cuerpo de Blandengues de la Frontera de Buenos Aires* (Frontier Corps of Blandengues of Buenos Aires). This unit endured a journey of Homeric dimensions. Apparently, there were about 600 soldiers that the British had taken prisoner during their attacks on Buenos Aires in 1806 and 1807. When the Peninsular War began, they were allowed to regain their freedom to go and fight for the patriotic army. Although some of them would return to their homes in the Viceroyalty of the Río de la Plata, as was the case of the former governor of Montevideo, Pascual Ruiz Huidobro, most of them decided to fight in Spain in the new Battalion of Buenos Aires, but other were distributed among various regiments. Ruiz (2016).

2. Chaudron-Rousseau, who fought in the battles of Medellín and Talavera, died in the battle of Barrosa. He was the son of Guillaume Chaudron-Rousseau, a humble farmer who, during the French Revolution, became a prominent *Montagnard*. He was a harsh repressor of the royalists and a firm supporter of the death sentence of Louis XVI. Robespierre's death marked the beginning of the end of his political career.

3. Álvarez García (2014), p. 54.

4. Rodríguez Díez (1909), pp. 416–31.

5. For his participation in the siege of Astorga, Valazé was promoted to colonel. This officer was a hero in the second siege of Zaragoza: he jumped into a breach, together with Engineer General Lacoste, who was mortally wounded at Santa Engracia. Valazé, at his side, tried to bring him out to the French lines, but could do nothing to save his life. He fought in Austerlitz, Liepzig and Waterloo, where he was Napoleon's chief engineer. He was the son of Charles Valazé, a leader of the Girondin party during the French Revolution. During the Reign of Terror he was accused of being a counterrevolutionary for his moderate ideas and sentenced to the guillotine. He committed suicide in his cell before being taken to the gallows.

6. Shortly after the conquest of Astorga, the French decreed the dissolution of its religious orders. The abbess of Santa Clara begged General Kellerman for an extension for her community, due to the large number of elderly nuns. Kellerman agreed. The abbess managed to lengthen the dissolution of the order, benefiting from the advance of Ferdinand's troops in the following years. Thus, after the war the reconstruction of the convent began, and it welcomed eighteen nuns in 1816, as indicated in the *Bulletin of the Royal Academy of History*, 1988, CLXXXV(II). After many vicissitudes, today the monastery is still open.

7. Martín Más (2008).

Chapter Twenty-Eight

The Siege of Tarragona

Date: from 4 May to 28 June 1811. *Place*: Tarragona, Catalonia.
Result: Napoleonic victory.

Order of battle

Spanish Army: Military governor Juan Senén de Contreras, in command of the following units: Regiment of Almansa, Regiment of Saboya, Regiment of América, Regiment of Granada, Regiment of Almería, Regiment of Ultonia, Regiment of Iliberia, Regiment of Grenadiers of New Castile, 3rd Battalion of Chasseurs of Valencia, Battalion of Volunteers of Zaragoza, Battalion of Volunteers of Girona, Battalion of Shooters of Tarragona, Urban Militia. Artillery Brigade. From the sea, HMS *Blake* (74 guns) and several gunships, under the command of Commodore Edward Codrington.[1] In total, near 14,000 men.[2]

Napoleonic Army: III Army Corps under the command of General Louis Gabriel Suchet with the following troops: the division of General Frere, comprising the Lorencez Brigade, with the 1st Regiment of Light Infantry and the 1st Regiment of Vístula; and the Callier Brigade, with the 14th Regiment of Line Infantry and the 24th Regiment of Line Infantry. The division of General Harispe, with the Salme Brigade, including the 7th and 16th Regiments of Line Infantry; the Palombini Brigade, with the 3rd Regiment of Italian Light Infantry and 4th Regiment of Italian Line Infantry; and the Balathier de Bragelonne

139

Brigade, with the 5th and 6th Regiments of Italian Line Infantry. The division of General Habert, with the Montmarie Brigade, with the 5th Regiment of Light Infantry and the 116th Regiment of Line Infantry; the Bronikoski Brigade, with the 117th Regiment of Line Infantry; the Abbe Brigade, with the 114th, 115th and 121st Regiments of Line Infantry. The cavalry brigade of General Boussart, with the 24th Regiment of Dragoons, the 13th Regiment of Cuirassiers, the 4th Regiment of Hussars and the Italian *Dragoni Napoleone*. Artillery Brigade, under the command of General Valée, including the 3rd, 6th, 7th and 8th Artillery Regiments. Engineers and Sappers Brigade under the command of General Rogniat. In total, 22,196 men.[3]

Background[4]

At the beginning of 1811 the Napoleonic Captain General of Catalonia, Charles-Pierre Augereau, controlled the territory between Barcelona and Girona. Furthermore, since 14 April Suchet had besieged the other great Catalan town in the north: Lleida. For this, he counted on the divisions of Musnier de La Converserie, Habert and the cavalry of Boussart, a total of about 14,000 men. His head of artillery was General Valée, who previously fought in Friedland and Eylau; Lannes brought him to Spain during the second siege of Zaragoza. The chief of the engineers was Colonel Haxo, whose dazzling record meant that, after the campaign in Lower Catalonia in 1810–1811, Napoleon Bonaparte himself took him along with his general staff in his invasion of Russia. At the battle of Waterloo, he was the chief engineer of the Royal Guard. Lleida, with hardly any defences, had General Jaime García Conde as governor, in command of a garrison of some 8,000 men. Despite the difficulties, the Catalans decided to resist until the end. On 13 May the Napoleonic forces managed to open a breach, which they fiercely assaulted. They fought street by street, house by house. In the end, the French superiority was overwhelming and finally García Conde surrendered. He would spend the rest of the war as a prisoner in France, along with 7,748 other men captured in Lleida.

The Captain General of Catalonia, the Spanish (though of Irish origin) general Enrique O'Donnell, understood that he could not beat the French in open battles on the field. His only chance was to surprise the enemy from the rear. A feasible target would be General Schwartz's headquarters at La Bisbal d'Empordà, on the northern coast, where he had dispersed his division among several fortifications, which were continually harassed by local guerrilla forces and Catalan corsair ships. Schwartz, who was one of the protagonists of the battles of Bruc, was described by the British historian Oman, as an 'always unlucky'[5] general. After his defeats at Bruc pass, he was sent to control the coastal fortifications of the rearguard, which would be a suitable destination for troops from the Confederation of the Rhine. On the face of it, it was a relatively quiet posting. It was almost boring. Together with the British general Charles William Doyle, O'Donnell devised a plan and together they attacked the towns defended by Schwartz's troops. Their attack was a success and O'Donnell received the title of Count of Bisbal. However, his continuing disputes with the junta of Catalonia meant he was replaced by the Marquis of Campoverde, who soon had the opportunity to confront the Napoleonic forces. But his only notable victory was the battle of Sant Quintí, on 21 October 1810, and his major failures included the loss of both Tortosa in January 1811 and Tarragona, which left Catalonia isolated from the rest of Spain.

There were also changes on the French side. General MacDonald replaced Augereau at the head of the Napoleonic troops in Catalonia. A few months later, the French general was ordered by Napoleon to head south and complete the conquest of Catalonia. However, MacDonald dawdled in the north in pursuit of guerrillas and the few, but extremely skilful, forces of the Catalan army. Thus the definitive fate of Tarragona began to be dictated on 10 March 1811, when Marshal Berthier delivered a dispatch from Napoleon to Suchet ordering him to conquer Tarragona, with the veiled hint that his success in the new mission would earn him the marshal's baton. The French were convinced that crushing the ancient city would put an end to the stubborn resistance of the Catalans.

The siege

Suchet wasted no time. On 3 May the Napoleonic Army appeared before the walls of Tarragona. Salme advanced along the Francolí river and positioned himself in front of the Fort Oliva; Harispe occupied the town of Constantí; Palombini occupied the hills of Llorito and Ermitaños; Balathier de Bragelonne cut off the road to Barcelona;[6] while Habert advanced to the mouth of the Francolí. Suchet had done his homework conscientiously. He had carefully prepared the siege and was now solidly situated on the ground. Tarragona was practically cut off, and it would be impossible for the city to receive help overland. The only corridor that remained open connected the city with the port, where various British and Spanish ships were able to bring in troops, supplies and food. The French dedicated the first days of the siege to carrying out the works and digging the trenches that would allow them to successfully undertake the conquest of Tarragona. In addition, every effort was made to destroy the corridor that connected the city with the port. After inspecting the walls, Suchet and his general staff concluded that the wall on the west side of the town was the weakest and this was where they would start to attack. Accordingly, they prepared for the conquest of Fort Francolí. But Suchet then changed his mind and instead concentrated his efforts on occupying Fort Oliva, where most of the forces defending Tarragona were concentrated; thus Fort Oliva's fall would mean the end of the city's resistance.

At the beginning of May the commander-in-chief of the city's forces was General Juan Caro Sureda, brother of the Marquis de la Romana. He appointed

Colonel Juan María Gámez López, commanding his Regiment of America, as governor of Fort Oliva.[7] In addition, he reinforced its defences with three battalions of the Regiment of Illiberia under the command of Colonel Casteras de Gauzan; several battalions of volunteers under the command of Colonel Aldea; and three artillery companies of the Urban Militia.[8] On 10 May further support came in the shape of Luis González-Torres de Navarra y Castro, Marquis of Campoverde and Captain General of Catalonia, who disembarked at the port accompanied by 3,000 fresh men.

On the night of 13/14 May Suchet ordered the conquest of the outer parapets of Fort Oliva by the *voltigeurs* and grenadiers of the 7th and 16th Regiments of Line Infantry, the 2nd Light Infantry and the Italian 4th Line Infantry, led by General Jean-Baptiste Salme. Despite a heroic defence, all the parapets fell, and attempts to recover them, ordered by Colonel Aldea, were unsuccessful. Then the Marquis of Campoverde ordered the battalions of volunteers to be replaced with units of the 1st Catalan Legion and the Regiment of Girona. On the 18th and the 23rd they made two sorties but both were repulsed, and the Spanish forces suffered heavy casualties. On 26 May, once the trenches were finished (they were partly dug through rock, which delayed the operation), Suchet moved forward the battery that he called the 'King of Rome' in honour of Napoleon's son, who had been born on 20 March. Seeing the French positioning their guns, the defenders of the Fort launched an improvised sortie; this forced the French 7th Regiment of Line Infantry to counter-attack, urged on by General Salme, who was supervising the battery's emplacement. At that moment a shell exploded near the general, who was killed by shrapnel. Salme's death caused enormous consternation in the French Army. He was a much-loved officer, although it could not be said that he had enjoyed much luck in his life. Salme's life had been full of ups and downs, partly due to his failure to choose the right friends, which cyclically caused Napoleon to lose confidence in him. For example, during the Wars of the First Coalition, he became close friends with his superior commander, General Jean-Charles Pichegru,[9] but when the latter's plot against Napoleon was discovered, Salme was stripped of his command. In 1802 he was pardoned and assigned to the expedition to Saint-Domingue led by General Charles Leclerc. Salme shone on the battlefield and Leclerc promoted him to major general, but after a few weeks he mysteriously dismissed him and sent him back to France. It is believed that Salme's affair with Leclerc's wife, who was none other than Pauline Bonaparte,[10] the Emperor's little sister, was discovered. And yet Salme was lucky, for shortly afterwards Leclerc's expedition suffered a yellow fever epidemic that killed Napoleon's brother-in-law, along with twenty-four other generals and 25,000 soldiers. No more fortunate was General Salme's marriage to his wife Jeanne Henriette. It would be an understatement to say that they did not get along. In fact, they hated each other. Their relationship had soured over property disputes, leading Jeanne Henriette to attempt to poison her husband. Only the timely intervention of a servant at the last moment saved the general's life. Not surprisingly, Salme began divorce proceedings. In 1804 another of his close friends, General Jean Victor Moreau,[11] was accused of conspiring against the Emperor and sentenced to exile, which led to Salme being interrogated and watched by the police. He later served in MacDonald's VII Corps in Catalonia, but his division was ceded to Suchet for the conquest of various Catalan towns. It is believed that his body was buried under one of the arches of the Tarragona aqueduct, while his heart was deposited in the Scipio Tower, where the two great Roman generals of that name were thought to have been buried.[12]

The assault on Fort Oliva began on 29 May at 8.30pm. Suchet ordered a mock attack to keep the entire Tarragona garrison distracted. Then he launched another feint on the left side of the fort, while on the right advanced a column led by Major Revel at the head of 300 men of the 16th Line Infantry, preceded by some twenty sappers under the command of Captain Papigny. A second column under the command of Major Miocque advanced towards the breach, comprising the 7th Line Infantry and about twenty Italian sappers under the command of Captain Vacani. Revel's column was stopped at the foot of the wall, trying to break down a wooden door with an axe, while a hail of bullets rained down on them from the few defenders who discovered them. Captain Papigny was killed in this action. The second column had more luck and, albeit with no little difficulty, advanced through the breach.

At that moment the Regiment of Almería came into the city through another gate to relieve the Regiment of Illiberia, which had been severely depleted after a month defending the Fort. Some French soldiers slipped into the Fort among the Spanish rearguard, and hand-to-hand combat began. General Harispe, wounded by the blast from a grenade, saw that he was now facing the critical moment of the battle and ordered the chief of his general staff, Major Mesclop, to advance with his reserve. Moving up in two columns, each one reinforcing those that had advanced as the vanguard, Mesclop was able to consolidate the conquered space and, above all, secure the key places of the Fort. Colonel Gámez tried to organize the defence of the left side of the fort, but was unable to stop the offensive of the Napoleonic soldiers advancing with fixed bayonets, giving no quarter. Harispe himself had to intervene so that the last resisters, cornered around the final bastion, would not be murdered. Spanish casualties numbered about 500 dead,[13] while those taken prisoner included Governor Gámez (a 26-year-old who received no fewer than ten wounds but somehow survived), his chief of staff, six lieutenant colonels and some 900 soldiers. A small group of Spanish soldiers managed to escape and took refuge behind the city walls.

As agreed, the military governor of the city prepared his troops for departure, but Campoverde did not appear. He stayed in Vilanova. In addition, some letters were discovered in which he gave permission to senior officials in Tarragona to dismiss Senén de Contreras if they considered it appropriate. Finally, on 28 June, the French opened a huge breach in the bastion of San Pedro. Senén de Contreras, waiting for the final attack, prepared a sortie to try to save the garrison of the city at least. But Suchet had got ahead of the defenders and at 5.00pm his forces began their assault on the breach. Suchet had promised his troops three days of unchecked looting, and the French forces were fired up. The fight through the streets was brutal and the thrust of the attackers unstoppable. The Spanish soldiers, unable to contain them, retreated from the Rambla to Portalet, and from there to Mayor Street, finally ending up on the steps in front of the cathedral, where most of the high-ranking officers fought and fell. Colonel González-Torres, brother of the Marquis de Campoverde, fought bravely until the very last moment and was bayoneted to death, while Senén de Contreras was wounded. When the city fell, many soldiers and civilians tried to flee, either by land or by sea. But on land the French troops were waiting for them, stationed strategically on the main exit roads. Men in uniform were captured, while those in civilian clothes were shot. At the port, desperate soldiers and citizens of Tarragona jumped into the sea and swam towards the British squadron, which had been forced to retreat out of the range of the French artillery. Many of the swimmers drowned, but the British rescued about 450 people. It should be added that all contemporary sources speak highly of Commodore Edward Codrington's role during the siege. They emphasize that he helped whenever he could and that he did not withdraw until the city was already lost.

Then the horror began: three hellish days in which Napoleonic soldiers looted, burned, tortured, raped and murdered. The slaughter began in the cathedral itself, which was filled with civilian refugees, but it did not stop there. It would not be possible to list all the atrocities committed by the rampaging assailants, intoxicated by their success. The death toll during the siege and subsequent looting was estimated at 10,000 people, a significant proportion of whom were civilians. In addition, 8,200 prisoners were taken. Among these was Senén de Contreras, whom Suchet reproached for his fierce defence of the city, which had provoked the wrath of his soldiers. The Spanish general was duly treated for his wound and, once he recovered, was imprisoned in Bouillon Castle. He would escape a few months later.

As for the French, their losses had also been heavy. Suchet admitted to having lost some 3,700 men, although contemporary calculations say that the figure was much higher. The Corps of Engineers, for example, lost 28 per cent of its strength. The Napoleonic eagles would not take flight from the old city until 18 August 1813. Its last Napoleonic governor, General Bertoletti, blew up a large part of the city's fortifications and walls when he left. The two years of French occupation had left the city in ruins and practically uninhabited, and it would take decades to recover from the tragedy.

As for the Marquis of Campoverde, after the fall of the city he had to defend his actions and his inability to fulfil his promise from the outside. Not surprisingly, like his colleague Sarsfield, he chose to publish a manifesto exonerating himself and blaming the rest of the world for the loss of the city. The text, entitled *Exposición de la conducta que ha observado el mariscal de campo de los Reales Exércitos Marqués de Campoverde, conde de Santa Gadea, en la época que obtuvo el mando en jefe interino del exército y provincia de Cataluña; y noticias de lo ocurrido en el sitio de Tarragona* ('Exposition of the behaviour observed by the General of the Royal Armies Marquis of Campoverde, Count of Santa Gadea, at the time he obtained the interim command in chief of the army and province of Catalonia; and news of what happened in the Tarragona siege'), served only to provoke in response a wave of manifestos published by officers who had been present at the siege, including Senén de Contreras, Caro, Eguagirre and Sarsfield, leaving the elusive Marquis isolated and condemned. Indeed, the Regency Junta instituted criminal proceedings against him, for which he was separated from the army.

Notes

1. Likewise, at one time or another during the siege, the British ships HMS *Centaur* (74 guns), HMS *Cambrian* (40 guns), HMS *Sparrowhawk* (18 guns), HMS *Termagant* (18 guns), HMS *Merope* (10 guns).
2. Redondo Penas (2011), p. 9. It should be noted that this figure was when there was a greater number of defenders in the city. As we will see, the entry and exit of troops was a constant feature at the beginning of the siege.
3. Pintado i Simó-Monnè (2013), pp. 9–10.
4. For the narration of this text we follow Rovira i Gómez (2019), among others. Other texts will be indicated throughout the chapter.
5. Oman (1903), Vol. 3, p. 295.
6. The ancient Via Augusta built by the Romans. Today the N-340, the longest road in Spain, has a practically identical route.
7. We find a detailed explanation about the attack on Fort Oliva in the article by Murillo Galimany (2011).
8. On the Urban Militia of Tarragona, Redondo Penas (2011).
9. Pichegru was one of the heroes of the Revolutionary Wars. He was a popular and charismatic general, but he sympathized with royalists who wanted to overthrow Napoleon. In 1797 the plot was discovered and Pichegru was able to go into exile in London. He returned to France in 1804 but was immediately imprisoned. A few days later he was found hanged in his cell. Officially, it was considered a suicide, but it was *vox populi* that it was a murder. It is believed that if Napoleon did not order it, he was informed of it.
10. The Emperor's favourite sister was known for her long list of lovers, which caused quite a few scandals. In 1803 Pauline was married to Camillo Borghese, Prince of Sulmona and head of one of the most important Italian families. Needless to say, Pauline continued her licentious life and the marriage was a disaster from the start. Borghese was a puppet in the hands of the Napoleon brothers.
11. Moreau was Pichegru's close friend. Although in 1797 he was not investigated, when he returned from London in 1804, they were both accused (among other people) of trying to overthrow Napoleon. Moreau had collaborated with Napoleon during his rise to power, and as a result of their close friendship his prison sentence was commuted to exile. It did not help Moreau that his politically ambitious young wife, Eugénie Hulot d'Osery, was a friend of Josephine de Beauharnais. Eugénie gathered around her the so-called Moreau Circle, which brought together a group of people opposed to the Emperor. After exile in the United States, Moreau ended up

fighting on the side of the allies. In 1813, during the Battle of Dresden, he was shot while talking to the Tsar of Russia, Alexander I.

12. At the foot of the Via Augusta was built a funerary monument known as the Scipio Tower. Tradition held that it was the tomb of the brothers Gnaeus and Pubius Cornelius Scipio, heroes of the Second Punic War and founders of Tarraco. However, archaeological studies carried out in the mid-twentieth century concluded that the tower was in fact built several decades after the death of the famous Roman generals, so it was ruled out as their tomb. Today, the Tower can still be visited.

13. The exact figure will never be known, as the French did not bother to count them and their reports are contradictory.

BATTLE MAPS

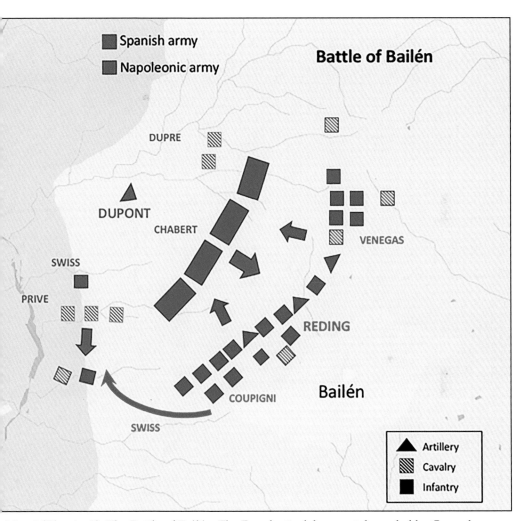

Map 1 (Chapter 7): The Battle of Bailén. The French attack began at dawn, led by General Chabert. He managed to occupy the Cruz Blanca hill, but the Spaniards recovered it after a bloody counterattack. At 6.00am General Dupont joined in and ordered three assaults on the Spanish lines, but all of them failed. However, the fighting on the French right flank was gruelling and General Reding had to send in a large part of his reserves. The large number of casualties suffered in the assaults, the exhausting heat, the lack of water and the danger of being attacked by another Spanish army from the rear, all convinced Dupont to surrender.

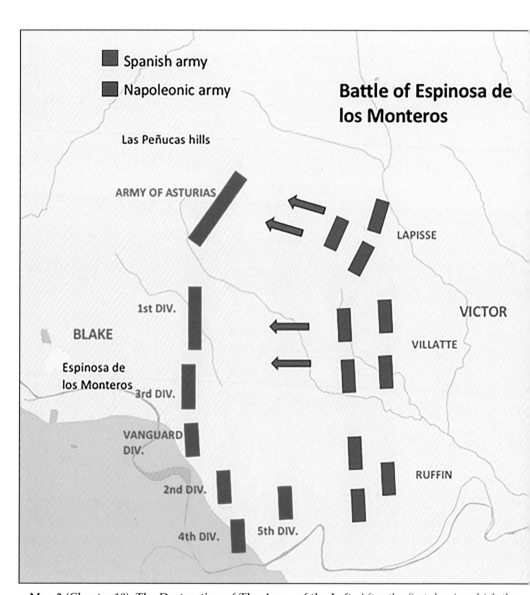

Map 2 (Chapter 10): The Destruction of The Army of the Left. After the first day in which the French assault on the Spanish lines failed, General Victor realized that the Spanish left flank (the Army of Asturias) was the weakest. While distracting the rest of the Spanish lines, Victor assaulted the Asturian flank, forcing it to disband. Shortly thereafter, the Spanish centre was assaulted on its left and also retreated, losing all its guns. General Blake had no choice but to order his right flank, the strongest, to retreat in haste. Victory belonged to Victor.

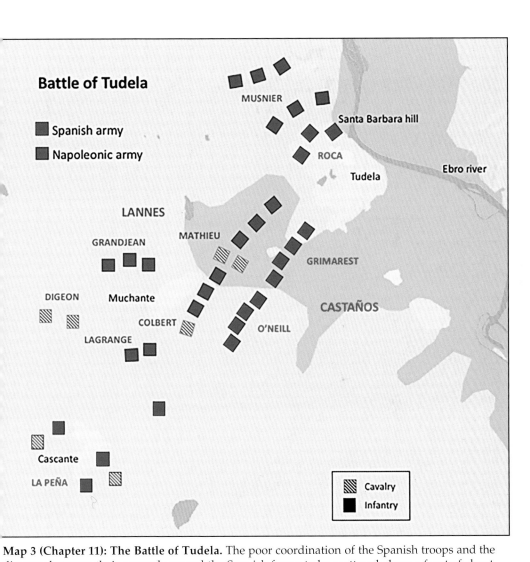

Map 3 (Chapter 11): The Battle of Tudela. The poor coordination of the Spanish troops and the disputes between their generals caused the Spanish forces to be scattered along a front of about 15 miles. Lannes focused his attack on the Roca's troops in Tudela, and Grimarest and O'Neill's troops in Tarazona. Towards noon, Marshal Lannes managed to occupy the hill of San Juan de Calchetas, between Tarazona and Tudela, breaking the Spanish lines and causing the disorderly flight of the troops of Roca and Grimarest. The soldiers fled towards Cascante, where General La Peña had remained. The disbandment was general and the defeat catastrophic.

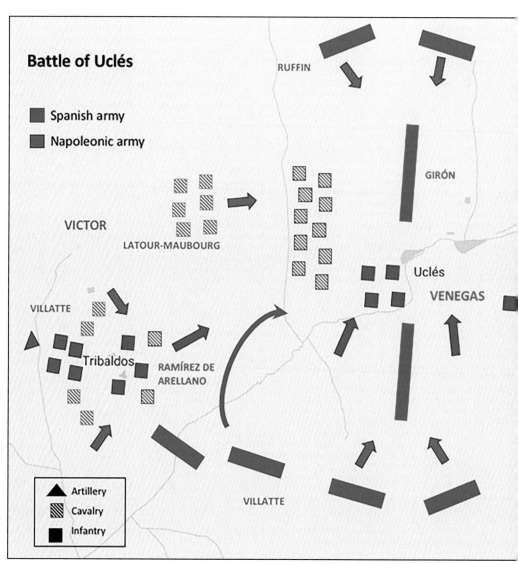

Map 4 (Chapter 14): The Battle of Uclés. General Vengas had placed the bulk of his army in front of Uclés, leaving an advance guard in Tribaldos. In the first phase of the battle, Victor sent General Villatte towards Tribaldos, pushing the troops of Ramirez de Arellano into retreating towards Uclés. In the second phase, Victor ordered Generals Villatte and Ruffin to attack with their cavalry the flanks of the Spanish infantry. The left side, under Venegas, soon collapsed, though Girón's troops resisted until they were surrounded. The Spanish cavalry, which had been fighting against Latour-Maubourg's troops, would later also flee.

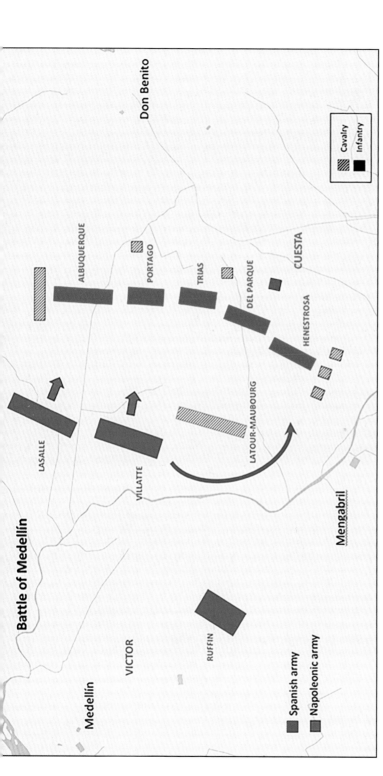

Map 5 (Chapter 17): The Battle of Medellín. General Cuesta took advantage of the fact that Victor's army was crossing the Guadiana by the Austrias bridge to get into battle formation. With much of the cavalry and the German division separated from the rest of his army, Marshal Victor had to ask these units to contain the Spanish army until the rest of his forces could get across. Once the French artillery crossed, the combat was equalized and the worst phase for the French seemed to be over. However, as the day went on, the French could not contain the thrust of the Spanish cavalry. In desperation, Victor ordered Latour-Maubourg's Dragoons to charge. The counterattack was successful, and they put to flight the Spanish cavalry, which caused the collapse of the Spanish infantry. The French Dragoons continued to hit the Spanish left flank, which eventually collapsed, dragging in its wake the rest of the army.

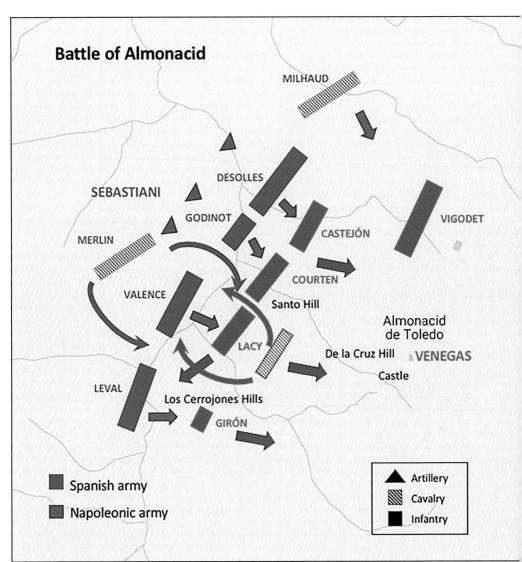

Map 6 (Chapter 21): The Battle of Almonacid. The key to the battle was control of Los Cerrejones hills, on the Spanish left flank. Sebastiani sent the Valence and Leval divisions against Lacy's and Girón's divisions, from which General Venegas had already transferred part of his troops, leaving the Spanish forces on the crucial point of the battlefield at a clear numerical disadvantage. Despite this, the troops of Lacy and Girón held out for most of the day despite suffering terrible casualties. When the left wing began to sink, Venegas ordered General Zolina's cavalry to charge, but the general's hesitant attitude caused the counterattack to fail. The Cerrajones were lost. At that moment, the centre of the Spanish line came under fire from the front and the left flank. On their right, Castejon's troops could not resist withstand an attack by Desolles' men and retreated towards Almonacid, along with Vigodet's division which had remained in the rear throughout, having received no orders from Venegas.

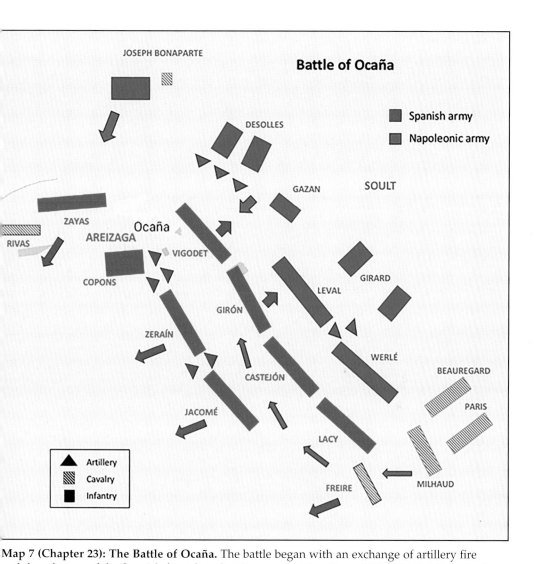

Map 7 (Chapter 23): The Battle of Ocaña. The battle began with an exchange of artillery fire and the advance of the Spanish front-line divisions against Leval's and Werlé's divisions. As the French weakened, Soult sent Desolles to hold the front and Milhaud's cavalry to counterattack the Spanish right flank. The French easily defeated the Spanish horsemen, who fled, abandoning the battlefield. Milhaud then led his men to attack the Spanish front line from the rear, provoking their flight, which infected the second line and the left wing of General Zayas. Meanwhile General Areizaga remained impassive in his command post until he decided that he too was abandoning the battlefield.

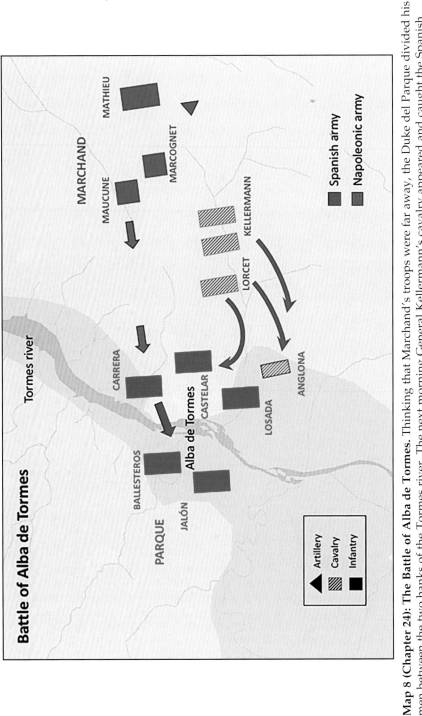

Map 8 (Chapter 24): The Battle of Alba de Tormes. Thinking that Marchand's troops were far away, the Duke del Parque divided his men between the two banks of the Tormes river. The next morning General Kellermann's cavalry appeared and caught the Spanish soldiers on the right bank totally off guard, causing carnage, especially among the soldiers of Castelar's division. Generals Carrera and Mendizábal managed to reorganize their men and finally repelled the repeated charges by Kellermann, but he continued his attack to prevent the Spaniards from crossing the river to safety. When Marchand's infantry arrived they launched a powerful attack but could not prevent the survivors of the three Spanish divisions, under Carrera and Mendizábal, from crossing the river. However, the French victory was complete.

Chapter Twenty-Nine

The Siege of Cádiz

Date: 6 February 1810–25 August 1812. *Place*: Cádiz, Andalusia.
Result: Spanish victory.

Order of battle

Spanish Army[1]: Regiment of Royal Guards (2 bns), one Regiment each of the
Provincial Militias of Sigüenza, Guadix, Córdoba, Ciudad Rodrigo, Trujillo and
Ronda, the 2nd Regiment of the Provincial Militia of Volunteers of Madrid, the
Battalion Imperiales de Toledo, the Battalion of Volunteers of the Fatherland,
the Battalion of Loyals to Fernando VII, the 2nd Regiment of Light Infantry
of Catalonia, the Regiments of Light Infantry of Campo Mayor and Valencia de
Albuquerque, the Battalion of Grenadiers of the Canary Islands, the Battalion of
the Canary Islands, a company of the Battalion of Ayamonte, the Infantry Company of Marbella, the 2nd and 4th Battalions of Volunteers of Seville, the Battalion of Distinguished Volunteers of Jerez, the Battalion of Shooters of Spain,
the Regiment of Loja (1 bn). Cavalry Division: the Regiment of Royal Carabineers, the Regiment of the King, the Regiment of Dragoons of Granada, the
Regiment of Calatrava, the Regiment of Dragoons of Villaviciosa, the Regiment
of Mounted Chasseurs of Spain (*aka* the 4th Regiment of Hussars) and the
Regiment of Perseguidores de Andalucia. Detachment of artillery, engineers and
sappers. Several ships of the Spanish Navy.

147

British Army: from Lisbon, under the command of General William Stewart (later replaced by General George Cooke) the 79th (Cameron Highlanders), 84th (Scotch Brigade) and 87th (Royal Irish Fusiliers) Regiments, and the Portuguese 20th Infantry Regiment (Campo Mayor). From Gibraltar, the 88th Regiment of Foot (Connaught Rangers). During the siege the city was also defended by various Royal Navy ships. In total, approximately 16,000 troops.

Napoleonic Army: I Corps of the Army under the command of Marshal Victor,[2] duke of Bellune, including the Ruffin's 1st Division, comprising the 9th Regiment of Light Infantry, the 24th and 96th Regiments of Line Infantry and a detachment of artillery; Leval's 2nd Division, comprising the 16th Regiment of Light Infantry, the 8th, 45th and 54th Regiments of Line Infantry and a detachment of artillery; Villatte's 3rd Division, comprising the 27th Regiment of Light Infantry, the 63rd, 94th and 95th Regiments of Line Infantry and a detachment of artillery. Artillery, under the command of General Sénarmont. In total, near 25,000 men.

Background

Previously we have seen how the Spanish defeat in the battle of Ocaña meant the fall of Andalusia. At the end of January 1810 the Central Supreme Junta was forced to withdraw from Seville, and moved to Cádiz. A few days later there was a political crisis, which saw the dissolution of the Central Supreme Junta, whose role in directing the war had proved so disastrous; it was replaced by the Regency Council of Spain and the Indies, which in September of that year decreed the creation of the National Congress and recognized the division of powers and national sovereignty: this was the birth of modern Spain. However, the city's defences were in a pitiful state and it hardly had a garrison large enough to withstand a siege. The almost miraculous appearance of the Duke of Albuquerque with the Division of Extremadura saved the city at the last moment, and with it probably also saved the patriot government.

The French made a serious mistake in spending too much time in Seville. Apparently the ambitious (and greedy) Marshal Soult openly disdained Cadiz's defences and preferred instead to take possession of a city as rich as Seville, wasting time there that was ultimately found to be crucial. Soult either distrusted or ignored Joseph Bonaparte, who endorsed the opinion of the Duke of Dalmatia that no time should be wasted, and when Marshal Victor's division was finally sent to Cádiz, the city had had time to begin preparing for its defence. On 4 February Victor arrived in Jerez de la Frontera and his advance party reached the outskirts of Cádiz the following day, verifying that Fort Matagorda and Fort-Luis had been demolished. Some 200 horsemen headed for the Zuazo bridge, which the last units of the Army of Extremadura had just crossed. The commanding officer of the bridge blocked the way to the French horsemen, who turned on their haunches. At the same time the Regency Council sent six boats to the Sancti Petri pass, since there were no fortifications to defend this vital route. The ship of the line *San Justo*[3] was located in the vicinity of the Trocadero. On the 6th the bulk of Victor's troops began to arrive and the longest siege of the war began. It was a long and vital battle that might well define the final outcome of the war.

The siege[4]

The French marshal tried to take the city by assault. To do so, he had to cross the Zuazo bridge, where the battle of Portazgo took place between 6 and 11 February, ending in a meritorious victory for the men of Albuquerque despite being exhausted from their epic journey and suffering from an alarming lack of material means. During the following days the Napoleonic authorities sent various surrender proposals both to the Regency Council and to the Duke of Albuquerque himself, all of which were turned down, the Spanish arguing energetically against any kind of capitulation.

The failure at the Zuazo bridge forced Soult to propose a blockade of the city by land, despite opposition from many high-ranking officials. Victor was in charge of organizing the blockade, although he found that Soult, with whom he was not on good terms, always dragged his feet when it came to sending him the resources he requested. But no matter how hard Victor tried, Cadiz and Leon Island were surrounded by marshes and swampy terrain that made a siege impossible. The French troops were entrenched in the several towns in the Bay of Cadiz that surrounded the blockaded city, specifically in Chiclana de la Frontera, Puerto Real and El Puerto de Santa María. From there, they established positions as close as possible to their goal, from where they bombarded Cádiz and León Island.[5]

The artillery was practically the only weapon the French could use to force the surrender of the stubborn besieged Spanish. And if there was one thing Victor's men had plenty of, it was cannon. In Seville they had captured the Royal Artillery Factory intact, obtaining some 300 cannon that the Supreme Central Junta had forgotten to order destroyed. However, these cannon could not reach the besieged city, so new cannon and mortar were built that were capable of firing at distances of over 3km (1.8 miles); this was quite a feat at the time.

The person in charge of producing these new cannon and mortars was the master foundryman Manel Pe-de-arrós, surely the best foundryman in Spain. This Catalan-born man had begun his exceptional career years before at the Royal Artillery Factory in Barcelona, which he brilliantly reorganized. His pursuit of perfection in the design and production of cannon did not go unnoticed by his superiors, who assigned him to the Seville factory. After the arrival of the French troops, Soult offered him the chance to stay in his post in exchange for advantageous conditions; the foundryman agreed and shortly afterwards King Joseph I named him a knight of the Royal Order of Spain. After the war, Pe-de-arrós accepted Soult's offer to accompany him to France, where he was appointed director of the prestigious Fonderie Royal de Toulouse (Royal Artillery Factory of Toulouse) and was awarded the Legion of Honour and the Order of Saint Louis. His son became a general, and later commanded the artillery of the Imperial Guard of Napoleon III during the Franco-Prussian War of 1870–1871.

During the following months of the siege the French had to content themselves with launching shells against Cádiz and León Island, but these hardly made a dent in the spirits of the besieged, who, as we shall see, curiously, were the ones who took the initiative in the combat during the siege. Furthermore, artillery fire was returned from Spanish positions, sometimes with surprising success. One of these successes took place on 26 October 1810, when Soult's artillery general, Alexandre-Antoine Hureau de Sénarmont, accompanied by Colonel Degennes and Captain Pinondelle, went to inspect the Villatte redoubt, which contained the most advanced French artillery. While trying to observe the performance of one of their new cannon, the redoubt was hit squarely by a volley from León Island, killing the three officers. Sénarmont was a veteran of Friedland and Eylau, among many other battles, and his unexpected death caused tremendous consternation among the high-ranking Napoleonic officers. In fact, such was the impact of his loss that Napoleon himself ordered that Sénarmont's heart be transferred to Paris to be buried in the Pantheon in France. The three officers were buried in the church of Santa Ana de Chiclana with the highest military honours. After the withdrawal of the French troops, however, their tombs were destroyed and the mortal remains disappeared.[6]

As mentioned above, much of the attacking initiative during the siege was shown by the Spanish. The mobile columns of Generals Copons and Ballesteros repeatedly attacked the French lines, and Victor was forced to organize numerous expeditions in pursuit of them, but the Spanish generals displayed superior skills and got away. All of this further distracted Victor from the siege and used up valuable troops. In addition, he also had to cope with Soult's constant requests for soldiers to go to other fronts in the south of the peninsula.

One of the most important factors in the French failure at Cádiz was the British contribution. Since the beginning of the war the British understood the importance of holding the city, and both Wellington and Dalrymple, the governor of Gibraltar, did everything they could to help the patriotic cause. Before the start of the siege the British contribution had consisted largely of the shipment of war material and funds, but a few days after the arrival of the French in the Bay of Cadiz Wellington ordered General Stewart to march to the city with a force of nearly 3,000 soldiers. They were received with open arms. Stewart himself was very popular in Cádiz. As soon as he arrived, he saw that Fort Matagorda had been demolished by the Spanish. It was a fortification of vital importance, so at the end of February a column formed by the 94th Regiment of Infantry recaptured it, and the defences were rebuilt by a brigade of British engineers. The 94th left there a garrison of 140 men, who for two months supported the constant French offensives. Finally, Victor's men managed to dislodge the garrison, by which time Matagorda was again in a ruinous state and the British had suffered almost 50 per cent casualties. The fort subsequently remained in French hands until the end of the siege. Weeks after its capture General Graham arrived; he maintained a policy of total understanding with the Spanish authorities, which resulted in the British military playing an essential role in offensives such as the battle of Barrosa and in the defence of Tarifa. To get an idea of the material support received by the British in Cádiz, the following list indicates the hardware supplied to the city from the United Kingdom:[7]

- 342 guns
- 128,040 shells
- 22,141 muskets
- 2,600 carbines
- 2,600 rifles
- 5,640 pistols
- 43,385,455 cartridges
- 28,924 barrels of gunpowder
- 87,229 spades

The Royal Navy also played an important role. The various ships that passed through Cadiz kept the French fleet at bay and effectively bombarded Victor's men. Under the orders of Admiral Richard Keats, ships of the line such as HMS *Implacable*, HMS *Marlborough*, HMS *Milford* and HMS *Centaur*, among others, passed through.

Mention must also be made of the proclamation of the Constitution of Cádiz on 19 March 1812, that is, in the middle of the siege. This gives us an idea that, despite the bombing and the militarization of the city, the people of Cadiz tried to keep their day-to-day life running with a certain normality. The debates were carried out by the deputies elected by decree in February 1810 and began at the end of August 1811 and ended in January of the following year, being proclaimed on the day of Saint Joseph, for which the Constitution was popularly known as the *Pepa*.[8] Surprisingly, its main inspiration was the French Constitution of 1791, and in it very radical postulates were agreed for the Spanish context of the time, such as attributing legislative power to a national assembly, excluding any aristocratic senate and limiting the royal power of veto. This, de facto, put an end to absolutism. (It should come as no surprise that Ferdinand VII, on his return to Spain, perpetrated what could be considered a veritable *coup d'état*, in which he suspended the Constitution, annulled the decrees passed by the Supreme Central Junta and the Regency and reinstated absolutism.)

The people of Cadiz passionately lived the political debates. The cafés became centres of improvised political discussions, although without forgetting that the common enemy was France and, even more so, the *afrancesados*. Indeed, at the beginning of the war they came to lynch the governor of the city, Francisco Solano, on suspicion of being *afrancesado*. The persecution and convictions continued during the siege. The castle of San Sebastián was set up as an improvised prison, and soon began to fill with Bonapartists. One such was Domingo Rico Valdemoros,[9] the former mayor of Madrid, who was kidnapped by the guerrilla group of Francisco Sánchez, known as Tío Camuñas. They took him on an epic journey to Cádiz, crossing the peninsula held by the enemy. In the city there was a heated debate about the penalty to be applied to Rico Valdemoros, but at the insistence of Tío Camuñas, and with the consent of some influential politicians, he was eventually sentenced to death in a public execution.[10]

After the battle of Salamanca on 22 July 1812, Soult feared he had been overrun and ordered the unsuccessful siege of Cadiz to be raised, which took place on 24 August 1812. And it must have been hasty, given that they had to abandon the almost 600 artillery pieces they had used during the siege, which in almost thirty months had fired just over 15,000 shells on Cadiz and León Island, although only a small number had actually done any real damage. Many of these weapons could not be rendered useless; and in addition the French canteens and infirmaries were found intact, together with a large quantity of foodstuffs and military effects in their warehouses. Cadiz had successfully resisted the French siege.

Notes

1. Throughout the siege the Spanish forces had different generals-in-chief. Its first captain general was José María de la Cueva y de la Cerda, Duke of Albuquerque, who had arrived in Cadiz with the Division from Extremadura. Political disagreements with the Superior Governing Junta of Cadiz led to his dismissal weeks later, and the command passed to General Blake. A few months later command passed to General Lardizánbal.
2. Napoleon later took Victor to the invasion of Russia, so the command of I Army Corps passed into the hands of General Villatte.
3. *San Justo* was a 74-gun ship of the line that had been built in the shipyards of Cartagena in 1779. In its long history its participation in the Battle of Trafalgar stands out, although it is true that it had only a secondary role there, since the incompetent Admiral Villeneuve's tactics saw his ship left behind and he barely entered the fight; this surely saved the ship from destruction. During the Peninsular War *San Justo* took part in the surrender of Admiral Rosilly's Squadron and during the siege of Cádiz starred in numerous noteworthy incidents under the command of Captain José Manuel de Villena. She was sunk at Cartagena in 1828, making her the last surviving Trafalgar ship.
4. Torrejón Chaves (2008).
5. Its full name was Real Villa de la Isla de León. Today this village is called San Fernando.
6. Torrejón Chaves (2010b).
7. Herson (1992), p. 159.
8. The feminine diminutive of Joseph in Spanish.
9. Porras Castaño (2012).
10. The judge who passed the sentence was Antonio Alcalá Galiano, son of Dionisio Alcalá Galiano, who died heroically in the Battle of Trafalgar commanding the ship of the line *Bahama*. The judge, who was only 22 years old, proved to be an excellent speaker. Later, he would enjoy an extensive political career, being appointed minister and deputy on several occasions.

Chapter Thirty

The Battle of Utiel

Date: 25 August 1812. *Place*: Utiel, Valencia. *Result*: Spanish victory.

Order of battle

Spanish Army: the 2nd Division of the 2nd Army under the command of General Pedro Villacampa y Maza de Lizana, with the 2nd Battalion of Volunteers of Aragon, the Regiment of the Princess (1 battalion), the Battalion of Volunteers of Molina, the Regiment of Soria (1 battalion) and the Squadron of Hussars of Aragon.[1] In total, near 4,000 men.

Napoleonic Army: A column under the command of General Louis-Joseph Maupoint with the 16th Regiment of Line Infantry (2 bns), a company of the 4th Regiment of Hussars, and two cannon with mounted artillery. In total, around 1,850 men.[2]

Background[3]

Marmont's defeat at Salamanca caused a metaphorical earthquake among the French troops stationed in Spain: Soult hastened to evacuate Andalusia, while Joseph Bonaparte left Madrid and headed towards Valencia. For his part, Suchet ordered Baron de Maupoint to withdraw to Valencia from Cuenca.

The occupation of Cuenca and its province in La Mancha had taken place between the end of 1811 and the beginning of 1812 as part of Suchet's campaigns to conquer the city of Valencia. Suchet appointed as governor of Cuenca General Jean Barthélemy Darmagnac, who began a brutal campaign of looting throughout his region, most notably in Utiel on 25 November 1811. This policy of terror was continued by his successors in office, Forumont as political governor and Colonel Lamay as military chief of the region. Darmagnac's abusive taxation and the looting of foodstuffs in the towns under his control plunged the people into a terrible famine.

In mid-June 1812 General Baron Louis-Joseph Maupoint[4] was appointed governor of Cuenca, and he too pursued an iron fist policy against the people of the town. Maupoint came from a wealthy Flemish family. In his youth, he was part of the bodyguard of Louis XVI and at the beginning of the French Revolution he remained loyal to the king. As a result, along with two companions, he was arrested by a group of *sans-culottes* in the Palace of Versailles. In fact, La Fayatte saved their lives when they already had a noose around their necks and were about to be hanged. Following this incident, Maupoint reconsidered his loyalty to Louis XVI and joined the revolutionary army. He soon distinguished himself as an excellent cavalry officer. He shone in the great Napoleonic campaigns in Central Europe, especially at Essling and Wagram, where Bonaparte himself awarded him the title of Baron of the Empire. In August 1811 he joined Suchet's army.[5]

Baron de Maupoint showed no more mercy to the people of Cuenca than his predecessors had done. Food was constantly requisitioned from the houses, and peasants were imprisoned or taken hostage if they demurred. In fact, this was the only way for the French to support their troops, who were also suffering hardship. In addition, they were constantly harassed by the guerrillas of Espoz y Mina and Villacampa's Division. The supply problem worsened at the end of July with the arrival of troops from Madrid. After the French defeat in Salamanca, the road to Madrid was clear for Wellington's army, which occupied the Spanish capital on 12 August. The French panicked and Suchet ordered his troops to withdraw. The last French soldier left Cuenca on 22 August, having blown up the castle and left the city in a ruinous state. Maupoint took the shortest route to Valencia, the road that leads through Caudete de las Fuentes, Utiel and Requena.

General O'Donnell, commander-in-chief of the 2nd and 3rd Armies, ordered General Villacampa to head towards the Utiel–Requena road to ambush the column that had left Cuenca.

The battle[6]

On 24 August Villacampa arrived at the town of Mira, where he ordered his men to leave their backpacks and supplies, in order to make the march to Utiel (about 30km (18 miles) distant) as quickly as possible. When they reached their objective, the Aragonese general saw that the terrain between Caudete de las Fuentes and Utiel was flat and hardly conducive to preparing an ambush. However, at dawn he hid his men among the vineyards, arranging them, according to his later war report, in the following way: on the right, the Volunteers of Aragon; in the centre, the Regiment of the Princess; on the left, the Volunteers of Molina; and in reserve, the Regiment of Soria and the Hussars.

Between 6.00 and 7.00am the French column appeared. As remaining hidden was difficult, the Volunteers of Molina opened fire against the advancing vanguard; unfortunately for the Spanish, the French found an advantageous position from which to defend themselves and were able to bring up their artillery pieces. Villacampa came forward with the reserve forces to support Molina's troops, and in a few minutes Maupoint's men were surrounded by the Spanish troops, suffering a large number of casualties in the process. Only the brave and determined action of Major Ronfort managed to break the Spanish line, allowing his men to break the encirclement and flee in haste to the castle of Requena, where they took refuge.

The battle of Utiel was over. The French left on the battlefield their two cannon, backpacks and supplies, and a number of carts loaded with weapons and ammunition; they also left behind some 400 casualties, either dead, wounded or taken prisoner. Among the wounded arriving in Requena was Maupoint himself.

In his report General Villacampa noted several officers for their bravery. Manuel de Latre, for example, the captain of the Volunteers of Aragon. A true veteran of the Peninsular War, he had fought in the second siege of Zaragoza, the siege of Girona, and the battles of Vic and Sagunto, among many others. He had also taken part in innumerable guerrilla actions in the province of Teruel. In mid-October 1811, while in Alcañiz, he was informed that a battalion of Neapolitan soldiers was resting in Muniesa. With his Volunteers of Aragon, he launched a surprise attack; several of the enemy troops were killed and large numbers taken prisoner.[7] Men like Latre made sure that the French soldiers could not enjoy a minute's rest during their occupation of Spain. Once the war was over, he remained faithful to the Constitution of 1812, to which end he supported Riego's uprising in 1821. He was awarded the order of Saint Ferdinand 4th class, with an annual pension of 20,000 reales. With the fall of the Riego government, he was discharged from the army. After the death of Ferdinand VII he would again hold important positions, until his death in 1840.[8]

For the action at Utiel (*aka* Tollo) General Villacampa was decorated with one of the first orders of Saint Ferdinand. In addition, a ditty was created that honoured his feat:

Villacampa ya no campa,
que en el Tollo ya campó
y a las águilas francesas
los cañones le quitó.[9]

Notes

1. See: https://iv.revistalocal.es/vuelven-jornadas-conmemorativas-accion-utiel-recreacion-batalla-tollo-1812/ (accessed 9 October 2020); Suchet (1828).

2. Suchet (1828).
3. Martínez Martínez (2009).
4. Villacampa cites him in his report as Baron de Mopos.
5. Mullié (1851).
6. General Villacampa's dispatch can be found at: https://www.boe.es/datos/pdfs/BOE//1812/014/C00124-00132.pdf (accessed 10 October 2020); Suchet (1828).
7. *Gazeta del Gobierno of Mexico*, 12 March 1812.
8. See the entry for José Luis Isabel Sánchez in the *Biographical Dictionary of the Royal Academy of History of Spain*.
9. 'Villacampa no longer camps, / who has already camped in the Tollo / and the French eagles / the cannon took away.'

Chapter Thirty-One

The Indomitable Guerrillas: the 7th Army

Date: from 20 February 1811 until the end of the war.
Place: Navarre, Basque Country, Cantabria, La Rioja and Old Castile.

Background

The phenomenon of Spanish guerrilla warfare during the Peninsular War is probably the most complex aspect of this period. Traditional historiography extolls its importance as fundamental to defeating the Napoleonic Army. However, modern historians, such as Esdaile,[1] have cast doubts on the traditional view by downplaying the guerrillas' influence on the conduct of the war, regarding them as military mediocrities at best, or bloodthirsty bandits at worst. It is not the aim of this book to participate in this historiographical debate. This chapter focuses on the so-called 7th Army, whose creation and development demonstrate the virtues and defects of this irregular army. (For this reason, we will leave aside the activities of other outstanding guerrilla leaders who did not form part of this new army, such as the Castilian Juan Martín Díez *el Empecinado* or the Catalan Joan Clarós, who have already been mentioned in previous chapters.) Two of the main problems in studying the guerrilla forces concern their composition and their motivation. There were many types of guerrilla units, since they could be made up of former soldiers, deserters or stray soldiers, civilians with a desire for revenge, fanatical churchmen, homeless people who had lost everything because of the war, but also criminals and bandits. Thus their motivation varied from unit to unit, according to composition, ranging from the honourable desire to fight an invading army, to simply robbing and looting (whether from the Spanish or the French), to the simple urge to survive. Whether for patriotism or for money, the kind of warfare they practised provoked contempt on the part of the French, but also among the British and indeed among a large proportion of the Spanish officers. Certainly their military tactics were in many cases disastrous; they resisted any kind of coordination with other fighting bands or with the regular army; and conflicts between guerrillas over territories of influence or booty were commonplace – but nevertheless they successfully carried out numerous missions in the French rearguard, as this chapter will describe.

A royal order of the Regency Council[2] dated 20 February 1811 formed the 7th Army under the command of General Gabriel Mendizábal. The aim was to integrate into the regular army the various guerrilla groups that were active in the north of the peninsula and which were becoming so numerous and well organized that the Regency wanted them to act as regular forces. By their own nature, these units did not participate in a coordinated way with one another and all of them were totally autonomous; their leaders were often ambitious and independent men as capable of fighting the French as they were of battling each other, if necessary. In some cases their attitude to the French differed little from their attitude to their compatriots. Thus Mendizábal's command, despite his efforts, was in some cases little more than nominal.

Just because the order was signed in February does not mean that the 7th Army was immediately created and on the move. Mendizábal's first mission was to convince the guerrilla leaders to join his army. This was no easy task, but with patience and diplomacy he succeeded, at least in most cases. For example, he managed to integrate the guerrillas of Juan López Campillo and Lorenzo Herrero[3] into the Battalion of Tiradores de Cantabria. It was also Mendizábal's task to define the territories in which each of his units would operate, since these invisible borders had been the cause of bitter disputes and rivalries between various guerrilla leaders when it came to hoarding food, recruits and money,[4] and had even provoked armed clashes between some of them.

The missions that were entrusted to the forces that made up the 7th Army included: to cut off communications between France and Madrid; to protect the civilian population from the excesses of the French (although, as will be seen, they sometimes overran the people they were supposed to be safeguarding); and, most important of all, to distract as many enemy troops as possible to prevent French reinforcements from reaching the Portuguese Army. This last task was more than achieved, bringing about a veritable insurrection in northern Spain that put on hold all the French ambitions in the Iberian Peninsula, earning the admiration not only of Wellington himself (who would take some of these troops with him on his campaigns in southern France) but also, astonishingly, of British historians, always so sparing when it comes to recognizing the merits of the Spanish armies during the Peninsular War.

Mendizábal was ordered to increase his troops to 40,000 men, but this was a totally unreasonable figure given that he was far from having sufficient weapons and uniforms for such large numbers, nor did he have time to adequately instruct his new troops. Thus, in the end Mendizábal was able to form five light divisions: the Vanguard Division commanded by Díaz Porlier; the Navarre Division commanded by Espoz y Mina; the Iberia Division commanded by Longa; the Castilian Division; and the Basque Division. It was not possible to find a general to lead the latter two divisions, so they were organized into brigades and sections that were practically independent. In the Castilian Division, these brigades were: the 'Burgos' of the famous priest Merino; the 'Rioja' commanded by Bartolomé Amor and Ignacio Zapatero 'Cuevillas'; the 'Bureba' of Francisco Salazar; and the 'Palentina' under Juan de Tapia and Santos Padilla. The Basque Brigade, meanwhile, was divided into the Biscayan Brigade under the command of Renovales; the Guipuzcoa Brigade under the guerrilla commander Jáuregui, the 'Pastor'; and the Alava Brigade under Espoz y Mina.[5]

The Vanguard Division (the Cantabrian Division)

The Vanguard Division was assigned to Juan Díaz Porlier. A native of Cartagena de Indias (then, part of the Viceroyalty of New Granada – present-day Colombia), Díaz Porlier came from a wealthy family. As a young man he joined the navy and, aboard the *Prince of Asturias*, fought in the battle of Trafalgar, among many others. Shortly after this, he requested a transfer to the army. At the beginning of the Napoleonic wars in Spain, he fought in the battles of Gamonal and Espinosa de los Monteros. Those wholesale defeats convinced him that the French could not be defeated by the tactics of conventional warfare, so with some of his former soldiers and volunteer civilians, he organized his first guerrilla force. In a daring *coup de main*, in 1809 he managed to capture more than 400 Napoleonic troops in the Castilian town of Aguilar de Campoo, which earned him enormous fame and promotion to brigadier, and brought queues of volunteers to join his unit. At that time he began to be known by the nickname *Marquesito*,[6] as it seems that in order to inspire confidence in his countrymen, he claimed to be the nephew of the Marquis de la Romana.

By early 1811 his forces had been organized into the following units: the Laredo Provincial Regiment; the 1st Cantabrian Regiment, commanded by Pedro Labastida; the Cantabria Shooters Battalion, commanded by Lorenzo Herrero; the National Guards; the Observers of Guipúzcoa, under the command of Captain José Gutiérrez; the Observers of Encartaciones, under the command of Mariano Cortés; and the Squadron of Hussars of Cantabria, under the command of Ignacio Alonso Remur, known as *Cuevillas Menor*.[7] In total, his forces comprised 4,247 men, with their base in the Cantabrian population of Potes.

Díaz Porlier's men had to deal with Régis Barthélemy Mouton-Duvernet, governor general and military commander of the province of Santander, and General Pierre Boyer, commander of the city of Santander. Against them, Díaz Porlier put into practice a low-intensity war, typical guerrilla warfare that drove the Napoleonic authorities mad, as they were constantly under attack and, in order to secure communications between Santander and Bilbao, they had to divide their forces into numerous garrisons along the road. In addition, the war led to a series of reprisals and counter-reprisals between the two armies, rivalling each other in such cruelty that General Pierre Boyer was nicknamed Peter the Cruel. The main victim of the barbarity in Cantabria was, of course, the civilian population, who were constantly punished for helping either side in the conflict. In most cases, this aid was provided under duress.

The main combat action carried out by the Cantabrian Division was the taking of the city of Santander on 14 August 1811. At dawn Díaz Porlier's troops fell on the city, whose garrison was mostly asleep. Boyer and most of his men could do little more than put on their boots and ride away on horseback. Less fortunate were the hundred or so Napoleonic soldiers who were imprisoned, and the fifty who died in the fighting. In addition, the patriots took advantage of the situation to take captive important characters such as the city's intendant, Joaquín de Barroeta-Aldamar. News of the capture of Santander spread quickly. General Caffarelli du Falga led a column to recapture the city, but by the time he arrived, Díaz Porlier's troops had already abandoned it. The year 1812 was one of frenetic activity for Díaz Porlier's troops. In March they confronted the French forces in the actions at Sasamón and El Tejo; on 2 August they returned to Santander, which was definitively liberated; a few days later, they took part in the capture of Bilbao; also in August actions were reported in Laredo, Castro and Miravilles; Díaz Porlier's last action as part of the 7th Army was at the Seros river on 17 October.[8] Probably the only blemish on his career was his inability to take the stronghold of Santoña (*aka* 'the Gibraltar of the north'), which the French held until the end of the war.

When the 7th Army was disbanded, in the new reorganization of military forces carried out by the Regency Council, it became part of the 6th Army. Later, serving with the 4th Army, Díaz Porlier participated in the battle of San Marcial, and after the war he was assigned to Corunna. A staunch liberal, he was arrested and imprisoned in the castle of San Antón in Corunna. The following year he rose against Ferdinand VII, receiving substantial civil and military support in the city, but when the absolutist troops arrived, the conspirators collapsed and Díaz Porlier was arrested, tried and hanged. He was 27 years old.

The Castilian (1st) Division

As mentioned above, Mendizábal was unable to achieve a single command that would unify the different guerrilla groups, so it was determined that each of them, called brigades, would act autonomously.

Cura[9] Jerónimo Merino, the parish priest of his native town, Villoviado, in Burgos, was probably the most popular brigade leader. He took command of the Burgos Brigade, as this was the province in which he spent most of his time, although he also carried out actions in other Castilian provinces including Soria, La Rioja and Palencia. Outraged to see how the French mistreated his parishioners, he decided to create his own guerrilla force. His first combat action was an attack on a post office in mid-January 1809. At the beginning he had the help of the Empecinado, who provided him with weapons and horses. This collaboration would continue throughout the war, during which they would carry out some major operations. During the first period of the war Merino's most famous action was the ambush he laid against a French regiment in the town of Dueñas. In 1811 he divided his men between the Arlanza Regiment and the Hussar Regiment of Burgos, bringing the total number of troops to 2,500. Harassment of the enemy forces was constant. The French response was to increase their repression of civilians, soldiers and guerrillas, which led to a whirlwind of revenge attacks against them. In April 1812, for example, Merino fell upon the 1st Battalion of the Vistula Lancers in Hontoria de Valdearados, shooting 110 of them in retaliation for the execution of four members of the Burgos Junta. In July he pursued Marshal Marmont's French troops as they retreated through the Esgueva valley after their defeat in the battle of Salamanca. Finally, he took part in the siege of the castle of Burgos. In 1813, after the final withdrawal of the French from Castile, he was appointed military governor of Burgos. When the war ended, Merino intended to continue his military career, but Ferdinand VII reserved a canonry in Valencia cathedral for him. Dissatisfied with this, he returned to his village. During the Carlist Wars he again took up arms, this time in favour of the absolutist pretender Charles of Bourbon. After Bourbon's defeat, Merino did not accept the amnesty of the liberal government and instead went into exile in France, where he died.

The Palentina Brigade was under the command of Juan de Tapia; like Merino, he was also a parish priest.[10] His area of action was the south of the province of Palencia and, according to the chronicles, he was as feared by the French as by the natives of the country, whom he did not hesitate to plunder as cruelly as necessary. Another of the leaders of this brigade was Santos Padilla, who had trained as a guerrilla in the heat of the departure of the priest Merino. Padilla remains infamous for his conquest of the town of Sasamón, known as the 'Bayonne of Spain' and reputed to be an *afrancesada* town. After his conquest of the town, on 21 and 22 July 1812, and supported by the Salazar and Longa guerrillas, his men set fire to most of the houses in the town and to the cathedral of Santa María la Real, with an incalculable loss of artistic and cultural heritage, given that they went to great lengths to destroy everything they could not steal. Padilla was also responsible for the destruction of several castles, such as Castrogeriz and Olmedillos, to prevent them from being used by the French troops.

The Rioja Brigade was commanded by Bartolomé Amor de la Pisa, a professional soldier. After the defeat in the battle of Gamonal, Díaz Porlier ordered him to raise a guerrilla force in La Rioja, a mission for which he gave him a detachment of Hussars from Cantabria. Amor's brigade stood out in the actions at Ezcaray and Navarrete. After the war he continued with his military career, though eventually his liberal ideas forced him into exile; indeed, during the First Carlist War he fought for the liberal army.

Another of the outstanding guerrilla leaders of this brigade was Ignacio Alonso Zapatero, known as 'Cuevillas' as he was a native of the Rioja town of La Cueva. At the start of the war he was a cavalry lieutenant. His eldest son, known as Cuevillas Menor, would enjoy a lengthy military career, and his second wife, Dominica Ruiz de Vallejo y Torre, also fought in his guerrilla. Cuevillas had numerous clashes with Mariano de Renovales, who got him removed from his guerrilla command. After the war, he would embrace the cause of absolutism, taking up arms during the First Carlist War.

Finally, the Bureba Brigade was commanded by Francisco Salazar, another former ecclesiastic.

The Basque (2nd) Division

As with the Castilian Division, here again Mendizábal was unable to agree on a single command, so the three brigades fought autonomously.

Perhaps the most notable was the Biscayan Brigade, under the command of the always charismatic, controversial and fearless Mariano de Renovales. An experienced Biscayan soldier of humble origins, before the Peninsular War he had distinguished himself in the defence of Buenos Aires. Once in Spain, he was one of the heroes of the two sieges of Zaragoza, where he was taken prisoner; he escaped in Pamplona, after being released on his parole.[11] From that moment on, he led a guerrilla band, but pressure from the French forced him to give up territory until eventually he had no choice but to retreat to Cadiz, where he was received as a hero; from there his fame spread throughout Josephine Spain and even to Central and South America, thanks to a press greatly in need of patriotic heroes and good news. This fame led to a collection being taken up in Cuba to finance a maritime expedition to the Cantabrian coast in 1810,[12] after Renovales had been appointed by the Regency Council as general commander of the Northern Provinces. However, the expedition ended in disaster when he tried to land in Santoña, where he lost two of his ships. He was finally able to dock in the Galician port of Vivero, where a large proportion of his troops deserted. Renovales was not discouraged by this, and with his remaining troops he set off for Cantabria, on a march that was as long as it was arduous owing to the adverse weather conditions. In early 1811 Renovales was dismissed and replaced by Mendizábal. He was not enthusiastic about the new organization, and dedicated himself to hindering many of the decisions made by his new superior; in particular, he was in constant conflict with Díaz Porlier. On 17 March the French built the Santa Lucía bridge over the Saja river in the Cabezón valley to control the road between Santander and Torrelavega, which Renovales attacked. The action failed and the intrepid Basque received a serious bullet wound in the neck, which kept him away from the front for several weeks. Once the commands and areas of action of each of the divisions of the 7th Army were consolidated, Renovales became a nightmare for the French in Biscay and even, at times, in the neighbouring provinces. (He also continued to be a headache for Díaz Porlier and Espoz y Mina.)

In 1812, in the vicinity of Orduña, he confronted and defeated the brigade of General Jean Antoine Soulier, who was wounded in the action. Then, with the collaboration of Commodore Home Riggs Popham, he assaulted Bilbao, seizing quantities of arms and supplies and freeing from the town's gaols numerous prisoners who then enlisted in his division.[13] Days later, in a coordinated action with troops from Cuevillas and Díaz Porlier, he repelled an attempt by General

Claude Pierre Rouget's brigade to recover the city, which remained in Spanish hands until 30 December.

Renovales' actions in Biscay were many. However, at the beginning of 1813, after a new disagreement with Mendizábal, he decided to visit Wellington to complain to the Duke about his superior. He was en route when he was captured by the French in Zamora and taken to France. Despite several attempts to rescue him, Renovales ended up in a prison depot in Normandy. In 1814 he managed to escape and fled to London,[14] but soon returned to Spain, from where he had to flee again after participating in a conspiracy to overthrow Ferdinand VII. Back in London, he contacted Simón Bolívar, offering to join his fight. The Spanish ambassador, aware of this, won him over to his cause, and convinced him to act as a double agent. After managing to irritate both sides, in 1820 Renovales ended up in Havana, where the captain general ordered his immediate arrest. Two days later he died in prison, presumably of yellow fever, ending the exciting life of an indomitable soldier whom Alcalá Galiano described as 'a man of courage, great presumption, little culture but such understanding' and Pío Baroja as 'small, dark and accustomed to swearing oaths; he used to repeat: *¡Hostias! ¡Se acabó la humanidad!'*[15]

The Alava Brigade depended on Espoz y Mina, discussed later, while the Guipuzcoa Brigade was led by Gaspar de Jáuregui, known as 'the Pastor',[16] as this was his profession before the war. He was one of the first Guipuzcoan guerrillas, joining the Corso Terrestre of Espoz y Mina, who gave him a contingent of guerrillas to lead in his province of origin, which he knew inside out thanks to his former profession. A very young Tomás de Zumalacárregui enlisted in his ranks, with whom he would maintain a close relationship. In fact, the future Carlist leader taught Jáuregui to read and write during the war. Jáuregui's Brigade participated in numerous actions throughout the war, some of the most notable taking place during the period in which it belonged to the 7th Army. On 17 April, for example, garrisons from various towns in Guipuzcoa joined forces to hunt down the Pastor, and there was a tough battle, after which the French had to take refuge in the fortification of Azpeitia. In mid-July a guerrilla band was surprised near Villarreal by a detachment of gendarmes. Outnumbered, the Guipuzcoans surrendered, but instead of being treated as prisoners of war, they were executed on the spot. The following month the Pastor returned to the same place in search of revenge, but his battle with the gendarmes ended in a draw. On 4 September he attacked the town of Villarreal again, but by now it had been reinforced by a column led by General Marie François Rouyer;[17] heavily outnumbered, Jáuregui suffered a defeat. On the 19th he fought with the Azpeitia garrison, suffering a gunshot wound to the leg. The battles in this town were repeated three more times during the course of the year. It was reported that sixteen French prisoners were executed by being thrown off a cliff; four of them survived, albeit badly wounded, and managed to return to their garrison.

The year 1812 began for Jáuregui with a serious gunshot wound to the chest suffered during combat at Anzuola, and there were fears for his life. But he recovered, and on 25 April attacked the escort of Colonel Pierre Cambronne.[18] In this action he was shot again, this time in the right buttock. On 14 June, in co-ordination with Commodore Popham's fleet, he attacked the defences of Lekeitio. The British bombarded the Napoleonic stronghold on Mount Lumentza and when one of its walls gave way, some 100 British soldiers and 400 of Jáuregui's men assaulted the fortification. The French resisted the first attack, but not the second one, abandoning the position and retreating towards the town of Lekeitio, where, together with 290 French soldiers from the 119th Regiment of Line Infantry, under the command of Major Guillot, they established strongpoints in two buildings. After a couple of days under siege and unable to be rescued, they surrendered. Jáuregui spared their lives thanks to the fact that Guillot had not executed a young *guerrillero* captured a few days earlier. Off the coast of Lekeitio lies the island of San Nicolás, where the French had built fortifications, but the garrison of the island surrendered to the British that same day. The British ships embarked all the prisoners and the strategic town of Lekeitio was left in the hands of Jáuregui and his men.[19] On 2 July, in Ormaiztegui, he attacked a French column that included a group of seventy prisoners. The French, who had almost 300 troops, resisted for as long as they could, but Jáuregui's men ended up crushing them. A few Frenchmen were able to reach Villarreal, but most of them were bayoneted. In August Jáuregui surrendered the garrison at Motrico, and in September the garrison at Deba. Although small detachments of the brigade continued to harass French columns and their couriers, Jáuregui's greatest efforts were focused on collaborating in the siege of Santoña. In 1813 he increasingly coordinated his actions with those of Espoz y Mina and the guerrilla fighter Dos Pelos of the Iberia Division. After the battle of Vitoria, he became a nightmare for Joseph Bonaparte's rearguard, and also took part in the battle of San Marcial and the siege of San Sebastián, the city where the war ended, forming part of its garrison. After the war, he soon took up arms again. A staunch liberal, he clashed with his former assistant Tomás de Zumalacárregui, who became the general in chief of the Carlist Army of the North. Jáuregui died in 1844 as commander general of the province of Álava.

The Iberian (3rd) Division

This division had its origins in a guerrilla band called the Corso Terrestre de Voluntarios de Castilla, created at the beginning of the war by Francisco Tomás Anchía y Urquiza (who adopted the nom de guerre Francisco de Longa, since Longa was the name of the Biscayan hamlet in which he was born), along with other fellow countrymen of his who would also become famous guerrilla fighters, such as Sebastián Fernández de Leceta, known as Dos Pelos, and Eustaquio Salcedo. Like practically all guerrillas, Longa began his career by attacking convoys or small Napoleonic detachments that ventured along Navarrese roads.

Success and notoriety soon followed. His band was gaining volunteers and began to grow at the same rate as the audacity in his actions increased. In 1811 Longa already had in his guerrilla band about 1,000 members, whom he took with him to form part of the 7th Army, which he officially joined on 28 October 1811, when he was promoted to colonel. The Iberia Division was born.

In 1812 a significant event took place that gives us a different picture of the guerrilla's actions. At the beginning of July, the French troops in Castro-Urdiales abandoned the town, which was immediately occupied by troops of the Iberia Division, with the help of the British navy under the command of Commodore Home Riggs Popham. Longa appointed as governor of the town Captain Juan Bautista Brodet, who began a reign of terror, demanding excessive taxes, arbitrarily imprisoning anyone who dared to oppose him, and turning his residence into a den of criminals. In one of his bacchanals, he ended up murdering an artillery commander, which led to his arrest.[20] He was temporarily replaced by Lieutenant Colonel Joaquín Gómez of the Iberia Division's general staff, but he in turn was soon replaced by Hussar Lieutenant Colonel Pedro Pablo Álvarez, who took up Brodet's despotism, perhaps even surpassing it. It should be noted that this attitude towards the Castro-Urdiales people was not only accepted by Longa, but encouraged. Castro-Urdiales also became the port of disembarkation for military supplies transported from Corunna by British ships. This became a point of conflict with other units of the 7th Army which came to claim by force what they believed was rightfully theirs. Thus, from Biscay the battalion of Renovales and Eguíluz appeared to take by hook or by crook a cargo of British rifles, and a real battle was about to break out between the troops of both sides.[21] From the moment of their arrival, Longa's men had planned the fortification of the town, which they considered of strategic importance. However, construction was much slower than planning, and when Napoleonic troops arrived in May 1813 the Iberian Division could do nothing to save the city, which they ended up abandoning to its fate. The town still remembers the *Francesada* (French invasion), marking the day when the French entered the city in blood and fire, looting and murdering in cold blood, with more than 400 civilians killed, including 82 children.

Another of Longa's outstanding actions took place in the Sedano valley on 29 November 1812, when he intercepted a column under the command of General Fremont made up of some 4,000 Napoleonic soldiers, with numerous prisoners and a convoy of supplies. In the ensuing battle, Longa won a crushing victory, resulting in over 700 French casualties and the release of Spanish prisoners. This battle was reported in the *London Chronicle* of 6 January and by the Count of Toreno,[22] but curiously it does not appear in any of the French sources consulted. Even the usually exhaustive *Victoires, conquêtes, désastres, revers et guerres civiles des Français, de 1792 à 1815*, makes no reference to this combat in vol. 21 in which this action should be found. Similarly, it is surprising that General Fremont (or Framont, as he is written in the *London Chronicle*) does not appear in any list of generals of the Napoleonic period or in the detailed work *Liste chrono-logique des généraux français ou étrangers au service de France, morts sur le champ de bataille, des suites de leurs blessures ou de mort violente, de 1792 à 1837*, edited by the French army in 1838 and listing all the generals from that period who died in action.[23]

Longa enjoyed the full confidence of his British allies. Thus his Iberia Division was one of those chosen by Wellington to participate in the battle of Vitoria and subsequently in the invasion of France. In the battle of Vitoria Longa's troops played a decisive role in taking Gamarra Menor, cutting off the French retreat. He also took part in the battle of San Marcial.

Once the war was over, Longa remained totally loyal to Ferdinand VII and supported his return to absolutism. This brought him promotions, honours and various posts in Biscay, but his corruption and abuse of authority put him at odds with the rest of the local authorities. Afterwards, Longa was appointed to other posts, ending up as Captain General of Valencia. In between, he left a trail of unparalleled embezzlement and rapacity, beatings and even indiscriminate execu-tions of those suspected of opposing the regime of Ferdinand VII. But after his scandalous mandate in Valencia, the king had no choice but to remove him from public life. It is worth noting that during the persecution of liberal leaders, he was entrusted with the task of arresting Mariano de Renovales. Longa must not have liked it, as he used very few means and gave his former comrade the opportunity to flee to France. Less lucky was another of his former comrades, the liberal Sebastián Fernández de Leceta, known as Dos Pelos, who in 1822 was inter-cepted, along with his men, by a guerrilla band of royalists; they were massacred in cold blood.

Finally, it is interesting to note the presence of a female guerrilla, Martina Ibaibarriaga, from Berriztarra. It seems that she joined the Manco guerrilla band to avenge the deaths of her father and one of her brothers, killed during the Napoleonic sack of Bilbao in 1808. Her role in this guerrilla movement was so notorious that the French authorities arrested her mother and sister, who were held hostage. She even commanded a party of more than 150 men. However, her band was also characterized by execrable acts of banditry, which could not be overlooked. Longa arrested them and killed all their leaders except Martina, who was spared because she was pregnant. Pardoned, she joined the Iberian Division as an officer and as such took part in numerous battles, including the battle of Vitoria. It is believed that many of the war reports in which a mysterious Captain Martínez is mentioned actually refer to Martina Ibaibarriaga. After the war she was tried for banditry but declared innocent, and Ferdinand VII granted her a life pension as a reward for her loyalty and bravery in wartime.

The phenomenon of guerrilla women is another of the aspects of the war that have yet to be studied in depth. In a society as emphatically patriarchal as that of the *Ancien Regime*, women did not have the option to form part of the regular army. However, the guerrillas gave them the opportunity to face the invader under the same conditions as their male compatriots. There were many such female guerrillas, and to judge from the cases that are known, they were extremely brave. One such was Catalina Martín López-Bustamente, second lieutenant in the band of her uncle, Toribio Bustamente, known as Caracol. Catalina stood out in the so-called 'Surprise of Valverde de Leganés' in Badajoz, when Murillo's troops, of which her party was a part, fell on a cavalry brigade that was spending the night in that town. General Charles Victor Woirgard died in this action, trying to organize a counter-attack. Woirgard has the dubious honour of being considered one of the worst cavalry officers in the Napoleonic army. Similarly, Juana Galán, known as Galana, was the symbol of the resistance against the invader in Valdepeñas, where she is still considered one of the region's greatest heroines; sadly, she did not survive the war, dying in childbed while giving birth to her second child in 1812. Other women included Damiana Rebolledo, who was one of the leaders of the anti-French uprising in Valladolid, and Lluisa Villalba, who took up arms in Catalonia, standing out in various actions in Molins de Rei and Mataró. She was taken prisoner in Montserrat, but was able to flee to Barcelona where, with the collaboration of Captain Vicenta Torres, she was able to steal important documents from one of Suchet's aides-de-camp.

The Navarre (4th) Division

The alma mater of this division was undoubtedly Espoz y Mina,[24] surely the most famous Spanish guerrilla along with Empecinado. His real name was Francisco Espoz Ilundáin and he was from a small Navarrese village called Idocín. During the first months of the war he is not known to have engaged in any military activity, but in the spring of 1809 he joined the Corso Terrestre de Navarra, whose leader was his nephew, Xavier Mina. In May 1810 Mina was captured by the French and the leadership of his guerrilla band passed into the hands of Francisco Espoz, who, in order to take advantage of his nephew's popularity, changed his name to Espoz y Mina. He soon distinguished himself for his extraordinary commanding qualities: his charisma, his ability to impose the discipline he demanded on his men; and his extreme cruelty towards the enemy made him a hero for the Spanish and a nightmare for the French, who came to know him as 'Le Petit Roi de Navarre' ('the little king of Navarre'). When he joined the 7th Army, his division was the largest and best organized. Such was his power that even Mendizábal feared that the Navarre Division would absorb the rest of the units in his army.

Espoz y Mina's first major successful action after joining the 7th Army was known as the First Surprise of Arlabán, and it took place on 25 May 1811 in the hills of Arlabán, located between the present-day provinces of Álava and Guipúzcoa. His brigade attacked a column of some 1,650 French soldiers escorting around 1,000 British and Spanish prisoners on their way to the French depots. The French defeat was complete. The French soldiers, from one of Masséna's divisions, suffered some 300 dead and 800 taken prisoner, the column of Spanish and British prisoners was freed, and booty worth more than 4 million reales was captured. Espoz y Mina became a hero to all of Fernandine Spain. The Regency Council, until then reluctant to grant too many favours to what it considered little more than a bunch of bandits, recognized his Navarre Division as a regular army unit by royal decree on 5 June 1811.[25] On 14 December he published his famous decree in which he declared 'War to the death and without quarter to chiefs and soldiers, including the Bonaparte of the French',[26] in response to the numerous executions carried out by the French against Spanish civilians and soldiers. He began to put this threat into practice on 11 January 1812 in the town of Rocaforte, some 45km (28 miles) southeast of Pamplona. Despite being greatly outnumbered, the Navarre Division, together with the cavalry of Mendizábal, who handed over command of the battle to Espoz y Mina, destroyed General Abbé's troops, the French ending the day with 600 casualties and a similar number taken prisoner, many of whom were executed.[27] The Navarrese general had become the terror of the French. His actions were celebrated as victories and his fame among the patriots grew in tandem with the terror he inflicted on his enemies.

The Navarre Division took part in countless actions and battles during the time it was attached to the 7th Army, notably the Second Surprise of Arlabán, which took place on 9 April 1812. On that day a Spanish force of some 3,000 men confronted a French column under General Caffarelli de Falga with a similar number of troops, which was transporting some 800 prisoners to France. The planned operation was again a complete success. After an hour of combat, the success of the Navarrese was complete: they put the Napoleonic troops to flight, and the French suffered some 600 casualties, compared to just 30 on the Spanish side. In addition, they captured 300 prisoners, freed the 800 Spaniards and British, and seized the very valuable French baggage comprising a large quantity of weapons, money and jewellery valued at almost 800,000 francs. The convoy also included a number of civilians. One of them was one of King Joseph's most trusted confidants, his personal secretary Jean Deslandes, an efficient, discreet and loyal man, who was killed as he tried to flee with his wife. Also travelling in his carriage was Carlota de Aranza, at the time the wife of the notable *afrancesado* Blas de Aranza, who held important positions in the Josephine administration. It is worth noting that in this case Espoz y Mina treated the captured women and the five children with them with exquisite care. In fact, he sent them all to Vitoria except Carlota de Aranza, due to the advanced state of her pregnancy. Later, Carlota de Aranza would be exchanged for Xavier Mina's mother, who was a prisoner of the French. The tragic end of Deslandes and his wife was a source of inspiration for various artists; for example, General Lejeune, a notable painter, dedicated an oil painting to them, and some authors, including the Count of Toreno and the Countess of Merlin, dedicated stories to them. Numerous letters from Joseph Bonaparte to his wife and siblings were also found in Deslandes' carriage. In them, he described the depressing political, military and personal situation in which he found himself. These letters quickly became the talk of Spain, as the Regency Council took it upon itself to publicize them as much as it knew how, which was a tremendous humiliation for King Joseph and greatly affected his already battered state of mind. The Navarre Division would not stop fighting until the complete liberation of their kingdom. It could be said that the war did not end for them until 3 May 1814.[28] That day, on the border between Navarre and France, Francisco Espoz and Xavier Mina embraced after four long years apart. Xavier Mina was able to see for himself how his ragged band of guerrillas had become a regular division of the Spanish army. His uncle was already a general and his former comrades were all colonels and majors, with their shiny uniforms and all. Together they mourned their former comrades who had not lived to see the end of the war, such as Lucas Górriz, who died while attacking a French convoy in the Etxauri valley in February 1811, and Gregorio de Cruchaga, who died after a clash with the French in May 1812. Both had been members of the Corso from day one, military men as brave as they were efficient, and personal friends of both Mina and Espoz.

But if one war ended for these men, another would soon begin. Mina and Espoz were to be deeply disappointed by the decisions taken by Ferdinand VII: his return to absolutism, and the dissolution of the Navarre Division, among other decisions, led them to speak out against the king. After this, they went into exile. After an eventful life, Francisco Espoz died in Barcelona in 1836, after receiving a pardon from the regent Maria Christina of Bourbon. Xavier Mina died fighting for the independence of Mexico in 1817.

Notes

1. Esdaile (2004).
2. Cabanes (1822), Vol. III.
3. García Fuertes (2016), p. 410.
4. Ibid., p. 411.
5. Ibid., p. 410.
6. 'The Little Marquis'.
7. Palacio Ramos (2008), p. 207.
8. Lión Valderrábano (1973), pp. 17–18.
9. Priest.
10. Numerous ecclesiastics led *guerrillas*. In addition to the aforementioned Merino and Tapia, we can list Lucas Rafael, Antonio Marañón *el Trapense*, Ramón Argote, Antonio Jiménez, Policarpo Romea, Antonio Temprano, Jacobo Álvarez, Juan Mendieta *el Capuchino*, Asencio Nebot and Francisco Salazar, who also headed one of the Castilian brigades.
11. Appealing to the sense of honour of the Spanish officers, the French authorities granted them a regime of semi-freedom in which they could move freely in a city, but never go absent without permission or take up arms against the Napoleonic troops. For Spanish prisoners this regimen was common in some French cities, but was rarely applied in Spain. Cases like Renovales explain why.
12. Ausín Ciruelos (2018), p. 26.
13. Letter from Popham to Admiral Keith dated 16 August 1812 and published in the *Gazeta de Madrid* dated 10 October 1812.
14. Ausín Ciruelos (2018), p. 27.

15. 'Damn! Humanity is over!' 'Artzentales bucea en la vida del militar local que plantó cara a Ferdinand VII', article by Elixane Castresana in the newspaper *Deia* dated 30 August 2020. Available at: https://www.deia.eus/bizkaia/ezkerraldea-enkarterri/2020/08/30/artzentales-bucea-vida-militar-local/1061430.html (accessed 9 January 2021).
16. Shepherd. In some sources his nickname in Basque, *Artzaina*, is also found. Most probably that was the language used in his guerrilla.
17. Rouyer was a veteran of the war on the Iberian Peninsula. In 1808 he was taken prisoner at the Battle of Bailén, although he was later released. Between 1810 and 1811 he was part of the Napoleonic troops fighting in Catalonia. In 1812 he was sent to Italy. During the Hundred Days he remained faithful to Napoleon, and after fighting at Waterloo he left the army.
18. Colonel Pierre Cambronne was one of the best *voltigeur* officers in the French army. At this time he was probably headed for the Russian campaign, where he commanded an elite infantry unit. He fought at Dresden and Leipzig, and was appointed brigadier general after the battle of Hanau on 31 October 1813. His enduring loyalty to Napoleon is demonstrated by the fact that he was the commander of the Imperial Guard that accompanied him to his exile on the island of Elba in 1814. On his return, Cambronne commanded a battalion of the grenadiers of the Old Guard. At Waterloo he led the last charge, and was seriously wounded by a bayonet. When General Colville (another veteran of the Peninsular War) ordered him to surrender, Cambronne replied: 'La Garde meurt, mais ne se rend pas' ('The Guard dies, but does not surrender'). Later, the children of General Claude-Étienne Michel, also from the Old Guard, claimed that the phrase was authored by their father, but it could never be proven. Colville, who was a civilized man, then ordered Cambronne to surrender, to which the Imperial general replied: 'Merde!' From then on in France and England it became fashionable to replace this expletive with the expression: *'le mot de Cambronne'* ('the word of Cambronne'). He would eventually marry his British nurse and return to France, where, after being acquitted of treason against the Bourbons, he was appointed to various military posts.
19. Goiogana (2013).
20. Reported in the newspaper *El Patriota* dated 28 July 1814.
21. Gómez Rodrigo (1976–77), pp. 302–3.
22. See *London Chronicle*, Vol. 113, p. 24; also *Historia del Levantamiento, Guerra y Revolución de España*, Vol. III, p. 128.
23. They do appear elsewhere, though, for example in 'The names and circumstances of their death of the twelve Napoleonic generals killed during the Peninsular War'.
24. Moliner Prada (2008).
25. García Fuertes (2016), pp. 427–8.
26. Ibid., p. 434.
27. Ibid., p. 438.
28. Miranda Rubio (2018), p. 45.

Chapter Thirty-Two

The Conquest of Monzón, Lleida and Mequinenza

Date: 13, 14 and 16 February 1814. *Place*: Monzón and Mequinenza (Aragon) and Lleida (Catalonia). *Result*: Spanish victory.

Background

The Spanish protagonist in these actions, Juan van Halen, is surely one of the most surprising and attractive characters of all the Napoleonic wars. Half soldier, half adventurer, his life could have been drawn from the imagination of Alexandre Dumas or Walter Scott. Born in San Fernando, near Cadiz, he came from a noble family of Belgian origin, whose ancestors included Charlemagne himself. At the age of 15, he enlisted as a midshipman and sailed aboard the frigate *Santa María Magdalena*. In May 1808 he was stationed in Madrid, where he participated in the popular uprising against the French in the Monteleón Park. After surrendering, as a 'sworn officer' he joined the Napoleonic army, with the condition of not having to fight against his compatriots. Thus, van Halen was appointed an officer of the King's Guard and accompanied Joseph Bonaparte to the baptism of the Emperor's son in Paris; in accordance with his wish not to fight against the Spanish, he was assigned to the Grande Armée in the campaigns in Central Europe, where he took part in the battles of Abensberg, Eckmühl and Aspern-Essling, among others, as a cavalry officer. In 1810 Joseph Bonaparte presented him with the Royal Order of Spain. He demonstrated his fiery and patriotic character by challenging the French officers Tiburce Sébastiani[1] and Montléger[2] to duels for making scathing remarks about his homeland; both left him at death's door.

After the French defeat at Vitoria and his subsequent dismissal, a frustrated Joseph Bonaparte took refuge in Mortefontaine Castle.[3] Van Halen followed him there to place himself at the service of the deposed king. But when van Halen was announced, Bonaparte threw him out of his chambers.[4] Enraged and humiliated, van Halen headed for Paris, where he contacted some Spanish agents who apparently offered an amnesty to Spanish officers prepared to serve Ferdinand VII. The disgruntled cavalry officer did not miss the opportunity to return to Spain.

At that time, few destinations were available since there was almost no Spain left to defend the Josephine party. Instead, van Halen managed to get the French Ministry of War to assign him to Suchet's general staff in Barcelona. The marshal welcomed him with open arms. He knew he was an excellent officer and, unaware of the episode at Mortefontaine, he still believed that van Halen was part of Joseph Bonaparte's inner circle. In Barcelona the cavalry officer managed to contact agents of Baron d'Eroles, who welcomed the transfer of van Halen's services to Ferdinand's cause, but at the same time told him that the stain of his Bonapartist past needed to be cleansed by some meritorious action. Between the two of them they devised a plan that was in keeping with their audacity: to obtain Suchet's secret codes and, with them, to liberate the strongholds that were still in the hands of the French. Van Halen's first objective was the city of Tortosa, in the extreme south of Catalonia, which had been blockaded for a few months by General Elío's troops. It should be added that this blockade was so ineffective that the governor of the city, General Baron Louis Benoît Robert, hardly considered it as such. However, this officer, defined by Elío as the most intelligent of the French generals he had come across, knew that his situation was untenable, regardless of the timid efforts of the Spanish troops to make life difficult for his garrison. Thus he had already begun to negotiate the surrender of the city.

Van Halen himself recounted the events in a book published at the end of 1814.[5] Determined to force the surrender of Tortosa, in early February he hatched a plan in the nearby town of Xerta, together with Eroles. The stratagem consisted of sending an emissary to the town with forged encrypted dispatches from Suchet ordering Robert to surrender. A fellow countryman volunteered to deliver the document. But the plan got off to a bad start almost from the very beginning. According to van Halen's account, Robert was apparently tipped off by a Napoleonic spy, and the countryman forgot the password with which he was to enter the city. Moreover, the dispatches contained gross errors and even a few spelling mistakes, which aroused the suspicions of the governor of the city; the man was arrested, and after a presumably unfriendly interrogation, he confessed to the clumsy manoeuvre. The next morning the man was shot, and Robert sent an emissary to van Halen to lure him to Tortosa in order to arrest him. But van

Halen was wary of the invitation and decided to withdraw.[6] The occupation of Tortosa finally came to an end thanks to the armistice signed between Wellington and Suchet on 19 April. On 3 May hostilities ended and Robert ordered preparations to begin for the evacuation of the city, which took place on the 18th of the same month. On 1 June Baron Robert and the so-called Ebro Division arrived in Perpignan without major setbacks.

Actions at Mequinenza, Lleida and Monzón

After the failure in Tortosa, van Halen and Eroles, with a small number of chosen collaborators, headed towards Mequinenza, on the border between Aragon and Catalonia. The plan to be executed here would be the same: they would try to deliver to the governor of the city some encrypted dispatches in which the terms of a fictitious armistice between Suchet and Wellington would be included. This agreement detailed that the French troops would keep their arms and baggage and, escorted by the Spanish army, would move on to Barcelona.

On 13 February an emissary, this time suitably trained, delivered the document to the governor of Mequinenza, General Charles-François Bourgois,[7] a veteran of the war in Spain. He had participated in the sieges of Tarragona, Tortosa and Valencia, as well as in the attack that had destroyed the abbey of Montserrat. From 11 September 1812 he was stationed in Mequinenza. Bourgois evidently saw nothing amiss in the delivered documents, for he ordered his relieved troops to begin their retreat towards Barcelona.

The next day van Halen and Eroles headed for Lleida. The city had been severely punished during the war. The rigours of the siege were followed by the despotic rule of General d'Henriot, a man whose cruelty shocked even his own countrymen. Greatly to the relief of the people of Lleida, in 1812 he was dismissed, being replaced by Baron Alban de Villeneuve-Bargemont,[8] only 28 years old but with a radically different idea of occupation from that of his predecessor, one based on dialogue and cooperation. In 1814 the city's governor was General Jean-Baptiste-Isadore Lamarque-d'Arrouzat,[9] in command of nearly 2,000 men from two battalions of the 42nd Regiment of Line Infantry. Van Halen repeated the plan, which worked once again, not least because Lamarque was aware of the preparations being made in Mequinenza to evacuate the garrison. He instructed his men to start the march towards Barcelona.

Next, van Halen and Eroles headed towards Monzón, another town of strategic importance in the border region between Aragon and Catalonia. After the withdrawal of the French troops, a garrison remained in the town composed of a detachment of the 12th Regiment of Gendarmes (93 men), plus an engineer, five artillerymen and a surgeon, all under the command of Captain Boutan; it is possible that this was a unit that had previously been stationed in Barbastro and specialized in the persecution and hunting of guerrillas.[10] At the time of van Halen's arrival, the town had been blockaded for about three months by some 3,000 men from Espoz y Mina's division. This attempted siege was proving to be a disaster for the Spanish. They had hardly any artillery, so they opted to use mines. But the French engineer Saint-Jacques,[11] using counter-tunnels, skilfully disrupted the mine tunnels dug by the besiegers, which cost the Spanish troops a huge number of casualties.

The arrival of van Halen and Eroles with their ingenious plan must have been a huge relief to the besiegers, who were unable to force the surrender of the town. Once again, van Halen's cunning stratagem worked. On this occasion, the cautious Boutan requested that one of his officers travel with safe conduct to Mequinenza and Lleida to verify that the document was true. After verification, Boutan surrendered the castle and set off with his men for Lleida.[12] From there they left for Barcelona, escorted by Spanish troops.

What the French did not expect was that just a few kilometres from the Catalan capital, near the town of Martorell, they would be surrounded by an Allied army of some 12,000 troops. There, General Copons appeared and informed Generals Bourgois and Lamarque of the trap into which they had fallen, and told them that from that moment on they and their troops could be considered prisoners of war. On hearing this, Bourgois remarked to van Halen: 'Truly, you have done your country a great service,'[13] adding 'I've been asleep for five days and I still haven't woken up!'[14] Lamarque complained bitterly. The generals had a furious argument, but they had no choice but to sign the surrender or fight against the overwhelming odds. To save the men's lives, Lamarque, as the senior commander, was the one to sign it, even though he knew he was signing his own death sentence.[15] The booty in cash, weapons and cannon was substantial. No fewer than two generals, eight superior officers, fifty subordinate officers and 2,385 soldiers and non-commissioned officers were arrested and taken to Tarragona. They would be released at the end of May, when the armistice between Spain and France was signed. In addition, van Halen had the pleasure of having a non-commissioned officer take a letter to Suchet explaining his ruse in detail.

As if this were not enough, this was only the beginning of van Halen's extraordinary life. His vicissitudes were innumerable, but at many moments of his life he also returned to glory. After the war, his liberal ideas led him to the prisons of the Inquisition. He managed to escape in 1818 and went to London, where he learned that Tsar Alexander I of Russia was hiring foreign military personnel. He left for St Petersburg and was duly hired as a commander in a regiment of dragoons in the Caucasus. In 1820, as part of a war against the Khan of Kasikumik, van Halen led a suicidal cavalry charge against Fort Joserek. Just when his commander, General Madatof, had come to believe that all his horsemen were dead, they appeared, raising the Tsar's standard on the castle tower. For this action, van Halen was awarded the Cross of the Order of Saint George, Russia's highest award for military valour in wartime, and the Cross of the Order of Saint Vladimir, which carried hereditary nobility in the Empire. On learning of his eventual disaffection, the Tsar ordered his execution, but the general in charge allowed him to leave Russia. On his return to his homeland, he was sent to

Catalonia, where he fought with royalist guerrillas. After a brilliant action at El Vendrell, he received his first Order of Saint Ferdinand. With the invasion of the absolutist 'Hundred Thousand Sons of Saint Louis' in 1823, he fled to Cuba and from there to the United States, where he spent two years surviving as a Spanish teacher. In 1826 he travelled to Belgium to attend to some family interests. But when the Belgians rose up against the Netherlands, van Halen was offered command of the Belgian army by the Belgian provisional government. It should be noted that his recently published memoirs had made him very popular and he was regarded as a champion of freedom. His actions were as frenetic as they were effective, and in just four days he managed to drive the Dutch out of Brussels and consolidate Belgian independence. King Leopold I showered him with favours and awarded him the Iron Cross and the Order of Leopold. In 1835 he was recalled to Spain. Although he led a regal life in Belgium, he did not hesitate to heed the call of his country. He was once again posted to Catalonia, where in 1840 he fought against the Carlist army of General Cabrera. For this, he received a second Order of Saint Ferdinand. He was also present at the battle of Peracamps, one of the bloodiest of the First Carlist War, where he was seriously wounded. A convinced defender of the Progressive Party, he supported the regent General Espartero until the revolution of 1843, which led to the regent's fall. After this, van Halen remained in Spain, but occasionally travelled to Belgium to visit King Leopold. He died in Cadiz in 1864.[16]

Notes

1. Brother of the famous General Horace Sebastiani.
2. Baroja (1998), p. 96. This is probably a transcription error by the writer and repeated by later authors. In fact, it probably refers to Gabriel Gaspard Achille Adolphe Bernon de Montélégier, renowned duellist and reputedly one of the best swordsmen of his generation. In addition, he was an excellent cavalry officer.
3. This magnificent castle, some 40km (25 miles) north of Paris, was purchased by Joseph Bonaparte from the French state in 1798, after its last owner had been guillotined a few years earlier. It soon became one of the favourite meeting points of the Bonaparte family. There, Napoleon signed important diplomatic treaties and his sisters got married: Caroline to Marshal Murat and Pauline to Camillo Borghese. In this castle Julie Clary, Joseph's wife and consequently the Queen of Spain, resided while her husband tried to act as king. After the fall of Napoleon, and to prevent the castle from being seized, Joseph transferred all his property to Mme de Villenueve, a cousin of his wife. Finally, when he was forced into exile, he sold the castle to the Prince de Condé.
4. Van Halen felt true affection for Joseph Bonaparte, so between his rancour and his desire for revenge, he also always wondered why his king had reacted in such a way. In 1826 the vicissitudes of life led the two men to meet again, in Philadelphia in the United States. Van Halen wrote to the former king asking for an explanation of what had happened that day at Mortefontaine. In the seven months that they both lived in Philadelphia, Joseph Bonaparte never sent an answer. But fate would give the stubborn van Halen another chance. Finally, van Halen got his answer during a lunch in a London restaurant in 1835. Through Juan Álvarez Mendizábal, a Spanish minister and mutual friend, Joseph Bonaparte and van Halen had the chance to talk for hours about what had happened during the war. Baroja (1998), p. 99.
5. Van Halen (1814), pp. 21–31.
6. Salvadó Poy (2016).

7. Lievyns (1845), p. 100.
8. Villeneuve-Bargemont was an interesting character. He came from an old noble family settled in Provence. After the French Revolution, Villeneuve-Bargemont joined the imperial administration. Leaving happy memories in Lleida, he returned to France, where he would continue to enjoy a successful political career. Villeneuve-Bargemont is considered one of the founders of French Christian socialism. Throughout his extensive political career, he expressed a sincere concern for eradicating poverty, to which he dedicated one of his best-known works, *Economía política cristiana o Investigación sobre las causas y naturaleza del pauperismo en Francia y el extranjero y sobre los medios de aliviarlo y proponerlo* (*Christian Political Economy or Research on the Causes and Nature of Pauperism in France and abroad and on the means of alleviating it and proposing it*). He should also be credited with introducing one of the first laws in Europe that regulated child labour.
9. Lievyns (1844), Vol. 4, pp. 300–1.
10. Sebastián García (2011), p. 264.
11. Despite the fact that in all the sources he is usually cited as such, he was not an engineer and nor was his name Saint-Jacques. He was a Piedmontese minelayer who was probably called Giovanni Antonio Pasquale, but who was called Saint-Jacques by his French comrades. He participated in the second siege of Zaragoza and later was assigned to Monzón. There he would stand out for his extraordinary intelligence and ability to disrupt the attempts of the Spanish to undermine the castle. French sources indicate that during the siege the French suffered just 10 dead, while the Spanish lost 160 dead, most of them as a result of the skilful traps set for them by Saint-Jacques. After the war he returned to France, where he was naturalized as a Frenchman. For his acts of war, he was awarded a 3rd class engineering degree. He died prematurely in 1833 due to an unfortunate accident in a mine. For his performance in Monzón he was awarded the Legion of Honour. Chaucard (1833), pp. 13–14.
12. The resistance in Monzón with such a striking inferiority of troops was considered a true heroic act in France. In fact, in 1823 Xavier Julien published in Montpellier the diary of the siege of Monzón written by the commander of the town entitled *Siège du fort de Monzon en Aragon, du 27 septembre 1813 au 14 février 1814*. It offers a detailed version of the fighting that took place in those months. It can be consulted at: https://gallica.bnf.fr/ark:/12148/bpt6k63564046/f7.item. texteImage.
13. Van Halen (1814), p. 46.
14. Ibid., p. 47.
15. Napoleon had strictly forbidden the surrender of an army in the field on pain of death. Baroja (1998), p. 106.
16. 'Juan van Halen y Sarti', by Juan Van-Halen Acedo, in the Biographical Dictionary of the Royal Academy of History of Spain. Available at: http://dbe.rah.es/biografias/15039/juan-van-halen-y-sarti (accessed 11 November 2020).

Chapter Thirty-Three

The Liberation of Catalonia

Date: 1812–1814. *Place*: Catalonia.

In the year 1812 the main Catalan cities were already under the wings of the French eagles. The process of assimilation into France that had begun the previous year, when *de facto* Catalonia was separated from the administration of Joseph Bonaparte, was accelerated with two decrees issued by Napoleon himself: on the one hand, the Principality was divided into four Departments (administrative units typical of France), and Catalonia was integrated into the French Empire, being definitively separated from Spain. The Departments were grouped into the regions of Upper and Lower Catalonia, and were administered by a regiment of civil servants from France. Two prominent political and intellectual figures were at the helm of each of these regions: Joseph-Marie de Gérando for Upper Catalonia, and the Marquis Chauvelin (the former chamberlain of Louis XVI) for Lower Catalonia. At the end of 1811 MacDonald ceased to be Captain General of Catalonia, being replaced by the General Count of Decaen, who had to deal with a military situation identical to that his predecessor had faced: he had control of the large cities and fortifications, but total lack of control of rural areas, where General Luis Lacy's men roamed freely.

The most controversial aspect of Lacy's military policy was the use of dirty warfare. The captain general bypassed all the laws of war as he saw fit to deal with the invader, whether through sabotage or assassination. One example of sabotage was the blowing up of the powder warehouse at Lleida castle in July. Since the proclamation of the Cadiz Constitution, the Josephine authorities in this city had increased repression against the patriots, multiplying arbitrary arrests and executions. This repressive policy was the perfect breeding ground for rousing anti-French sentiment among the citizens. Eroles took advantage of this and arranged with one of the warehouse guards, a certain Azequinolaza, to prepare the explosion of the castle's powder reserves. It was to take place on 16 July, when the French officers of the garrison were holding a reception in the courtyard adjacent to the powder warehouse. After the explosion, taking advantage of the confusion and the casualties among the French, Eroles would occupy the city with his troops. But Azequinolaza was too hasty and caused 1,500 quintals of gunpowder to explode too soon: the officers had not yet reached the courtyard. But the explosion was so violent that it collapsed an adjoining building in which an artillery detachment was stationed. There were no survivors. The people of Lleida fared little better. Several houses collapsed, killing more than 200 residents. Many other buildings were severely damaged. After the explosion, Eroles did not believe he could hold the city with the troops he had, and withdrew. On another occasion Lacy tried to poison a shipment of brandy that was headed for Tarragona, another of wine for Mataró and the waters of the fortifications of Hostalric. In May three people were arrested in Figueres accused of trying to poison the city's garrison with arsenic. After a hasty trial, the two men were executed the next day, while the woman, who was pregnant, was imprisoned indefinitely.

The most famous mass poisoning attempt took place in Barcelona in July in the so-called 'Conspiracy of the Poisons'. On the advice of the presbyter Coret, Lacy ordered his chief apothecary, Juan Ortiz, to prepare twelve packets of an arsenic derivative to be added to the bread that was to be eaten by the garrison of the Barcelona citadel. It is believed that the pharmacist Josep Antoni Balcells, one of the most famous pharmacists of his time, was also involved in this poisoning attempt. As the bread was tested by the bakers themselves before being delivered to the French soldiers, the precaution was taken of using a delayed-effect poison. The operation resulted in the deaths of three French soldiers and a large number falling ill to varying degrees, but the outcome fell far short of the conspirators' expectations. General Maurice Mathieu, the governor of Barcelona, called in the pharmacist Balcells himself to analyse the loaves; Balcells confirmed his suspicions, and the French authorities resolved the matter by making several arrests.

This kind of dirty war did not only outrage the French, and Lacy also made many enemies within his own ranks. The members of the Catalan Junta did not understand this dishonourable conduct in the war. But this was not their only point of friction with the general: they also criticized him for limiting himself to guerrilla actions rather than engaging in a major action. Also, he was a markedly liberal military officer, whereas the Junta was guided by a rancid absolutism. As we have seen, he did not have the sympathies of Codrington either, who would have preferred to see Eroles as Captain General of Catalonia. The constant disputes ended when Lacy was dismissed in December. His replacement was General Copons, who had earned a well deserved reputation as an extraordinary military man. Copons, whose vision of war was more conventional than that of his predecessor, sent a letter to Decaen announcing that from then on, the laws of war would be respected and that the era of poisoning and sabotage was over. The French general replied by announcing that, in that case, he would stop shooting the Miquelets he captured and henceforth they would be treated as prisoners of war.

Lacy's later life was interesting. He was appointed Captain General of Galicia, where he did not have to fight the French, as the region had already been liberated. Once the war was over, he vehemently opposed the absolutist abolition of the 1812 Constitution, so much so that in 1817 he returned to Catalonia and, together with Milans del Bosch and other prominent liberals, attempted to promote a *coup d'etat*. However, the plan was discovered and General Castaños, the Captain General of Catalonia, arrested him. Other conspirators, such as Milans del Bosch, fled to France. Ferdinand VII ordered Lacy's execution, which raised many complaints in Catalonia, as the common people had an excellent memory of the Andalusian soldier. Fearing a revolt, Castaños spread the rumour that Lacy would be pardoned, and then secretly transferred him to Palma de Mallorca, where he was shot. But this would not be the general's last journey. In 1820, with the arrival of the new Liberal government, his remains were returned to Barcelona. He received a tribute in the church of Santa Maria del Mar and was buried in the military chapel of the Citadel. A popular subscription was opened to finance a tomb in Barcelona cathedral, but the money was eventually spent by Barcelona city council on other matters. In 1823 the ineffable Count of Spain was appointed Captain General of Catalonia and one of his first decisions was to order Lacy's remains to be exhumed and thrown on the dunghill of a parish house. The priest who lived there collected the remains at night and buried them in his garden. In 1881 the remains were found and the notary Maspons put them in a box and took them home. Twenty years later the notary died and his widow asked the civil authorities to take over the box. In 1901 Lacy was reburied in a modest niche in Montjuïc cemetery. In the 1940s a military pantheon was built in the Sant Andreu cemetery, where the remains of the Andalusian general were transferred and where they still rest today.

By 1813 much of Spain had been freed from Napoleon's yoke, but a large part of Catalan territory was still occupied. The French were reluctant to abandon their strongholds, hoping for a miracle to reverse the difficult situation. Although Suchet was in effective command of the territory, it was General Decaen who held the title of Captain General of Catalonia. In just a few months his forces had been reduced by half and he was practically unable to leave the strongholds he still held, especially Barcelona (General Maurice Mathieu's division), Girona (General Lamarque's division), Tarragona (General Bertoletti's Italian brigade) and Tortosa (General Habert).

But the winds of war were blowing against the Napoleonic forces. The British victories at Salamanca and later Vitoria forced the French to abandon most of their possessions in Spain. In addition, Napoleon himself was constantly pulling back the troops fighting in Catalonia for his campaigns in Central Europe. Decaen was dismissed and cedes his post to Marshal Suchet. With the Anglo-Spanish army pressing from the south, and with hardly any soldiers with which to defend Catalonia, Suchet decided to begin an evacuation of the territory, leaving garrisons in some strongholds, such as Tortosa, and marking a line of defence along the Llobregat river. On 13 August 1813 the marshal ordered General Bertoletti to evacuate Tarragona. What would be the last Napoleonic victory in Spain took place at Ordal on 13 September. In mid-October Napoleon's defeat at the battle of Liepzig only worsened Suchet's situation. He must send more troops back to France as the Napoleonic Empire was crumbling.

Suchet had no choice but to withdraw to Girona, practically abandoning to their fate the garrisons of Tortosa, where the efficient General Robert was heroically resisting, and Barcelona, where General Habert was sheltering. The Allied armies immediately took advantage of the French retreat to begin a blockade of these two cities, which they hoped to starve into surrender. The novel loss of Mequinenza, Lleida and Monzón convinced Suchet that the war was already lost. Moreover, he received orders from Napoleon to negotiate the capitulation of the strongholds still in his power, and then return to France. Suchet reluctantly obeyed. From then on, events began to accelerate. On 9 March Olot, Besalú and Palamós were liberated. The following day, Girona. On 11 March Ferdinand VII left Valençay. On 31 March the troops of the Sixth Coalition invaded Paris. The days of Napoleon's rule were coming to an end. On 6 April Napoleon abdicated, and in the middle of the month, as the Emperor was on his way to exile on the island of Elba, the last battle of the Peninsular War – known as the 'Action of Barcelona' – took place. In mid-May the garrisons of the last fortifications held by the French on the Valencian coast, Dénia and Sagunt, met in Tortosa. On the 18th General Robert led the column that evacuated the city. In the rest of Spain, the last French positions were being liberated one by one: Benasque, Jaca and Santoña. Barcelona was liberated on 28 May. The last towns to be recovered were Hostalric on 3 June and Figueres and the castle of San Fernando on 4 June.

Chapter Thirty-Four

The Military Prisoners

Date: 1808–1814. *Place*: France.

Military prisoners

The Peninsular War was a catastrophe for Spanish society. To the destruction of towns and cities, their infrastructure, historical and religious heritage, must be added the worst of misfortunes: that inflicted on people. It was a ruthless war, in many cases without quarter, in which it is estimated that between 500,000 and 600,000 Spaniards died, half of them civilians, as well as some 250,000 to 300,000 Napoleonic soldiers. As for the British troops and their allies, it is assumed that the number of deaths was considerably lower, amounting to approximately 11,600 men.[1] The number of wounded is probably at least three times more. There were also large numbers of people taken prisoner. There is no record of the number of prisoners captured by the French, and nothing to indicate how many of these were held in France. And, in fact, as Zozaya[2] points out, there is a great information gap regarding the number and activities of the vast majority of the prisoners – so much so that it is not possible to know the exact numbers of Spanish prisoners and deportees. The figures that have been put forward range from 50,000 according to Aymes, to the 100,000 reported by Gregorio Marañón,[3] while a more recent study by Arnabat Mata estimates that 65,000 were deported.[4]

Surprising as it may seem, the first people to want to draw a veil over their stay in France were the ex-convicts themselves who returned to Spain. To begin with, their stay was in most cases, and as we shall see below, not necessarily negative. In Spain during the war there was only hunger, death, misery and epidemics, while the captives in France enjoyed relative comfort. Of course, any positive expression in favour of what had happened in France could bring with it the accusation of being *afrancesado* or might lead to an appearance before one of the 'purge' tribunals, widely feared for their arbitrariness and injustice. It should be borne in mind that at the beginning of the reign of Ferdinand VII there was a veritable wave of repression against any element suspected of Bonapartism or liberalism, and even his closest collaborators, such as Joaquín Blake, among many others, underwent agonizing 'purification' processes.[5]

At the beginning of the war, especially from the campaigns of the autumn of 1808 onwards, the Napoleonic armies were surprised by the large number of soldiers they captured in their battles. It was unthinkable to keep them in Spain:

there were no prisons large enough and there was a risk that the soldiers would escape and take up arms again. Thus, their transfer to France was no mere act of cruelty. The Spanish arrived in France on foot marches, although some officers hired horses or carriages. The journeys covered about 30km (18 miles) a day, which took a toll on troops who typically started out exhausted and poorly fed.[6] Normally they travelled by pre-established routes, taking in cities where spaces had been set aside for them to rest during the journey. The most important of these cities was Bayonne, where the hospitals were full of Spanish soldiers sick or exhausted from long marches and poor food. But where were the French to keep them in France? The same problem of prison overcrowding that would have occurred in Spain also occurred on French soil. Thus the imperial authorities built what they called *dépôts* (depots), which would evolve into a kind of internment camps. It should be clarified that these were nothing like the concentration camps created later in Spanish Cuba by Weyler, in South Africa by Lord Kitchener or in Germany and Poland by Hitler; in the French camps the treatment of prisoners (both Spanish and those of other enemy nations of the Empire) was largely correct. All the sources consulted and cited affirm that the prisoners were provided with food, health care and welfare.[7] In fact, their treatment was infinitely better than that meted out to Napoleonic prisoners in Spain. As the numbers of prisoners continued to rise, the next dilemma for the imperial authorities was to find the right location for new *dépôts*. Some regions were not considered. For example, Brittany and the Vendée were notorious for their sympathies to the royalist cause, so it did not seem a good idea to send thousands of men there, who might rise in support of the Bourbon king; in the coastal regions the risk of escape was obvious, given the Royal Navy's maritime power; the southern French departments were too close to Spain; Paris was a 'sensitive area'; and they could not be placed near the Château de Valençay, where Ferdinand VII lived. So there remained the departments of the Massif Central, the Alps, Lorraine, northern France, the left bank of the Rhine and some regions of Belgium and the Netherlands. The best-known camps were those at Périgueux and Mâcon, although there were many others in these regions. It should be added that as the war progressed, some prisoners were placed in camps near the sea, for example in Normandy, as the *dépôts* in the Dordogne or at Nancy were at full capacity.

Prisoners were initially given the option of being released if they swore loyalty to King Joseph and took up arms in the armies fighting in Central Europe or Russia. This option was taken up by a minority of the prisoners, which Aymes puts at about 7 per cent. If they did not accept it, they were confined in the *dépôts*. Those who did accept included the engineer colonels Luis Rancaño de Cancio and Manuel Caballero y Zamorategui, both captured after the second siege of Zaragoza.[8] The volunteers were grouped into the four battalions of the Regiment Joseph Napoleon, which was sent to fight in the campaigns in Central Europe and Russia. Their presence on the battlefield was generally highly valued by most of their superiors, such as Marshal de Castellane and Colonel Tschudy, although other officers despised them for their indolence and tendency to desertion. Be that as it may, the two battalions that took part in the Russian campaign fought valiantly and were virtually annihilated. Many Spanish soldiers also joined the so-called Portuguese Legion, which also took part in the Central European campaigns, or the sapper brigades.[9]

Later, the Napoleonic authorities had to address the 'profitability' of these camps. The huge number of prisoners ended up causing an ever-increasing expense to the public purse, so it was decided that the prisoners would carry out the creation or maintenance of public works and infrastructure, such as roads, bridges, canals or the dredging of marshes. It should be noted that this work was voluntary and was compensated either financially or by improving the living conditions of the workers. Later, when the capacity of the *dépôts* was overwhelmed by the arrival of new prisoners, other types of buildings were adapted to house them, such as deconsecrated churches or convents. Another of the measures taken to alleviate the demographic pressure on the *dépôts* was to allow private companies or individuals to hire Spanish prisoners to work in textile workshops, handicraft workshops, farm work, etc., in towns far from the *dépôts*. These workers (who could practically no longer be considered prisoners) were even given permission to live outside the *dépôts*, being housed in the homes of the people who hired them. These Spaniards forged social networks that meant they never returned to Spain, and many new families were founded. Eventually, as the war progressed and the number of prisoners increased, living conditions in the *dépôts* worsened. In 1813 the Spanish were no strangers to the economic crisis that hit France,[10] although the hardships they suffered were mitigated by the possibility of receiving packages or money from relatives who remained in Spain. Zozaya[11] cites the case of the Nancy *dépôt*, which housed José Antonio de Aragón-Azlor y Pignatelli, Duke of Villahermosa,[12], whose mother regularly sent generous amounts of money which the young duke distributed among his neediest companions.

When the prisoners arrived at their destination, the non-commissioned officers and officers were separated from the other ranks. The officers, whom Zozaya calls *elite prisoners*, were sent to surrounding cities, and were granted the same rights and salary as French soldiers of the same rank. They stayed in castles, barracks or private houses. The surveillance regime was lax and they could move freely throughout the city. The officers of the Napoleonic wars were still governed by the old codes of honour, so it was enough for them to give their word of honour that they would not try to escape and to appear before the competent authority once a month.[13] But some did take their chance to escape, and so, as the tide of war seemed to be turning against the French, the conditions of captivity began to be more severe and prisoners were forced to report daily. In Spain there is only one documented case of such prisoners being held 'on their word of honour'. This took place during the siege of Pamplona in 1813, when General Cassan discovered five Spanish officers living in the city. Although he officially arrested them, he allowed them to move freely around the city in exchange for not taking up arms against the French. The pact was scrupulously fulfilled.[14]

The very highest echelon of the prison hierarchy was made up of generals and other high-ranking officers, who were known as state prisoners. Their living conditions were not exactly comfortable, but could vary according to the castle in which they were held and the strictness with which each was managed. The conditions under which these commanders had been captured also played a role: those who had fallen on the battlefield or in a siege without surrendering were allowed few or no personal possessions, while those who had capitulated had usually negotiated advantageous conditions that allowed them to enjoy personal possessions and certain comforts. The most famous detention centre is surely the Château de Vincennes, about 10km (6 miles) from Paris, whose governor was the legendary General Pierre Daumesnil, known as *Jambe de Bois* ('Wooden Leg') since he lost one of his lower extremities in the battle of Wagram. This building had its origins in a hunting lodge erected by King Louis VII in 1150. Subsequently, more buildings were added until it was completed with its emblematic keep, which, at 52m (57 yards), is the tallest in Europe. Louis XIV stopped using it (he had built Versailles) and it fell into disuse until it was converted into a prison at the end of the eighteenth century. Illustrious prisoners such as Mirabeau, Voltaire, Diderot and the Marquis de Sade all passed through it. In 1804 it was here that the Duke of Enghien was tried and executed.[15] Generals such as José de Palafox, Joaquín Blake, Xavier Mina, Carlos O'Donnell and José Pascual de Zayas, to name but a few of the most prominent, lived in this castle. There they met with not only European military men of the same rank but also opponents of Napoleon's regime,[16] including the Baron de Kolly, the protagonist of one of Ferdinand VII's escape attempts in Valençay.

In his biography of Espoz y Mina,[17] Guzman recounts the stay in this prison of the former guerrilla leader. Apparently, after his arrival, he spent a few days locked up alone in a cell. Afterwards, he was interrogated and then transferred to Paris, where he was offered the chance to fight under Napoleon's flags. He declined the invitation and was taken back to his cell. The regime for him was often severe, but he was allowed to maintain contact with other prisoners. Those considered exceptionally dangerous, such as Palafox, were kept in solitary confinement for most of their captivity. In Palafox's case, the French authorities were so terrified of him that they registered him under the false name of Pietro Mendola to prevent his real name from being leaked in case enemy agents tried to free him.

Another of the most famous castles was Bouillon, on the border between Belgium and the Netherlands. Here, were imprisoned General Senén de Contreras (the governor of Tarragona during the siege) and Colonel Antonio Lechuga Reynoso (commander of the Volunteers of Castile, who was captured in the second siege of Zaragoza). Lichtengerg castle housed Brigadier Felipe Perena (commander of the Huesca Volunteers, captured during the siege of Lleida) and

Brigadier D. Francisco Ruíz Gómez (head of the artillery during the siege of Ciudad Rodrigo).

Despite the strict confinement, there was no shortage of escape plans. Some managed to escape on the way to the *dépôts*; Baron d'Eroles, for example, after being captured at the siege of Girona, managed to escape when his string of prisoners arrived in Perpignan. Senén de Contreras,[18] imprisoned in the castle of Bouillon, managed to escape in October 1812. After a journey lasting eight months, he reached the English coast, then embarked for Spain. The following year Lieutenant Colonels José de la Serna y de Hinojosa and José Román y Herrera Dávila,[19] among others, escaped from their *dépôt* in Normandy. However, many escape plans were thwarted. Prisoners who had tried to escape were then sent to fortresses where security was tighter or where the geographical location made escape virtually impossible. One of the most feared prisons was the Château de Joux in the Bourgogne-Franche-Comté region. This ancient castle (dating back to the eleventh century) stood on the top of a cliff; it was difficult to access and impossible to escape from. It was also the place of a sad legend dating back to the time of the crusades, when the lord of the castle, Amauri III of Joux, took the cross. A few years later another crusader, Amé de Montfaucon, appeared at the castle and announced that Amauri had been mortally wounded in battle. His wife, Bertha de Joux, disconsolate, gave shelter to Montfaucon for a few days, which turned into months when the guest became the lover of the lady of the castle. Then one day, Amauri III appeared, alive and kicking, and out for revenge. On learning of the adultery, he had Montfaucon executed and Bertha was thrown into the castle dungeon, from which she only emerged to enter a convent. These dungeons would later be occupied by characters such as Mirabeau, Heinrich von Kleist and Toussaint-Louverture, known as the 'Black Napoleon', who led a slave revolt in Santo Domingo in the early nineteenth century. Among the Spanish prisoners here were Captains Salvador Manzanares, Joaquín Alvistur and Fernando de Alcocer, and Second Lieutenant Pedro Verástegi. All of them had at least one escape attempt behind them.[20] Aymes reports that more than 300 Spanish officers were confined in Joux, where living conditions were so harsh that in 1813 more than a hundred fell seriously ill and were transferred to other centres for recuperation.

An extreme case of attempted escape was that of artillery major Carlos Espinosa de los Monteros y Ayerdi, who had been captured at the beginning of the war during the siege of Rosas, in northern Catalonia. In 1811 he was put in Joux castle after four escape attempts. Despite the extreme security measures, Espinosa de los Monteros managed to escape. Recaptured near the Spanish border, he was sent to Saint Venant in the far north of France. From there he escaped again but shortly afterwards was captured again. This time he was sent to Bourges in Flanders, and from there, on 13 February 1814, he escaped again. This time he reached the coast and managed to reach the port of Pasajes on 15 March 1814, after a sea voyage.[21]

At the beginning of 1814 it seemed clear that the Napoleonic regime was breaking up. In February 1814 the armies of the Sixth Coalition were getting dangerously close to Paris and, by extension, to Vincennes. The military authorities decided to turn the château into a large storehouse for arms and military equipment, and most of the prisoners housed there were transferred to the Château de Saumur in the Loire Valley, some 60km (37 miles) to the southwest, where the Comte de Saint-Simon had been imprisoned since the beginning of the war. At the end of March Paris fell to the Allies, and on 6 April Napoleon Bonaparte was forced to abdicate. The war was over. One of the logical consequences of this was that the prisoners of war had to be released. On 13 April Talleyrand signed the decree to release all prisoners of war. However, their return was neither quick nor easy. The precarious French provisional government was obliged to return thousands of soldiers and civilians. They had to be provided with food and accommodation along the way (and in some cases they had to cross almost the entire country from Normandy or even from the Netherlands), to avoid causing huge problems in the towns through which they passed. Convoys of up to 300 prisoners at a time were organized and taken to the cities of Bayonne and Perpignan. However, there were some groups of soldiers who did not want to spend a day longer in France than necessary and so organized their own return. In some cases the living conditions the prisoners had endured were so poor that the authorities now had to give them new uniforms and footwear in order for them to make the journey. This was the case for the 872 *miquelets* from Northern Catalonia who had been divided between *dépôts* in Brest and Rochefort. As for those known as Spanish prisoners of state, in 1814 they numbered about sixty. On 16 April they were released and a large number of them requested passports to go to Paris and from there to Spain.

Just as we do not know the total number of military prisoners deported to France, it is impossible to know the number who died during their captivity, either in work-related accidents or from illness. Nor do we know how many stayed behind, either of their own free will or because they had been convicted of common crimes and were imprisoned. In any case, the process of return would take several months. The former prisoners found themselves in a country in ruins and were forced to undergo a cleansing process, as many were suspected of treason or having French sympathies. Fortunately, the vast majority of them would see their honour restored.

The fate of non-commissioned officers and soldiers is less often known. In 1810, however, there was a bizarre case which was later recounted by its protagonist, Sergeant Fernando Mayoral, and verified by the French historian Jean-René Aymes. It is a story that deserves to be told. Sergeant Mayoral had been captured during the French siege of Ciudad Rodrigo. After a hard journey on foot, he arrived in Bayonne with a group of prisoners. Most of them were soldiers, but there was a few friars. Mayoral was indignant to see that while the soldiers were fed poorly, the friars received rich delicacies and new clothes.

So he resolved to pose as a friar. In the next village he feigned illness, and when his comrades-in-arms had left him alone, he revealed to his guards that he was a friar. From then on his luck changed. He was taken to a civil prison and a few minutes later a nun appeared; she brought him new clothes and ordered the gaoler to provide him with a good bed, saying that she would pay for his expenses. He was in this prison for ten days, during which time he was visited by priests and nuns, who left him a total of 200 francs in alms.[22] Once recovered, he was sent with a group of Spanish religious to Cahors, where he was unable to prosper in the cathedral, and from there he went to the village of Brives la Gallarde. He was taken in by the sweet and innocent Miss Malvis, who showered him with attention. When they began to trust each other, Miss Malvis confessed to him that she was the bastard daughter of the former bishop of Limoges, from whom she had inherited great wealth. Mayoral, for his part, confessed that he was 'not a friar, but a person of great distinction', but not revealing his true identity. The bold Mayoral then conspired with a Spanish barber named Martin to deliver a letter (written by Mayoral himself) to Miss Malvis at a time when he was absent from the house. So, at the agreed time, the barber Martín handed Miss Malvis's maids the letter warning 'Cardinal Bourbon' of a plan by a group of Spanish agents to procure his return to Spain.[23]. One can only imagine the anguish that young Miss Malvis must have suffered. On Mayoral's return, she confessed to him that she knew, and would keep, his secret. It should come as no surprise that over the next few days pious ladies from all over the county visited 'Cardinal Bourbon' and pressed on him lavish gifts ranging from money to jewellery. These were used to establish a lifestyle in keeping with his cardinal status. He also made donations to the Spanish prisoners convalescing in the town's hospital and rented a villa in a nearby town, where he spent a few days' holiday with one of Miss Malvis's maids. Obviously, the presence of such a high-born person in such a small town could not be hidden, and in the following months he was visited by a general and several noble ladies who showered him with attention, but who tested his nerves by asking him to say mass in the cathedral (Mayoral did not know how to say mass, let alone in Latin), and to correspond with his cousin, the Empress Marie-Louise of Austria . . . and Napoleon's wife answered him! Sent to Sedan, he lived in a convent, where he broke the heart of a novice. But the wily soldier managed to avoid all misfortunes – until he was recognized by soldiers from his old regiment. He was imprisoned in terrible conditions, but managed to trick his gaolers again, improving his situation. When the war was over, the French authorities still did not know his real identity, but they suspected he was someone of importance, so they escorted him to the border of La Jonquera in Gerona. There, the border official, seeing the confusion of identities in the documents Mayoral presented, arrested him and sent to Barcelona. The Diocesan Archive of Barcelona preserves the documentation of the trial that the Inquisition opened against him. He was sentenced to six years in prison for blasphemy and was banished to Ceuta. After his release in 1820, he disappeared.

Notes

1. Available at: https://www.napoleon-series.org/research/abstract/military/army/britain/casualties/c_britcas.html (accessed 15 November 2020).
2. Zozaya (2014), p. 81.
3. Aymes (1992), p. 42.
4. Arnabat Mata (2009), p. 167.
5. Zozaya (2014), p. 82.
6. Patinaud (2017).
7. In fact, these *dépôts* were an evolution of medieval hospitals. Despite their name, these were not places to treat the sick, but rather places where beggars or passing travellers were given shelter.
8. Sala Valdés (1908), pp. 125, 127.
9. Aymes (1982).
10. Ibid.
11. Zozaya (2014), p. 87.
12. Aragón-Azlor was the nephew of the Palafox brothers. He distinguished himself for his bravery in the second siege of Zaragoza. He ended up imprisoned and deported to France. At the time of his capture he was 24 years old. Following the deaths of his father and older brother, he had inherited their titles at age 3.
13. Zozaya (2014), pp. 88, 100.
14. Espinosa de los Monteros y Jaraquemada (2014, 2018).
15. Just over a century later the legendary Mata-Hari was also executed in that same castle.
16. Alboise du Pujol (1844), pp. 334–5.
17. Guzmán (2003).
18. Captured after the fall of Tarragona.
19. Captured during the second siege of Zaragoza.
20. Espinosa de los Monteros y Jaraquemada (2014), p. 36.
21. Ibid., pp. 34–5.
22. The salary of a soldier was 4 reales.
23. Archbishop of Toledo and Seville Luis María de Borbón y Vallabriga was Ferdinand VII's uncle (although they called themselves cousins for protocol reasons) and the only Bourbon who remained in Spain. Of liberal bent, he was the president of the Regency Council. When Ferdinand VII returned to Spain and repealed the Constitution of 1812, he imprisoned all the members of the Regency except his uncle, who was forced to resign from the archbishopric of Seville.

Chapter Thirty-Five

The Navy at War

Date: 1808–1814. *Place*: Spain.

Background

The role of the navy during the Peninsular War was entirely secondary. The main reason for this was that the French were aware of their navy's clear inferiority to the British fleet, so they did not engage in naval combat and their use of the navy was limited to small operations such as transporting soldiers, arms and mail; on occasion they also engaged in privateering, especially in territories that were, at least on paper, under their control. In 1793 the Royal Navy had some 400 warships (115 of which were ships of the line), compared to the French navy's 246 ships (including 76 ships of the line).[1]

This subsidiary role was also influenced by the calamitous state of the Spanish navy, resulting from the country's very poor economic situation. For decades, the Royal Navy no longer shone with the splendour of previous centuries. Thus, the fateful battle of Trafalgar should not be considered so much the cause as the symptom in which the Spanish navy found itself. At Trafalgar in 1805 nine Spanish ships of the line and some 4,500 men were lost; however, this was a drop in the ocean compared to the disaster of 1588, when Philip II's *Grande y Felicísima Armada* (literally the 'Great and Most Fortunate Navy', *aka* the Invincible Armada), lost no fewer than sixty-three ships and more than 20,000 men during its expedition to England. The difference is that in 1588 Spain had the resources to make a rapid recovery, while in 1805 there were no funds to carry out even the most minimal repairs, let alone build new ships of the line. At the beginning of the war, the navy already had a debt of some 410,139,246 reales,[2] but in addition there were also fifteen payments owed to officers and sailors,[3] who lived in conditions of utter misery.

An example of this dire situation can be seen in the letters that the Lieutenant Commander of the Navy, José María Jalón y Bañuelos, sent to his father, the Marquis of Castrofuerte, and to his administrator, Antonio Ballesteros.[4] In a letter dated 1 October 1800, he said:

> For two years I have been on this [*San Agustín*, the ship of the line on which he served] without having received from the king a single maravedí of my wages; in addition to this, of the 22 duros that we are given to eat while embarked, we are already owed 5 months, so that I have been reduced to

eating only rice and crackers[5] ... at the expense of the few clothes I had, and I have been selling ... but having been left almost naked, the day after tomorrow is the day I do not know where to get my sustenance; in this town one can only breathe misery and only find women, daughters and relatives of naval officers and people working in the Arsenals begging for alms in the streets.

In a letter sent to his father on 17 July 1801, he gave a brief account of the battle of Algeciras, in which he was involved on board *San Agustín*, and in which two other ships of the line, *San Hermenegildo* and *Real Carlos*, were lost, with the loss of almost 2,000 men. Jalón also described how, on arriving at the port of Cádiz, the naval officers, 'after each one had done his duty in accordance with the principles of honour', were insulted and stoned by the people of Cádiz. In addition, naval officers were often frowned upon by the towns where they were based, as they were often forced to take fishermen from the Cádiz coast by force owing to the lack of crews to sail the warships, to the detriment of their families.

This awful situation provoked numerous protests and some mutinies, the best known being one that took place on 10 February 1810 in Ferrol, where a desperately hungry mob assaulted the residence of the Commander General of the Department, Squadron Commander José Ramón Vargas y Vargas, cruelly murdering him. It so happened that a few days earlier Vargas had resigned in despair at not being able to get the salaries owed to the seamen, and he was only waiting to receive his replacement.[6] The hardships became endemic, so in 1816 was reported the death by exhaustion and starvation of the ship's lieutenant José Lavadores and her commander, Pedro Quevedo.[7]

The Spanish navy during the Peninsular War

Given this background, it should come as no surprise that, perhaps paradoxically, where sailors shone the most during the Peninsular War was on the mainland, where a large proportion of them were transferred. Excellent navy officers such as Díaz Porlier, Jado Cagigal, Francisco de Riquelme and Mariano de Renovales served in the 7th Army, and Domingo de Monteverde in the Army of the Centre; General Ricardo de Álava, who later became the Duke of Wellington's most trusted Spanish officer, was also a distinguished sailor. Likewise, the marine infantry went to fight on land, shining in countless battles, such as Bailén, Espinosa de los Monteros, Uclés, Tamames, Medina de Rioseco and Ocaña, among many others, as well as defending besieged cities such as Cádiz, Zaragoza, Girona and Tarragona.

As for the ships, few saw action in the conflict. The ships of the line, those perfect machines of war, did not participate directly. In 1808 the few that remained seaworthy were dedicated exclusively to travelling to the American colonies to bring back funds to keep the war going. However, the condition of the ships was so dire that in many cases they barely had enough gear to withstand a transatlantic crossing. Thus, in September 1810 the British authorities had to provide cables, rigging and even sailors so that the ships *Santa Ana* and *Príncipe de Asturias* could travel to Havana,[8] as well as supplying other ships destined for the port of Mahón in the Balearic Islands. It was precisely in this port where, a few months earlier, some ships had had to be scrapped, including the ship of the line *Conde de Regla*, because they lacked the means to carry out repairs; broken up, they were used to supply the local population with firewood.[9] Their lack of seaworthiness also meant that many ships were used as floating gaols for prisoners of war, the best known being those fitted out in the Bay of Cadiz. On occasions, however, Spanish ships also fell victim to fate. For example, on 6 March 1810 several allied ships were anchored at the mouth of the port, sheltering from Napoleonic artillery, when a terrible storm broke their cables and dragged the ships towards the coasts of Puerto de Santa María and Puerto Real, near Cadiz, where they ran aground. This territory was under fire from the enemy, who wasted no time in opening fire on the ships. Fires broke out, and it was impossible to save them. On that day the ships of the line *Purísima Concepción*, *Montañés*, *San Ramón*, *Castilla* and *Argonauta*, as well as the frigate *Paz*, were lost. It so happened that *Castilla* and *Argonauta* were occupied by French prisoners. Those on *Castilla* were able to be rescued by their compatriots, but those on *Argonauta* barely had time to flee and most of them burned to death with the ship.

The Spanish navy's actions were largely limited to helping the British in the following operations: transporting, evacuating or supplying weapons to the army, supplying besieged cities and bombarding enemy positions, normally within the framework of operations coordinated with the land army. In this regard, several actions carried out by the navy during the siege of Cadiz are worth mentioning. Thus, Captain Francisco Mourelle de la Rúa, in command of the fleet 'Fuerza Sutil de Reserva', comprising the corvette *Príncipe* and six gunboats, prevented the arrival of two French frigates that were attempting to enter Rota.[10] Another outstanding operation was carried out by Lieutenant Lorenzo María de Parra y Villalba, when in March 1810 he led an expedition of gunboats to the coast of Huelva, where they sank two French corsair ships. Parra had previously been fighting on land, having participated in the battles of Talavera, Puente del Arzobispo and Ocaña. After the disaster in La Mancha, he had to return to Cadiz with Copons' troops and was re-embarked, subsequently taking part in various battles. The navy played an important role in the battle of Pontesampaio, with the participation of the frigate *Ifigenia*,[11] commanded by Captain Juan José Carranza, and the schooner *El Tigre* being particularly noteworthy.

One of the navy's main tasks was to transport troops. Along the Catalan and Valencian coasts, the role of transport from the Balearic Islands was particularly important. Certainly the navy played a crucial role in the transport of troops that enabled the Spanish victory in the battle of Barrosa and in the nearby county of Niebla, where the Napoleonic troops were harassed by land, but with the invaluable collaboration of the navy. No less important was the so-called 'Cantabrian

Expedition' in October 1810, commanded by the naval captain Joaquín Zarauz, which took General Mariano de Renovales and his division to the Cantabrian coast with the mission of conquering the strategic town of Santoña (the Gibraltar of the north) and subsequently disembarking his division to conquer other towns on the Cantabrian and Biscay coasts. The fleet comprised the frigate *Magdalena*, commanded by the naval captain Blas Salcedo; the brig *Palomo*, commanded by the naval lieutenant Diego de Quevedo; the schooners *Insurgente Roncalesa* and *Liniers*; the gunboats *Corzo*, *Estrago*, *Gorrión* and *Sorpresa*; and fifteen transports. They were accompanied by a British fleet under the command of Captain William Roberts Mends, which included the frigates HMS *Arethusa*, HMS *Amazon*, HMS *Narcissus* and HMS *Medusa*, and the brig *Puerto Mahón*, along with 800 marines. After a stop in Asturias, the fleet continued with favourable winds to Santoña. But on 23 October a violent storm hit the Cantabrian coast, forcing the allied ships to withdraw. Four of the gunboats went down. Fortunately, they were close to the coast and their crews were saved. The surviving ships headed for the town of Vivero in Galicia. Once again, the weather took an unexpected turn for the worse on the night of 1/2 November. The British frigates had time to weather the storm by going out to sea and unstepping their masts, but not so the Spanish ships. *Magdalena* almost collided with HMS *Narcissus*, but the latter escaped through skilful manoeuvring. Then the mast of the Spanish frigate collapsed, destroying part of the hull and opening up numerous holes; battered by the waves, she ran aground near Covas beach. Meanwhile, the brig *Palomo* became a toy in the hands of a furious Poseidon, who threw the ship against the rocks of some nearby cliffs. The next morning the spectacle there was Dantesque: the bodies of 500 crew members of *Magdalena* washed up on the beach, only three of them having escaped with their lives. As for the *Palomo*, fifty of her seventy-five crew members were lost. Among the dead were the head of the squadron, Captain Zarauz, *Magdalena*'s captain, Salcedo, and *Palomo*'s captain, Quevedo. Tragically, Salcedo was found hugging the corpse of his son, who was part of the crew as a midshipman and had also drowned.[12]

This expedition also witnessed a heroic episode that demonstrates the unwavering self-sacrifice of Spanish sailors, whatever the circumstances. The protagonists were the crew of the gunboat *Estrago*, commanded by Ensign José Aguiar y Mella. After *Magdalena* was destroyed by the storm in Santoña, *Estrago* tried to reach one of the ports on the Biscayan coast, but all of them were controlled by French troops, so disembarking would mean being taken prisoner. Finally, they anchored in the Elantxobe inlet, between Getxo and Lekeitio (i.e., east of Bilbao) – in other words, in the middle of territory dominated by Napoleonic troops. Ensign Aguiar then led his crew to Santoña, hoping to meet with the Spanish troops there. Seeing that the fortifications were still held by the French, the group began an epic journey through enemy territory that culminated in their arrival in Ferrol on 2 December. They were greeted with a mixture of astonishment and enthusiasm. Ensign Aguiar had managed to hold his men together and reach Galicia without suffering a single casualty. All the crew members of *Estrago* were rewarded with double pay, although we cannot be sure that they actually received it, given the parlous state of the navy.

Finally, one aspect of life at sea that was no less important was the maritime corsairs. If corsairs on land, i.e. guerrillas, were of fundamental importance in the war, so too were the maritime corsairs. Both on the Andalusian coast and on the Cantabrian coast, the few French ships that ventured to transport arms, supplies or mail were in extreme danger, either from the presence of the British fleet or from Spanish privateers. As mentioned above, the Josephine authorities also issued privateer's patents, although they were of little significance. Privateers gained greater relevance on the Catalan coasts.[13] At the beginning of the war the Junta of Empordà, for example, registered no fewer than thirty-two ship captains who asked permission to carry out privateering against French ships. Josep Bajandas, captain of the frigate *Místic Sant Josep*, stood out in this task. He managed to put together a small fleet that was a terror to French ships, especially during 1808 and 1809. His numerous achievements included the capture of numerous ships carrying food to the garrison and population of Barcelona and of numerous vessels carrying imperial mail, as well as the kidnapping of numerous personalities, such as the famous spy and scientist François Arago.[14] The constant corsair activity in ports such as Palamós, Roses and Sant Feliu de Guixols caused the French authorities to make their conquest a priority objective. One after another, these ports fell into the hands of Napoleon, who promoted the arrival of French merchants and corsairs. From that moment on, it can be said that a group of privateers from Marseille took possession of the Catalan coast, including the famous Jean-Baptiste Durande, whose presence encouraged numerous merchants to come from the south of France, the most important of whom was François-Bernard Boyer-Fonfrède,[15] who became lord and master of the port of Palamós. However, Catalan privateers continued to operate, albeit to a lesser extent, from their other bases, such as the Medes Islands. On occasions, they resold the booty captured from French ships back to their compatriots. The Spanish regained control of the coast at the beginning of 1813, at which time most of the French merchants returned to their homeland, as the losses in their businesses became unsustainable and the French fleet was no longer able to defend them.

The end of the war did not mean a revival of the Spanish navy. During the war up to thirty ships of the line were lost due to lack of maintenance or abandonment. From 1816 onwards an attempt was made to remedy the lack of ships, but in addition to the scarcity of money to build new ships, there was also the deplorable state of the Spanish shipyards, where there were no materials or workers to launch new ships. It was therefore decided to cede the shipyards to private shipbuilders, but these were interested in building smaller vessels, smaller than corvettes, for their private business. So there was no choice but to buy warships from abroad, usually with disastrous consequences, as was the case with the famous Russian squadron that Ferdinand VII wanted to buy in 1817. In all, five ships of the line and three frigates were acquired at an exorbitant price of some 70 million reales.[16] In fact, the operation was already a bit of a squeeze, even among those closest to the king, who found it difficult to find someone who dared to sign the decree for the purchase. In the end, the always docile and faithful Lieutenant General Francisco de Eguía agreed to sign it, a man anchored in the last century, who still wore a ponytail, face powder and clothes that would have seemed old-fashioned to Charles IV; the cursing circles of the court knew him as the 'Coletilla'. The Russian squadron arrived with difficulty in Cadiz in 1818, and was soon found to be in a terrible state of disrepair, with the rigging in very poor condition and the timbers largely rotten. In response to the complaints, Dmitriy Tatistcheff, then the Russian minister plenipotentiary in Madrid, stated that the agreement was for eight ships, without specifying that they had to be in good condition. Tatistcheff was a Knight of the Order of the Golden Fleece. None of the ships of the Russian squadron continued to sail after 1823. In 1834, at the death of Ferdinand VII, the Spanish squadron had only three ships of the line, all in poor condition.[17]

Notes

1. Diego Garcia (2009), p. 60. By 1809 the Royal Navy had increased its fleet by 844 ships, including 160 ships of the line.
2. Using the summer 2022 exchange rate, this would be equivalent to £1,175,957,300, US$ 1,383,471,040 or CAN$ 1,802,074,485.
3. Diego García (2009), p. 63.
4. This correspondence is unpublished and is preserved by the descendant of both, Mr Joaquín Ibáñez, who has given it to the author for this book. José María Jalón y Bañuelos (1778–1824) left the navy at the beginning of the war, joining the army, where he became general in 1815. He ended his duty in the king's Halberdiers Regiment. We have seen his father, the Marquis of Castrofuerte, in command of the 5th Division of the Army of the Left in the battles of Tamames, Medina de Rioseco and Alba de Tormes.
5. Also known as 'sea cake', it was made with white flour, well kneaded with water and a little yeast. It was cooked to be dry, without crumbs, hard and brittle, in the shape of a hemispherical bun. To eat the biscuit, it had to be soaked for a few minutes in water or wine, the latter being the preferred drink. González-Aller Hierro (2005), p. 202.
6. Fernández Duro (1903), p. 54.
7. Ibid., p. 142.
8. Ibid., p. 30.
9. Ibid., p. 26.
10. Juan y Ferragut (2008), p. 126.
11. *Ifigenia* was a frigate captured from the French navy in 1793. It sank in Campeche (Mexico) in 1818, after a storm.
12. The Salcedo family was marked by tragedy. After the death of the father and son, both named Blas Salcedo, three more of his sons were killed in action. Ensign Toribio Salcedo died in 1804 on board the frigate *Mercedes*, which was blown up while fighting a British ship. Ensign José Salcedo died in 1823 in the battle of Venta de Armentia, serving in the 6th Regiment of Marine Infantry, when he was surprised by a column of royalists during the short war that brought absolutism back to Spain. Commodore Eusebio Salcedo died suddenly in 1863 on his way back to Spain after being stationed in the Philippines for a year. Even one of his grandsons died in combat, the naval lieutenant José Bedoya y Salcedo, who, in command of a gunboat, died of wounds during the siege

of Bilbao in the First Carlist War. Ana Reguera, Blas Salcedo's widow, had to make numerous requests to be paid the promised pension, as she was living in the most abject poverty and still had eight children to feed. Information from Marcelino González Fernández, *Biographical Dictionary of the Royal Academy of History*. Available at: http://dbe.rah.es/biografias/6125/blas-salcedo-y-salcedo (accessed 16 January 2021).

13. Martín Roig (2010a).

14. Arago's exciting biography is full of important scientific achievements, but his political side is no less interesting. In 1848 he became President of the Republic and in that same year he signed the decree that put an end to slavery in France and its colonies. Incidentally, on this trip he was escorted by the then Captain Pierre-Augustin Berthemy, who would reappear as one of the military governors of the Valençay castle-palace during Ferdinand VII's stay there.

15. His brother Jean-Baptiste Boyer-Fonfrède was an important leader of the Gironde who was guillotined during the French Revolution.

16. As a reference, the cost of ships of the line at the end of the eighteenth century was between 2 and 4 million reales, some being cheaper and a few, exceptionally, more expensive. So that price, by all accounts, was outrageous.

17. Anca Alamillo (2009), p. 267.

Chapter Thirty-Six

The *Afrancesados* and the Spanish Army of King Joseph

Date: 1808–1814. *Place*: Spain.

In the spring of 1808 Spain took up arms against the new Napoleonic regime, but not all Spaniards opposed Napoleon. A large section of the nobility and elites stood by and watched. After all, Charles and Ferdinand had renounced their crown in favour of Joseph Bonaparte. This was the case, for example, with the Duke of Infantado, one of Ferdinand VII's closest collaborators, who did not decide to embrace the patriot cause until he saw that the majority of the population was against the Napoleonic rulers. Others took up arms after seeing how some authorities, accused of collaborating, were lynched by angry mobs: Francisco Solano in Cadiz, Antonio Filangieri in León, José de Marquina and the Marquis of Perales in Madrid, among many others. A small group of enlightened nobles, ecclesiastics and intellectuals embraced the new Napoleonic system in the hope that it would be able to reform a society that had missed the train of modernity. And they sincerely believed that the new Napoleonic government would be able to deepen the timid enlightened reforms that the governments of Charles III had tried to carry out in the eighteenth century. These people were known as *afrancesados*, literally 'Frenchified'. López Tabar estimates that there were around 4,000 *afrancesados*, although in reality there were many more who, to a greater or lesser degree, collaborated with the new regime. In any case, they were a small minority in a population of over 10 million people. Among the French supporters were mainly civil servants, high-ranking military officers, nobles with liberal tendencies and, above all, scientists and intellectuals, such as Leandro Fernández de Moratín, the most important playwright of his generation. In the towns where Napoleonic rule was consolidated, such as Madrid, Barcelona, Zaragoza and Seville, civil servants, judges and the police were obliged to swear loyalty to the new king. Those who did not accept the new government had no choice but to flee or end up in prison, and their posts were filled by many opportunists who saw an opportunity to enrich themselves, as in the case of the obscure Barcelona police chief Ramón de Casanova.

King Joseph was aware that he could not impose himself by force alone. It was necessary, as far as possible, to persuade the Spanish people to accept his new government. To this end, he made use of a powerful propaganda apparatus through the publication of numerous Napoleonic-style newspapers, such as those edited by Alberto Lista in Seville and Manuel Antonio Ygual in Barcelona. Checa Godoy[1] put the number of these newspapers at thirty throughout Spain, In addition, King Joseph endowed the Royal Order of Spain[2] with a substantial pension, which could reach 30,000 reales a year (the basic salary of a Spanish citizen was usually around 4 reales a day) in the class of commander, with which he rewarded the loyalty of his closest collaborators, but which also served to attract new supporters to his cause. Among those who received this prized decoration were his most loyal ministers, such as Cabarrús and O'Farrill, artists such as Francisco de Goya, writers such as Fernández de Moratín and military men such as Juan van Halen (who, as we have seen, changed sides at the end of the war) and the Marquis of Castelar, who, having been repudiated by the patriots, was welcomed by Joseph Bonaparte.

One of the great failures of the new government was the plan to set up a Napoleonic army made up of Spanish troops.[3] The man in charge of carrying out this project was the Minister of War, Gonzalo O'Farrill, a Spaniard born in Cuba but of Irish descent. He had the collaboration of a large number of generals who had sworn allegiance to Joseph Bonaparte, including Admiral José de Mazarredo, considered one of the best sailors of his generation in Europe, the artillery general Tomás de Morla and some curious cases, such as José de Moctezuma, a descendant of the last Aztec emperor. But the biggest problem O'Farrill had to face was finding soldiers willing to fight under the Napoleonic flag. Despite generous pay, the advantageous conditions offered to Spanish soldiers to join the Napoleonic army and the release of Spanish soldiers captured on the battlefield, the battalions could hardly be filled. In January 1809 the first regiments began to be organized, No. 1 in Madrid and No. 2 in Toledo, with prisoners captured in the battle of Uclés. However, the first regiment had only 800 men, and the second had little more than 600, which meant that they did not even comprise a battalion. Despite this, they took part in the battles of Almonacid and Ocaña, in a secondary role. In the latter battle they managed to recruit prisoners for the Seville Regiment No. 3, but this never numbered more than 500 men. Moreover, these soldiers deserted at the slightest opportunity. On paper, the Minister of War had organized a total of twelve line infantry regiments, but of these, eight never even had a colonel in charge and in many cases existed only on paper. He was never able to complete a single battalion. O'Farrill also 'created' four regiments of light infantry, five regiments of cavalry and several companies of artillerymen and engineers, as well as a corps of Royal Guards; the latter came closest to resembling a fighting force. These units never really managed to be combatant and only took part in a very few battles, most notably those of Almonacid, Vitoria and San Marcial. After these last two defeats, the Spanish Josephine army practically disappeared, either dead, missing or deserters.

Likewise, the territories controlled by Napoleonic troops had carabineer or militia units that used to act against the guerrillas, and to guard or escort prisoners. Corps of *gendarmes* and a kind of volunteer corps ('Cuerpos Francos'), whose main mission was to act against the guerrilla bands, were also created. In fact, technically we could say that they were Napoleonic guerrillas, although they never accepted this name. Gil Novales[4] and Sorando Muzás have studied them in depth, listing more than eighty of these units. Their origins were diverse, but they tended to be recruited from among people living on the margins of society. The common denominator of the vast majority of them is that they were renegades from the patriot army. Many of them were former bandits, thieves or smugglers. In Aragon, specifically in the province of Huesca, perhaps the best known were Gerónimo Rocatallada and Domingo Brun, alias Chandón, who had gone from defending the city of Zaragoza during the sieges to becoming guerrilla fighters for the Napoleonic army, sowing death in the Echo valley. In Andalusia, after the arrival of Soult's troops in 1810, a great part of the population decided to collaborate with the invaders, and a large number of counter-guerrilla units were set up. In the Sierra Morena, for example, Antonio Ariza commanded the Company of Guides of Córdoba.[5] In Malaga the former smuggler Tomás Villarreal stood out at the head of the Malaga Squadron of Chasseurs Guides, and P. García, a former friar, commanded a squadron of Spanish gendarmes called the Lanceros de Dalmacia (presumably in honour of Marshal Soult, Duke of Dalmatia). In Castile there was the curious case of the Marquis of Barriolucio, founder and president of the Junta of Burgos. Because of his inflexible and authoritarian character, he ended up being expelled from the Junta and decided to join the Josephine side. Shortly afterwards, in the spring of 1810, he was captured by the guerrilla band of El Empecinado, who decided to set him free. Barriolucio returned to his guerrilla activity, but this time against the French. Guerrilla activity was particularly intense in Navarre, so the Napoleonic authorities did everything they could to counteract it, either with the regular army or with the counter-guerrilla forces. Among the many supporters of King Joseph, we should mention José Chacón, who, in command of the so-called Battalion of the Chacones,[6] wreaked havoc among the patriotic guerrilla bands until his death from wounds received in the battle of Tiebas.[7] A former guerrilla of El Empecinado, Saturnino Gómez Abuín, alias El Manco, changed sides after being captured and King Joseph appointed him commander of the Free Company of Hussars of Guadalajara, and he also received the Royal Order of Spain. Catalonia boasts perhaps the most famous example, in the shape of Josep Pujol, alias Boquica, a former smuggler who, at the head of the Distinguished Chasseurs of Catalonia, terrorized the north of the province of Girona. In fact, his numerous crimes were so cruel and abject that, once the war was over, and in a totally unprecedented act, the French authorities extradited him to Spain, where he was tried and executed.

Napoleon's defeat in the battle was a turning point in the fate of the *afrancesados*. A large number of them followed King Joseph in his flight to France, where they witnessed in terror the battle of Vitoria. Most of them managed to leave Spain. Considerable numbers left their country in small groups until the end of the war. Checa Godoy states that some 12,000 people left Spain because of their collaboration with King Joseph's government. Among those who were forced to flee were practically all the tax collectors, policemen and others who had been part of the repressive apparatus of the Napoleonic state. Once in France, most of them were confined in *dépôts*, such as those in Dax, Gers, Toulouse, Bayonne and Orthez.[8] Their life was not always easy, especially with the accession to the throne of Louis XVIII, who was wary of the presence of Napoleonic allies on his territory. Shortly after the end of the war some of them asked to return to Spain. All of them underwent a process of 'purification', which consisted of a kind of trial in which the actions of each individual during the war were assessed, including the Fernandist officers who were held captive in France. Some of the people mentioned above were pardoned, such as Gerónimo Rocatallada; his colleague Domingo Brun was not so lucky and was forced to remain in France, as was Ramon de Casanova, chief of police in Barcelona. The Spanish government decreed an amnesty in 1817 and again in 1820, but the absolutist regime through which Ferdinand VII ruled dissuaded many from returning, such as the ministers Gonzalo O'Farrill and Mariano Luis de Urquijo, or second-ranking politicians like Domènec Badia.[9] Of the same opinion were many of the liberal noblemen, such as Carlos Miguel Fitz-James Stuart, Duke of Alba and Berwick. Other nobles chose to return, such as Cipriano Palafox Portocarrero, Count of Montijo.[10] As for the intellectuals, some, such as Goya, decided to stay in Spain, although later, disenchanted with Ferdinand's policies, they took the path of exile. Others, such as Fernández de Moratín, initially returned to Spain but ended up going back into exile in France.

The *afrancesados* have gone down in history as traitors to their homeland. However, their only desire was to modernize Spain, to put an end to the oppressive influence of the Church, and to promote a true industrial revolution. But their project failed. There were too many factors working against them. Probably, they were the true patriots.

Notes

1. Checa Godoy (2013).
2. Boguñá (2022).
3. Sorando Muzás (2018).
4. Gil Novales (2009).
5. *Gaceta de Madrid* dated 20 December 1811, no. 354, p. 1,443. Among his most notable actions we find the capture of a *guerrillero* called the Monk, who was tried in Seville and hanged on 11 November 1811.
6. Previously called the Catalan Volunteers Battalion, after a group of Catalan prisoners that it escorted and who decided to change sides, and before that the King's Volunteers Company.
7. On 21 August 1813 General Abbé had left Pamplona with 1,600 men, including the Chacones Battalion, to escort a food convoy to the city, when they were attacked near Tiebas by some 2,400 guerrillas under the command of the legendary Espoz y Mina. The patriots managed to put

the Napoleonic forces to flight, resulting in General Abbé being slightly wounded and Chacón seriously so, among many other casualties.

8. Sánchez García (2008), p. 23.
9. Domènec Badia (1766–1818), popularly known as Ali Bei, was an adventurer, explorer and spy with a romantic life. He was the first non-slave European to visit Mecca.
10. Cousin of the famous José de Palafox and his brother, the Marquis of Lazán, both heroes of the Spanish Army. His daughter Maria Eugenia de Montijo later married Napoleon III and became Empress of France.

Chapter Thirty-Seven

Ferdinand VII in Valençay

Date: 1808–1814. *Place*: Valençay, France.

Background

The abdications at Bayonne seemed to put an end to the Bourbon dynasty in Spain. After the signing of the treaty, Charles IV and Ferdinand VII, father and son but irreconcilable enemies, renounced the throne of Spain and began an exile that would separate them for ever. Napoleon arranged for Charles IV to go and live in the Compiègne palace, some 80km (50 miles) north of Paris in the Picardy region, while Ferdinand VII would go to the Valençay palace, about 230km (143 miles) south of Paris in the Loire valley region. They each left with their large entourage and never met again.

An old palace for a new court

On 18 May Ferdinand arrived at Valençay.[1] He was accompanied by his brother Carlos María Isidro and his uncle, Prince Antonio Pascual, as well as a large entourage. His court was headed by the Duke of San Carlos, who functioned as the chief steward; other high-ranking members included the Marquis of Ayerbe, Blas de Ostolaza, chaplain and confessor of Ferdinand and Carlos, the Duke of Híjar, the Duke of Feria, the Marquis of Guadalcázar, Antonio Correa and Pedro Macanaz. Their servants included Isidoro Montenegro (Ferdinand's valet), Domingo Ramírez, Ignacio Molina and Pedro Sisternes; Ignacio Jáuregui and Francisco Vulliez (doctors); Antonio Moreno, Fermín de Artieda, Ignacio Menéndez (Ferdinand's hairdresser), Manuel Moreno, Pedro Basadre, José Vazquez and Domingo Larraondo as service personnel; José Gomezo, Antonio Cobos, Vicente Feijoo, Pedro Pelaez, Francisco Otero and Antonio Oliver y Cozina as lackeys; and Agustín Feito, Antonio Miranda, Juan Guischot, Pedro Sierra, José Villar, Juan Peus and José González de Rivera as confectioners. Days later the indispensable Juan de Escoiquiz and the servants Pedro Collado and Juan Aldavín arrived. In addition, all the aristocrats were accompanied by a servant. There was also a group of grooms.

In other words, the princes were accompanied in their exile by their closest clique, as well as by their most trusted servants. In the case of Ferdinand, for example, he had two of the three members of his private council,[2] as well as Blas de Ostolaza, his confessor for a few months, but whose loyalty always proved to be bombproof. The other ecclesiastic, Escoiquiz, on the other hand, had known Ferdinand since his childhood, when he had been his tutor. Ferdinand counted on the company of his great friend and crony Pedro Collado. Known as Perico Chamorro, he was working as a water carrier at the Berro fountain[3] when he met Ferdinand, then Prince of Asturias, although they also met in more murky circumstances. Chamorro was a handsome young man, quarrelsome and a womanizer like few others; he lived with a famous prostitute known as Lola la Naranjera or La Tirabuzones, a woman of unparalleled beauty and endless clientele. Such was her fame that the young Ferdinand decided to meet her;[4] this could not have made Chamorro happier, as Ferdinand became his best companion in his nocturnal escapades. There was no slum or prostitute that Chamorro did not know and that the Prince of Asturias was not fully satisfied with after his visit.[5] But beyond his nocturnal escapades, he also formed part of the prince's political clique, as he was imprisoned after the Escorial trial. It should come as no surprise, then, that Ferdinand called on Chamorro to accompany him to Valençay.

The cortège caused some astonishment among the welcoming committee, as the carriages in which they arrived were very old and did not seem to them suitable for Ferdinand's dignity. They were received by Talleyrand himself. Charles-Maurice de Talleyrand-Périgord was one of the most important political figures in France. Despite living through a time of conflict with the Emperor, he was still his Minister of Foreign Affairs and therefore someone to whom Bonaparte listened carefully. In 1803 Napoleon had asked Talleyrand to buy this château-palace, where various international treaties had been negotiated and which had hosted the highest European authorities. Valençay had many advantages for hosting such distinguished guests: it was sufficiently isolated to be free from outside interference, easy to guard, far from the main roads and close to a small, peaceful town.

Life in Valençay

Talleyrand was ordered to do everything he could to ensure that Ferdinand and his court had a pleasant stay to dissuade them from any heroic temptation. They knew exactly what the 'Felon King' was like. So, the minister arranged for his noble guests to be accompanied by a group of distinguished ladies, headed by Catherine Noël Worlee, his own wife. A woman of troubled existence, she had been the minister's lover for many years, but Napoleon forced them to marry, after which love gave way to indifference. For years they had lived civilly apart, but Madame Talleyrand knew how to do her duty when she was called by her husband – perhaps a little too much. Likewise, the minister was very scrupulous with his service when it came to strictly observing etiquette, something to which the Spanish princes were not really accustomed; if it shocked them at first, it later bored them. The princes had complete freedom of movement around the castle and its gardens, but were not allowed to leave it without permission.

Thus, their programme of activities could be considered both routine and controlled. The princes woke up at approximately 9.00am and took an hour to get dressed and eat breakfast. The rest of the morning was occupied by hearing mass and performing spiritual exercises. Afterwards, Ferdinand used to dispatch his correspondence with the Marquis of Ayerbe, and they read and commented on the press. The three princes met to have lunch together, with the chaplain Ostolaza and the gentleman of the bedchamber whose turn it was. After a brief rest, in the afternoon, when the weather permitted, the princes would go out, on foot or on horseback, except Ferdinand, who did not like to ride and usually went in a carriage. The alternative was to stay in the palace to play cards, billiards (contrary to common belief, Ferdinand was an excellent billiards player) or board games. Around 6.00pm Ferdinand, Carlos and Ostolaza would retire to read for about an hour, apparently preferring the works of Saavedra Fajardo.[6] The Spanish princes procured an exceptional library, made up of not only pious Spanish writers but also classics of Greco-Roman literature and philosophy, in their original language, and a multitude of works on the most varied subjects. According to the police, some French illustrated books ended up in the chimney. After dinner, they used to join the rest of the gentlemen of the bedchamber to share a board game or listen to a concert by the guitarist Salvador Castro de Gistau, a Spaniard who had lived in Paris for many years and who knew how to win the esteem of the princes, or by the eminent pianist Jan Ladislav Dussek, with whom they never got along.[7] Talleyrand had a sincere interest in ensuring that the princes received an education commensurate with their rank. He also ordered Castro to give them music lessons, an activity in which Ferdinand showed himself to be an acceptable interpreter of the pianoforte, and dance lessons, at which he was less gifted. In addition, among the reforms he carried out to adapt the palace to his guests was the construction of a small theatre, in which various operatic and theatrical performances were staged. But neither of these were to the princes' liking, as they tended to find the shows impious. The French members of the court discovered with astonishment and disapproval that the first opera that Ferdinand had attended was in Valençay. As for the other nobles, they spent much of each day on their own. Their life was less strict and pious than that of the princes. It was hardly a dissolute life but they did spend more time with Madame Talleyrand and her companions, with whom they apparently maintained excellent relations. Indeed, the Marquis of Guadalcázar married the young Ernestine Godeau d'Entraigues.[8] The relationship between the Duke of San Carlos and Madame Talleyrand was more troubled.

The first months in Valençay were happy for Ferdinand and his court, but it wouldn't last. In September 1808 Talleyrand returned to Paris, which saddened both Ferdinand and Carlos, who had come to really appreciate him. In that same month part of the allowance the princes were supposed to receive ceased to arrive, Napoleon excusing it on the grounds that no money was coming from

Spain for their upkeep, so part of the service had to be dispensed with. In addition, the Napoleonic police were suspicious of some of Ferdinand's friends and servants, so Pedro Macanaz, Isidro Montenegro and Ignacio Menéndez, all of whom he held in high esteemed, were expelled, which plunged him into great sorrow. The Marquis of Ayerbe, who acted as the chief steward after the expulsion of the Duke of San Carlos, decided to dispense with the services of the musician Salvador Castro in order to reduce the costs of the stay. It is a matter of supposition, but it seems that Castro was a master not only of the guitar but also of palace intrigues, and on his return to Paris it would not be unreasonable to think that he met with Fouché or one of his henchmen. The fact is that the much-feared head of the Parisian police took the drastic decision to expel practically the whole of the court of the former King of Spain.

It happened in March 1809, when Valençay was preparing to celebrate Holy Week. Only the accountant Antonio Moreno; Pedro Collado (Chamorro) as Ferdinand's valet; Manuel Moreno as Carlos's valet; and Antonio the barber were spared the irrevocable expulsion. From the general servants there remained only a sweeper, two cooks and three footmen, plus Dr Francisco Vulliez. It was at that moment that a figure appeared who would be transcendental for Ferdinand. Juan Gualberto de Amézaga[9] arrived in Valençay as a simple groom. Charismatic and with a gift for people, he gained Ferdinand's trust to become first his *caballerizo mayor* (great equerry) and later the intendant of the palace: the man who controlled everything. But where had he come from? At the time of his arrival in Valençay Amézaga was about 40 years old. He hailed from the Basque country and his family was relatively wealthy. He had worked in his brother-in-law's trading house, which must have been very dynamic, as it maintained a fluid traffic in products from the Spanish colonies. After the death of his first wife, he married a niece of Escoiquiz. Shortly before the start of the war the company went bankrupt. Escoiquiz's departure to Bayonne was a golden opportunity for Amézaga to avoid the lawsuits his company was facing and he doubtless saw that by getting closer to King Ferdinand's inner circle, he would be able to prosper at court.

After the departure of their closest confidants, the Spanish princes spent a few weeks of real sadness. Ferdinand hardly ever left his chambers. Prince Antonio Pascual, who had always lived somewhat on the fringes of the world, had practically no relations with anyone except his servant Sisternes, with whom he spent the day praying or playing board games. When Sisternes left, he spent most of the day wrapped in clouds of solitude, sewing or embroidering pieces of cloth (his only known pastime) that he would later donate to churches in the surrounding area. The situation was ripe for Amézaga to take over as the palace intendant. However, in June Amézaga was also expelled. Surprisingly, in December, he returned. From that moment on the former groom not only recovered his functions as intendant, but also took control of practically everything that happened in the palace: he controlled income and expenditure, checked correspondence, and controlled the staff, and Ferdinand even gave him permission to act on his behalf in different matters, from making arrangements for the purchase of a palace (Ferdinand wanted to move), to requesting donations from his loyal followers or loans from bankers. Amézaga was omnipresent and became the king's best friend and confidant. There was only one person who could overshadow him: Chamorro, Ferdinand's most trusted servant, who was surly towards the upstart groom. It should come as no surprise that Amézaga plotted some mischief, for within a few weeks Chamorro was expelled from Valençay and forced to live in Montbrisson, some 300km (185 miles) southeast of the palace. The situation began to worsen for Amézaga with the departure of the governor of Areberg, who was replaced by Pierre-Augustin Berthemy,[10] with whom he had a very bad relationship (the new governor reproached the new intendant for spending all day trying to seduce his own wife!). Moreover, the princes eventually realized that Amézaga was taking advantage of Ferdinand's trust for his own benefit. By the end of 1810 Prince Antonio Pascual was already openly accusing him of having enriched himself at the monarch's expense, and the relationship between the princes and Amézaga became strained to the point that the latter was expelled from Valençay in March 1811. The real reasons for the rise and fall of the intendant, whose life remains shrouded in mystery, will never be known, but it may have been linked to the failure of the Tassin affair. He was undoubtedly a man with *savoire faire*, a trickster who knew how to win the confidence of his interlocutor. After his expulsion, Charles d'Arberg de Valangin, the military governor of Valençay (and Napoleon's former chamberlain) recommended to the minister of police, Savary, and to Fouché that Amézaga be hired for his good services at the palace. Was he a spy in Napoleon's service? That would certainly explain his return to Valençay. What seems clear is that Amézaga was a survivor, someone capable of doing anything to survive and, if possible, get rich. When he failed to get a job as a police commissioner, he returned to Spain, where he swindled people of good faith, asking for donations for the princes of Valençay.

The Tassin affair brings us to one of Ferdinand's obsessions during his stay in France: money. Did the Spanish princes in Valençay have financial difficulties? On the basis of the information available, it does not seem so. The Treaty of Bayonne established an annual rent of 1 million francs for Ferdinand, in addition to the rents from the château of Navarre in Normandy, and 400,000 francs apiece for his brother and his uncle. It was stipulated that the rent of Valençay, 50,000 francs a year, would be paid by the Treasury of France. And if it is true that Ferdinand was a compulsive buyer, the accounts reveal nevertheless that every month he enjoyed a surplus. In fact, during their stay in Valençay, the princes spent exorbitant sums of money on books, watches, decorative items, mechanical objects, weapons (sabres and pistols), a great deal of jewellery and a multitude of paintings. It is worth noting that Talleyrand had his palace decorated with exquisite taste and filled with works by artists of the stature of Rubens, but the princes found these paintings impious and replaced them with religious oil paintings (much to the minister's displeasure). However, we must also comment on Ferdinand's sincere generosity towards the underprivileged, as he regularly donated a large amount of money to the priest of Valençay for charitable works. Another of his objectives was to acquire a new palace and leave Valençay, so Amézaga took numerous steps that never came to fruition. However, the largest sum of money went on allowances for his gentlemen of the bedchamber and service personnel.[11] Ferdinand always feared that he would be short of funds, and he worked hard to raise new income, especially after Napoleon soon stopped paying the agreed amounts, excusing himself on the grounds of the dire war situation in Spain. At this point the banker Louis Tassin de Messilly came into the picture. He contacted Ferdinand in Bayonne when he arranged a loan requested by the French state to pay the first instalment of the princes' pensions, through the Franco-Spanish banker Francisco Cabarrús.[12] His diligence won the royal confidence, and Ferdinand commissioned him for various tasks to raise funds. In 1812, for example, Tassin was sent to London, with various safe-conducts signed by Ferdinand, to obtain a million pesos from the Crown's funds in Lima and another million from the funds in Mexico. But the Duke of Infantado, ambassador in London, refused the transfer. The following year Tassin was commissioned to garner funds from various trading houses in Madrid and the Basque provinces. At the same time Ferdinand demanded more money directly from the Basque authorities. In his letters the king extorted money from the merchants and blamed the Spaniards ... for winning the war! As a result, Napoleon did not send him enough money 'to preserve our decorum and dignity'. The documents were carried by two of Tassin's workers, Duclerc and Christoph. It was soon suspected that they might be forgeries, as they showed the king in a very bad light. So, while Duclerc and Christoph were in Madrid in early 1814 they were arrested, and Amézaga was accused of having forged the letters, for which he was arrested in Zaragoza, where he lived. The matter was not resolved until 1817, when the Crown satisfied Tassin, Duclerc and Christoph with extravagant sums of money to help them forget the episode and, above all, keep quiet.

The people who shared Valençay with Ferdinand had a lot to keep quiet about, not least the king's disloyal (if not outright treacherous) attitude towards his fellow countrymen. While the country was bleeding to death, in all respects, defending the dynastic rights of the Bourbons, Ferdinand showed Napoleon an attitude of shameful submission and obedience. Thus, from Bordeaux, on his way to Valençay, on 12 May (just ten days after the Madrid uprising) he sent an exhortation to the Spaniards to keep calm and follow Napoleon's orders. Back in Valençay, when he heard of Joseph Bonaparte's coronation, he hastened to write to congratulate him. He also wrote to Napoleon to congratulate him on his military victories and on numerous occasions to ask him for the hand of a princess from among his relations, as he was obsessed with becoming a member of Bonaparte's family.[13] Some of these letters were published by the Emperor, but the news spread in Spain that they were false. Blas Ostolaza, who had managed to reach Cadiz, had launched an effective propaganda campaign, presenting

Ferdinand as a martyr living in Valençay with little more than torture and misery. The originals of the letters eventually fell into the possession of a lady of the Spanish nobility, who made them disappear with the help of a chimney.[14] Needless to say, the Bonaparte brothers turned a deaf ear to any request from Ferdinand, such as in December 1809 when he asked King Joseph for the Grand Band of the Royal Order of Spain,[15] or in December 1811 when General Kindelán fell ill while in command of the 2nd and 3rd battalions of the Joseph Bonaparte Regiment[16] and Ferdinand wrote to Napoleon begging him to appoint his brother Carlos general of that regiment. Neither was granted. Nor were his requests to be invited to the wedding of 'his father, his protector, his sovereign'[17] Napoleon to Marie-Louise of Austria,[18] held in Paris on 15–16 August 1810. However, this did not prevent the wedding from being celebrated with all possible pomp and ceremony in Valençay, where a military parade, concerts, theatrical performances, fireworks, various religious events and banquets were held, to which the princes invited various military and political authorities from the town. A police report described how Ferdinand had raised numerous cheers to Napoleon. A similar celebration took place to celebrate the birth of Napoleon's son, the King of Rome. Thus, while the Spaniards fought tooth and nail for their 'captive and virtuous' king, Ferdinand simply assumed that he would never be king again; moreover, concerned exclusively with his economic well-being, and gripped by the fear in which he always lived – above all, fearing for his life – he took care not to take any step that his captors might interpret as an act of rebellion. This even led him to denounce outside agents who came to Valençay with plans for his escape.

There had been several attempts to rescue Ferdinand since his stay in Bayonne. Many of them were carried out but all of them invariably failed. The first serious attempt was hatched by Palafox and Tomás de Veri, a member of the Supreme Central Junta, at the end of 1808. Their plan was to send Ventura Malibran,[19] a French spy in the service of Spain, to Valençay to rescue the princes. To achieve this, Palafox provided Malibran with two mules and six boxes full of gold and silver, totalling 820,000 reales: a veritable fortune. On 12 January Malibran tried to pass through the Catalan town of Organyà, but the locals were suspicious of the mysterious traveller and when they discovered the contents of his boxes, they tried to rob and murder him. Malibran managed to explain his true mission, saved by a safe-conduct signed by Reding, who was then Captain General of Catalonia. Finally, members of a local Junta arrived in Organyà and cleared up the mess, but they did not allow Malibran to continue with his extremely risky mission. The boxes with the gold were deposited in the cathedral of La Seu d'Urgell and later sent to Tarragona to contribute to the war effort. In vain Palafox demanded his money back. For his part, Malibran continued to carry out missions in southern France in favour of the Spanish cause, some of which were extremely dangerous. He had an extensive network of spies and collaborators ranging from noblemen to police commissioners. It seems that he carried out some successful rescues, such as that of the diplomat Pedro Gómez Labrador y Havela, Marquis of

Labrador.[20] The protagonist of the second attempt came to a worse end. After being expelled from Valençay, and knowing the castle and Ferdinand's habits, the Marquis of Ayerbe devised a plan to rescue him. He finally managed to find the means to travel to France, accompanied by Captain José Wanestron of the Regiment of Osuna and a muleteer called Francisco Lacámara. Disguised as traders, in June 1810 they took a route that led them from Corunna to San Sebastián, from where they entered Navarre. Their journey ended in October. Near the town of Lerín they were surprised by a guerrilla band; when they were found to have 41,000 reales concealed in their transport, the Marquis of Ayerbe and Wanestron were killed, their bodies being abandoned in the farm of Miguel Cabrera.[21]

Probably the most famous escape attempt was made by the Baron de Kolli. It all began in January 1810, when the alleged baron arrived in London accompanied by his secretary, Albert de Saint-Bonnet. Kolli's real name was Louis Collignon and, contrary to what he later revealed in his memoirs, he was in fact a deserter from the French army who escaped from prison after being accused of robbery. With excellent English language skills, pompous manners and some nerve, Kolli managed to meet one of the sons of King George III and, through him, the foreign minister, the Marquis of Wellesley (brother of the Duke of Wellington), and convinced them of his plan to free Ferdinand VII. In March the two agents set out on their journey and at the end of the month arrived in Paris, where they stayed with a trusted friend of Kolli's named Frédéric Richard. However, Richard immediately denounced the spies to the police and they were arrested. Fouché saw the propaganda potential of Kolli's documents and, using his usual persuasive techniques, convinced Richard to pose as Kolli and go to Valençay to find out how Ferdinand VII would react to an attempt at liberation. Fouché knew that any reaction from the Spanish prince could be exploited for Bonaparte's end: if he accepted the invitation to escape, it would justify tightening the conditions of captivity of the Bourbon princes; if, on the other hand, he refused, it could be presented to European public opinion that Ferdinand did not wish to flee Valençay. At the beginning of April Richard/Kolli arrived in Valençay, posing as a merchant, and managed to meet Prince Antonio Pascual, although he did not pay much attention to him. His aim was to reach Ferdinand; instead he was met by Amézaga. Richard lost his temper and rushed in, becoming violent. The palace intendant (whom we suspect was also acting as an imperial agent) denounced him to Berthémy, who arrested the intruder. Richard managed to clear up the misunderstanding over his identity and returned to Paris. Berthémy obtained a letter from Ferdinand VII in which he stated that his greatest wish was 'to be the adopted son of HM the Emperor, our sovereign' and declared his 'submission and entire obedience to his intentions and wishes'. Unsurprisingly, the letter was published in the French press as another of Fouché's great successes, while in Spain and the UK the letter was treated as a crude forgery. It is impossible to know if the letter was genuinely written by the king, but it at least seems plausible. The real Baron de Kolli (an invented title) and Saint-Bonnet spent the rest of the war imprisoned in Vincennes. After the war Kolli became part of Ferdinand's inner circle and represented the king at various European courts.

In the end, military developments ended up benefiting Ferdinand VII. After Napoleon's defeat at the battle of Leipzig in November 1813, some voices in the imperial cabinet began to look for a negotiated solution to the war in Spain. The foreign minister, Maret, even proposed the possibility of arranging a marriage between Ferdinand and Joseph Bonaparte's first-born daughter Zenaide, but the plan was soon rejected, not least because the princess was only 12 years old. Finally, negotiations began to arrange Ferdinand's return to Spain, recognizing him as king. Napoleon hoped to resume the old alliance with Spain, even at the cost of establishing an absolutist regime. The negotiations, which on the Spanish side were conducted by the Duke of San Carlos, Escoiquiz and Macanaz, culminated in the signing of the Treaty of Valençay on 8 December 1813. The Regency Council, which was expressly ignored in the negotiations by both Napoleon and Ferdinand, did not ratify the agreement, by virtue of the decree of 1 January 1811 that invalidated any act of the king outside Spain. This did not prevent Ferdinand's arrival on 22 March 1814. The strength of the absolutist party among the generals and the enthusiastic reception of the Spanish people for Ferdinand set in motion the countdown to the end of the constitutional regime born of the Cortes of Cadiz. The shadow of absolutism was once again looming over Spain.

After Valençay

It is easy to suppose that Ferdinand VII, no matter how heartless he was, felt little pride in his time in Valençay and much less in his servile attitude towards Napoleon (and, indeed, towards Joseph Bonaparte). It should come as no surprise that he tried to cover up everything that had happened during his days in Talleyrand's palace, from the destruction of documents to the elimination of witnesses, either through exile or ostracism or, more directly, through their physical disappearance. Quantities of compromising documentation, especially letters, went up in flames.

As for the testimonies, Ferdinand did not have to worry about some of them. The Marquesses of Ayerbe and Guadalcázar had died during the war. Among those who survived, the vast majority received posts far from Madrid. Blas de Ostolaza was appointed dean of the cathedral of Murcia, where he soon fell out of favour with Ferdinand because of his incendiary sermons criticizing the king's dissolute life. In 1817 he was accused of abusing the orphans at the hospice he managed and then began a series of imprisonments or confinements in monasteries that did not end until 1824, when he was acquitted of the accusations. He clearly had not learned his lesson, since he continued with his impassioned speeches against the king's clique, while unreservedly embracing the cause of the pretender Carlos. The outbreak of the First Carlist War surprised him in

Valencia, where he was immediately arrested by the liberal authorities and later shot.[22] Less eventful was the life of Juan de Escoiquiz, who at first not only stayed close to Ferdinand, but was appointed by him to various ministerial positions. However, he ended up the victim of a palace conspiracy and was exiled to Ronda in southern Andalucia, where he died in 1820, not before having written to Ferdinand informing him of General Riego's plans for a *coup d'état*. A similar fate was suffered by another of the king's closest advisers, Pedro Macanaz. After carrying out a policy of repression against the Bonapartists, he too fell victim to a palace conspiracy. On the morning of 8 November 1814 he was visited by Ferdinand VII, accompanied by the Duke of Alagón and a detachment of the Royal Guard. He was arrested and imprisoned in the castle of San Antón in Corunna. Two years later he was released and spent the rest of his life in his birthplace in Hellín (La Mancha). Better luck attended the Duke of San Carlos, who was fêted with various posts, such as the directorship of the Royal Spanish Academy and the Bank of San Carlos, as well as numerous ministries. However, he ended up losing royal favour and was forced into exile, dying in Paris in 1828. Juan Gualberto de Amézaga posed a potential risk to the king. The former groom and palace intendant, who had controlled everything in Valençay for several years, was a man who knew too much. Luckily for Ferdinand, he had been in a prison in Pamplona since 1814, accused of fraud. A normal trial would have lasted a few weeks, but after three years in prison Amézaga still had not been tried. Any statement Amézaga might make in a public trial could be a danger to the monarch's image. The problem was solved in 1817 when Amézaga was mysteriously found dead in his cell.

One of the most serious threats to Ferdinand VII was posed by his own brother, Carlos. Talleyrand comments in his memoirs that in Valençay, for the first time in their lives, they were able to behave like true brothers, demonstrating a close relationship. Their friendship ended abruptly when Ferdinand signed the Pragmatic Sanction of 1830, by which the heir to the Spanish crown became Isabella, the king's first-born daughter, who was then only a few months old. Carlos felt betrayed. He had been the victim of a shady palace conspiracy carried out by the liberal faction of the court and Ferdinand's fourth and last wife, Maria Christina of the Two Sicilies. Ferdinand, once again, betrayed those who had supported him in his years as king. Carlos moved away from the court, although he would not take up arms until the death of his elder brother in 1833, giving rise to the First Carlist War, the first of the three civil wars that the supporters of absolutism waged in Spain during the nineteenth century.

The only one of the Valençay clique who never lost royal favour was Perico Chamorro. This was perhaps the king's longest-lasting friendship and it endured until the death of the former water carrier in 1827. After his return to Madrid, Chamorro resumed his duties as the king's procurer. They were joined in their nocturnal revelries by the king's new best friend, the Duke of Alagón (*aka* Paquito de Córdoba), who was at the time the commander of the Royal Corps of Guards and was a rascal on a par with his king. The three of them became regular clients of the famous brothel owned by Pepa la Malagueña, with whom Ferdinand is said to have fallen madly in love. Her real name was Josefa Montenegro, and Ferdinand ordered her to marry an officer named Francisco Marzo, who was always stationed far from Madrid. From that marriage two children were born, Manuela and Francisco, whom Ferdinand planned to appoint as heir and Prince of Asturias. Only strong opposition from the church, and especially from his second wife Isabel de Braganza and his brother Carlos, prevented the legitimization of the young Francisco. Eventually Ferdinand stopped visiting Pepa la Malagueña (but not other brothels), although he tried to leave her in a solid financial position.

In conclusion, it is clear that Ferdinand's particular mentality, as an absolutist king appointed by the Grace of God, gave him a patrimonial concept of Spain (and of the Spanish), for which he felt he did not need to show gratitude or loyalty to his subjects. To his way of thinking, the members of his court in Valençay, by propping him up in power and keeping his shameful secrets, were merely doing their duty. Those who dared to contradict him were expelled from court and ended up dying far from the monarch to whom they had dedicated their lives. The exception was Chamorro, his pimp, his prankster, his chattering rascal, his wicked rogue, perhaps the king's plebeian alter ego – and perhaps the only man who understood Ferdinand and accepted him as he was, a Felon king.

Notes

1. This chapter uses verious sources, but is primarily based on Parra López (2018), surely the best biography of Ferdinand VII written to date.
2. The third one was the Duke del Infantado, who stayed in Bayonne to serve Napoleon. Later he would go over to the patriot side.
3. Repullés (1842), p. 63. Since the time of Philip IV, it was thought that the water from this fountain had healing properties and was even aphrodisiac, so it was said that the Spanish kings drank more water from the Berro fountain than wine.
4. On a certain occasion, Ferdinand wrote 'those of my blood are not a model of abstinence, and everyone hates celibacy', Villa-Urrutia (1922), p. 102.
5. Deira (2012).
6. Diego de Saavedra Fajardo (1584–1648) was a diplomat and writer at the time of Philip IV, and one of the most illustrious intellectuals of his generation.
7. Matrat (2015), p. 24. Dussek, whose career was in frank decline when he arrived in Valençay, had been a true *avant-la-lettre* rock star in Europe at the end of the eighteenth century. Born in Bohemia and a descendant of a famous dynasty of musicians, he stood out for his virtuous interpretations and Apollonian beauty, which opened for him the doors of the great European courts; there were rumours that he became a lover of both Catherine the Great of Russia, and Marie Antoinette. During the French Revolution he fled to London, where he abandoned his wife and son because of his debts (which sent his father-in-law to prison). Talleyrand claimed the debt and Dussek, bankrupt, put himself at his service. But by then the pianist was already a shadow of his former self. Obese and typically drunk, watching him play the piano had become a sad exercise in mercy.
8. Rafael Alfonso de Sousa of Portugal, Marquis of Guadalcázar, was 39 years old and a widower. His first wife was María Isidra de Guzmán, famous for having been the first woman with a

doctorate degree in Spain: in fact, she is known as the 'Doctor of Alcalá', having obtained her doctorate at the Faculty of Arts and Literature of the University of Alcalá in 1785. The couple had three children. María Isidra's health was very fragile and she died at the age of 35 in 1803. For her part, Ernestine Godeau was a 19-year-old girl whose father was a wealthy businessman. Her parents were enthusiastic about becoming part of the family of a Grandee of Spain, while the Marquis of Guadalcázar, who had serious money problems, could count on a large dowry and the support of the Godeaus. After their expulsion from Valençay, the couple moved to live in Burgos, where their only son Ferdinand was born. The marquis died the following year. Ferdinand VII, godfather to the child, did not avoid his obligations and made sure that the young man had an excellent education in the United Kingdom.

9. Franco de Espés (2019).
10. Berthemy had just recovered from a personal journey worthy of a novel. In July 1808 he accompanied the scientist François Arago on a mission to Catalonia. The ship they were travelling on was boarded by a Catalan corsair, and they were transferred to a prison on Majorca. In August he obtained permission to travel to Algiers, but the Turkish merchant ship that was transporting him was intercepted by other corsairs, who sent him to a prison in Catalonia. There he fell seriously ill; as his condition dramatically worsened, he was given permission to return to Marseilles. However, the ship carrying him was swept away by two terrible storms to Bougie, near Algiers, where Napoleon's old *dey* of Algiers had been overthrown; in his place, the new *dey* was hostile to the French, so Berthemy was once again imprisoned. In mid-June 1809 the *dey*, as a measure of grace, embarked forty French citizens and sent them to Marseilles, but when the ship was already in sight of the French coast, it was seized by a British frigate, which escorted it to Minorca. Luckily, the captain of the Turkish ship was able to get rid of his watchman at night and managed to land his passengers on the French island of Pomègues, opposite Marseille. On 2 July Berthemy finally arrived in Marseilles. He was still seriously ill, and spent a year recovering. Finally, he appeared before Napoleon, who, admiringly, sent him to Valençay.
11. We find these expenses minutely detailed by Franco de Espés (2019), pp. 56–7. Thus, Ferdinand had assigned his gentlemen of the bedchamber, the Marquises of Ayerbe and Guadlacázar, 24,000 reales a year; Domingo Ramírez de Arellano and Isidro Montenegro, 33,000; Fermín de Artieda and Antonio Moreno, 15,000; and Pedro Collado, 8,800. For his part, Carlos assigned his gentleman of the bedchamber, the Duke of Feria, 24,000 reales a year; Ignacio Molina, his wardrobe, 33,000; and his hairdresser and barber, Ignacio Mendoza, 20,000. Similar figures were assigned by P Antonio Pascual, although he paid them in monthly instalments.
12. A prestigious financier, Francisco Cabarrús was a close associate of Napoleon and by extension of his brother Joseph Bonaparte, who had awarded him the highest rank of the Royal Order of Spain. He was finance minister until his death, which happened unexpectedly in Seville in 1810, when he was buried in the cathedral. After the war his tomb was desecrated and his bones were probably thrown into the Guadalquivir river. His daughter was none other than Teresa Cabarrús, known in France as Notre-Dame de Thermidor; during the French Revolution she contributed decisively to the fall of Robespierre (the 9th of Thermidor, hence her nickname) and was a close friend of Josephine de Beauharnais, Napoleon's first wife.
13. At that time, Ferdinand was the widower of his first wife, his cousin Maria Antonia of Naples, who had died in 1806, after four years of marriage, without issue.
14. Villa-Urrutia (1922), p. 102.
15. Franco de Espés (2019), p. 36.
16. Sorando Muzás (2018), p. 412.
17. Villa-Urrutia (1922), p. 116.
18. To whom the royal princes were related, since Ferdinand and Carlos were cousins of her mother, Maria Theresa of Bourbon, daughter of Ferdinand I of Sicily and granddaughter of Charles III of Spain.

19. Cassinello Pérez (2005), pp. 61–4. This is undoubtedly the most complete work on the Malibran missions; details on the attempted rescue of Ferdinand VII are also given in Goméz de Arteche (1880), pp. 20–5, and Parra López (2008), p. 193.
20. The Spanish representative at the Congress of Vienna. Historiography usually describes him as haughty, mediocre and stupid.
21. Gomez de Arteche (1880), pp. 36–41; Parra Lopez (2008), p. 193. This area was dominated by the men of Espoz y Mina, but when questioned, the guerrilla leader denied knowing the identity of the merchants or the destination of their valuable cargo.
22. Lores Altuve-Febres (2007) is a detailed biography of Ostolaza. It can be criticized for its excessively laudatory tone.

Conclusion

Throughout the chapters of this book, I have tried to explain the causes of the defeat of Napoleon's army in the Peninsular War from a Spanish perspective. How, since the beginning, the majority of Spaniards rose up against the invaders to defend the dynastic rights of a king who had just been proclaimed and whom they hardly knew. Incidentally, while that king, Ferdinand VII, lived non-chalantly in Valençay trying to curry favour with Napoleon, his subjects died by the thousands in his name. This massive support was the key to resisting what was probably the world's best army in the early nineteenth century. Thoroughly well trained, with excellent officers, it was an army with experience gained at the great European battles such as Ulm, Austerlitz, Jena, Eylau and Friedland. When Napoleon took the decision to invade Spain, however, he did not take into account various aspects that would ultimately lead to his defeat there, which would necessarily be associated with the fall of his regime.

The first aspect to consider is the geography of the Iberian Peninsula. Spain is not an easy country to traverse, nor is its orography helpful to travellers. The Greek philosopher Strabo, in his work *Geography*, long ago warned that in Iberia 'most of the inhabited country consists of mountains [and] forests'. Many mountain ranges and rivers serve as natural borders. At the beginning of the nineteenth century, the infrastructure to cross them was scarce and many of the roads and bridges dated back to Roman times – for example, the Despeñaperros pass in Sierra Morena, the only road connecting Castile and Andalusia or, to put it in other words, Madrid and Seville. Thus, to conquer and maintain Andalusia it was necessary to conquer the plains north of the Sierra Morena. This explains why the battle of Ocaña was so decisive: it opened the way to Despeñaperros. But it also explains why, when Wellington defeated Marmont at the battle of Salamanca, Soult's first decision was to evacuate Andalusia by force: he feared being trapped between the allied armies in the north and south. Similarly, the few bridges crossing some of the main rivers were commonly military objectives and the scene of battles, such as at Alcántara in May 1809, where the fight was to control passage over the bridge crossing the Tagus river in this town. In the case of road junctions, such as at Tudela, they have been the subject of numerous battles throughout history, and the Peninsular War was no exception. This combination of countless mountains, lush forests and scarce roads had serious consequences for the Napoleonic troops: not only could the imperial divisions not move through Spain as quickly as they could in Central Europe, but also they became easy targets for the guerrilla bands, who had their best refuges in the mountains and could easily harass slow-moving convoys and couriers. Controlling passes, bridges and road junctions meant committing numbers of troops and resources in a war of attrition that the French could not withstand indefinitely.

Then there were the economic aspects. Napoleon claimed that the only general who won every battle was General Gold. In 1808 Spain was bankrupt. Overwhelmed by debts, Spanish governments were unable to get out of a situation of economic hardship, despite the gold and silver from the American colonies. The economic structures were obsolete and condemned a large part of the population to poverty. But in the war, to try to bridge the gap, Spain had a kind of Lend-Lease Act *avante-la-lettre* from the British government. From London, first the Supreme Central Junta and later the Regency Council received weapons, ammunition, uniforms, boots and all the material necessary to equip the armies that stoically faced the French. Without this support, it is very likely that Spanish resistance would have collapsed, especially from 1810 onwards. As for Napoleon's army, its attempt to feed itself on the ground caused numerous problems. The local population, with virtually no food for themselves, were unwilling to hand over what little they had to the invaders, who were forced instead to requisition and loot, which only increased the people's hatred for them in the territories they occupied. The situation caused many French soldiers to starve. Poorly fed, they soon fell ill, drastically reducing the number of soldiers available to fight. Particularly bitter in this regard were Masséna's complaints during the invasion of Portugal in 1810, but there were numerous examples in Spain. In Barcelona the French garrison also suffered hardship, which General Augereau could only alleviate by bringing in food convoys from France, but at the price of having to devote virtually 20 per cent of his available force to protecting them. Moreover, as the war wore on, the French economy was increasingly stretched for resources. With so many young men on the front lines, economic indices were stagnant at best, and the financing of campaigns became increasingly difficult. The preparation of the Russian campaign was an unprecedented economic and logistical effort, and its failure would contribute to the collapse of the economic plans drawn up by Napoleon and his trusted men, such as Mollen, Petiet and Daru.

Of course, it is impossible to ignore the military aspects of the war. Here, there are three factors to consider. First and foremost, once again, is British assistance. The Spanish alone could not have defeated Napoleon and Wellington's contribution was decisive. It has been extensively studied and little more can be added to those studies. Less frequently mentioned is the role of the Royal Navy, which made it possible to maintain resistance in many parts of the Peninsula that were cut off by land, such as Catalonia, where the collaboration between the British and the Catalans was particularly fruitful.

On the French side, Napoleon probably did not expect such a fierce reaction from the Spanish. He therefore had to make the most of it the situation, sending not only his best troops but also his best officers to the Peninsular War. After the unsatisfactory campaign of 1808, Napoleon Bonaparte himself led the best troops of his *Grand Armée* to ravage northern Spain during the campaign of 1809, when it seemed that the war might be concluded. In fact, nothing could be further from the truth. After the massacre of the Army of the Left and the heavy defeats in battles such as Tudela, the war was most definitely not over and the Emperor was forced to continue sending men and resources to Spain. For example, nineteen of the twenty-six marshals of the First Empire saw service in the Peninsular War at some point in their careers. Lannes, Soult, Masséna and Suchet, among others, won great victories, but despaired at the price they had to pay for them. Moreover, time was against the Emperor. One important milestone was the Russian campaign, for which Napoleon employed nearly 650,000 men. Since soldiers were also a limited resource, many of them, including their excellent officers, left the Peninsular War to start the new conquest. This drawdown of troops meant that many territories could not be defended, which contributed to the imperial forces being forced to retreat northwards.

Thirdly, there was the Spanish army, perhaps best described by the family motto of General Pérez de Herrasti, governor of Ciudad Rodrigo during the French siege of 1810: 'the thumb breaks, but it does not bend'. In 1808 the Spanish patriots had to raise an army from scratch. Many of these units had no chance of defeating the veteran imperial troops. Casualties numbered in the tens of thousands and many soldiers deserted in despair. But while some returned home or went back to the regular army, many others, fed up with their inexperienced or inept officers, went over to join the controversial guerrilla bands. Some of these newly created regiments, such as the bombastic Victory or Death or Union regiments, after initial defeats, eventually became elite units. Even some of the giddy guerrillas managed to become militarized, such as those commanded by Longa, and were even appreciated by Wellington himself. Despite some surprising early victories, such as Bailén and the first siege of Zaragoza, the campaigns of 1809 and 1810 meant only death and destruction for the Spanish armies. But if from a British point of view the turning point for victory was the battle of Salamanca in 1812, from a Spanish perspective the turning point for resistance can be found in the retreat of the Army of Extremadura in 1810, after the defeats in the battles of Ocaña and Alba de Tormes. The journey of the Duke of Albuquerque's troops demonstrates the stubborn resistance of the Spanish, their will to continue fighting, and their unshakeable faith in their ultimate victory. There can be no doubt that without this infinite fighting spirit, without the Spanish contribution, Napoleon could not have been defeated. To resist was to win. And they resisted.

Finally, there were the social aspects of the war. Obviously, Spanish society in the early nineteenth century cannot be judged through twenty-first-century values. It was a backward and largely illiterate society, as well as a deeply religious one. In fact, it was in the churches where most Spaniards not only heard the word of the Lord, but also where they were taught … regardless of the bias of the priests. Thus, a society had been formed that was allergic to the changes proposed by modernity, a society that rejected the timid reforms proposed by Godoy; in contrast, the figure of Ferdinand VII was magnified, presented from the pulpits as a hero and martyr. The accession to the throne of Joseph I seemed to confirm the worst fears of the defenders of the *ancien régime*. Alarmed by the anti-religious policies of the French, and fearing that they wanted to subvert the traditional social order, the masses reacted by rising up against the invaders, dragging into their maelstrom all those members of the elite who had maintained a neutral or expectant position at the beginning of the invasion, many of whom ended up being lynched by the enraged population. The French failed to adapt, to change this outlook. Despite Joseph I's initial goodwill, a climate of extreme violence developed in Spain between the two sides. The French committed all sorts of crimes and outrages in Spanish towns, some of which were wholly defenceless, and on several occasions shot prisoners of war, as happened after the battle of Medellín, while the Spanish responded by massacring any imperial soldiers who fell into their hands, whether they were couriers, convoys of wounded or small isolated garrisons. And then, of course, there were the collaborators. This climate of extreme violence was best captured by General Lacy during his time as Captain General of Catalonia. However, it is no less true that some of the Spanish elite were of a liberal bent and they hoped that the young King Ferdinand would side with them once the war was over. Surprisingly, the Spanish liberals knew how to play their cards right during the Cortes established in Cadiz during the siege and managed to promulgate the first Spanish Constitution in 1812, giving birth to modern Spain, although this was abrogated by Ferdinand VII as soon as he returned to Spain.

I hope to have shown throughout this book the Spanish point of view on the Peninsular War, concluding that it was not just Wellington who defeated Napoleon, but nor was it the Spanish army by itself, much less the disorganized guerrillas. It was a combination of them all, working together, bridging the differences and mistrust that separated them, and taking advantage of Joseph I's inability to assert himself as king and the Emperor's overweening ambition to conquer all of Europe. It was a long, bloody, ruthless war that created many of the popular myths that survive today in Spain, with its defeats and victories, its acts of cowardice and heroism, a war that, more than 200 years later, continues to fascinate and surprise us. It was a war that saw the birth of a modern nation.

Bibliography

Adzerias i Causi, Gustau (2006). *Conquesta de Montserrat (25 juliol de 1811)*. Available at: https://www.inh.cat/data/files/files/conquesta_montserrat.pdf (accessed 28 September 2020).

Alboise Du Pujol, Jules Edouard (1844). *Le donjon de Vincennes depuis sa fondation jusqu'à nos jours*. Paris: Administration de librairie.

Alcaide Ibieca, Agustín (1830). *Historia de los Dos Sitios que Pusieron a Zaragoza los años 1808 y 1809 las Tropas de Napoleón*. Vol. 1. Madrid: M. de Burgos.

Alonso, Gregorio (2015). *Imaginando a Fernando VII, el rey católico y felón*. University of Leeds, England.

Álvarez de Toledo, Pedro, Duque del Infantado (1809). *Manifesto de las operaciones del exercito del centro desde el día 3 de diciembre de 1808 al 17 de febrero de 1809*.

Álvarez García, Manuel Jesús (2014). 'Astorga y su ayuntamiento bajo la ocupación francesa, 1812' in Arsenio García Fuertes, Francisco Carantoña Álvarez and Óscar González García (eds), *Más que una Guerra: Astorga y el noroeste de España en el conflicto peninsular (1808–1814)*. Astorga: Edita Centro de Estudios Astorganos Marcelo Macías, pp. 41–72.

Anca Alamillo, Alejandro (2009). 'Pérdidas de Buques de la Armada Española durante las Guerras de Emancipación Americanas', in *Revista General de la Marina*, 257:253–70.

Ancely, Jean-Luc Waterloo (2015). *La marche à l'abîme*. Paris: Le Cri.

Aquillué Domínguez, Daniel (2020). 'Castaños: el odiado. Propaganda y opinión pública tras la batalla de Tudela' in *la revista Locvber*, 4:97–111.

Aquillué, Daniel (2021). *Guerra a Cuchillo*. Madrid: La esfera de los Libros.

Artaza, Ramón de (1888). 'La Reconquista de Santiago en 1809' in *Boletín de la Real Academia de la Historia*, XII. Madrid: Imprenta de Tejada.

Ausín Ciruelos, Alberto (2018). 'Propaganda, Periodismo y Pueblo en Armas: Las Guerrillas y sus Líderes según la Prensa de la Guerra de la Independencia (1808–1814)' in *la revista Aportes*, 97(XXXIII):7–43.

Aymes, Jean-René (1982). *La déportations ous le premier Empire: les Espagnols en France (1806–1814)*. Paris: Publications de la Sorbonne.

Aymes, Jean-René (1992). 'Les Espagnols en France (1789–1820)' in *Exils et émigrations hispaniques au XXe Siècle*, 1:34–49.

Baroja, Pío (1998). *Juan van Halen*. Vol. 233 Biblioteca EDAF. Editorial EDAF.

Boguñà, Jaume (2022). Las medallas españolas de las Guerras Napoleónicas [The Spanish Medals of the Napoleonic Wars]. Barcelona: self-published.

Bonne, Paul (1899). *Les Espagnols a la Grand Armée: le Corps de la Romana (1808–109) et le Regiment Joseph-Napoleon (1809–1813)*. Paris: Berger-Levrault et Cie.

Brown, Anthony Gary (2006). *The Patrick O'Brian Muster Book*. London: MacFarland & Co.

Burnham, Robert (2011). *Charging Against Wellington: The French Cavalry in the Peninsular War, 1807–1814*. Barnsley: Frontline Books.

Cabanes, Francisco Javier (1815). *Historia de las Operaciones del Exército de Catalunya en la Guerra de la Usurpación*. Barcelona: Brunt.

Cabanes, Francisco Javier (1822). *Explicación del Cuadro Histórico-Cronológico de los Movimientos y Principales Acciones de los Ejércitos Beligerantes en la Península*. Barcelona.

Calpena, Enric and Junqueras, Oriol (2003). *Guerres dels Catalans*. Barcelona: Pòrtic Panorama.

Calvo Albero, José Luis (1809/2014). *La Campaña del Tajo*. Biblioteca GESI, Grupo de Estudios en Seguridad Internacional/Departamento de Ciencia Política y de la Administración, Universidad de Granada. Granda.

Campos y Fernández de Sevilla, Francisco Javier (2007). 'El Monasterio de San Lorenzo el Real en la época del "Proceso del Escorial, 1807–1808" in *Cuadernos del Pensamiento*, 19:269–313.

Casanova Honrubia, Juan Miguel (2009). *La Minería y Mineralogía del Reino de Valencia a Finales del Período Ilustrado (1746–1808)*. València: Servei de Publicacions de la Universitat de València.

Cascorro Moreno, Manuel (2006). *Los Franceses en Chinchón (29 de diciembre de 1808)*. Chinchón.

Cassinello Pérez, Andrés (2005). 'Aventuras de los Servicios de Información durante la Guerra de la Independencia' in *la Revista de Historia Militar*, Extraordinary edition.

Castrillo Mazares, Francisco (2000). 'La historia del Museo de Ejército en sus hombres' in *la Militaria*. Revista de Cultura Militar. Madrid: Servicio de Publicaciones del Ministerio de Defensa.

Ceballos-Escalera y Gila, Alfonso de (2002). 'Los Primeros Caballeros Españoles de la Orden de la Legión de Honor' in *Cuadernos de Ayala*, 10. Madrid.

Ceballos-Escalera y Gila, Alfonso de (2011). 'El Teniente General Duque de Alburquerque Salvador y Defensor de Cádiz en 1810', in *Cuadernos de Ayala*, 48:3–7.

Chaucard, C. (1833). 'Le siége du fort de Monzón' in, Jean Maximilien Lamarque and Francois Nicolas Fririon (eds), *Le Spectateur militaire: Recueil de science, d'art et d'histoire militaires*, Vol. 16. Paris: Bureau de Spectateur militaire.

Checa Godoy, Antonio (1848/2013). 'La prensa napoleónica en España (1808–1814). Una perspectiva' in *Varia*, 10. Available at: https://doi.org/10.4000/argonauta.1848 (accessed 6 March 2023).

CISDE (2014). *La División del Norte, los soldados españoles a disposición de Napoleón*. CISDE Observatorio.

Clonard, Conde de (1858). *Historia Orgánica de las Armas de Infantería y Caballería Españolas desde la creación del ejército permanente hasta el día hoy*. Vol. XI, Part 1. Madrid: Don Francisco del Castillo.

Cobbett, William (1808). *Cobbett's Political Registers*. Vol. XIV. London.

'Comunicación de Bartolomé Muñoz dirigida al Diputado General de Álava remitiéndole la sentencia del Proceso de El Escorial', dated 8 April 1808. Archivo de la Diputación Foral de Álava/Araba. Signatura: ATHA-FHPA-DH-267-46-06 (del folio 7 al folio 8). Available at: http://www.araba.eus/arabadok/doc?q=%28*%3A%29+&start=65&rows=1&sort=msstored_title%20asc&fq=norm&fv=*&fo=and&fq=mssearch_people&fv=Fernando+Vii%2C+Rey+de+España&fo=and (accessed 6 March 2023).

Deira, José María (2012). 'Perico, la Tirabuzones y Candelas' in *La Voz de Cádiz*, 19 February 2012. Available at: https://www.lavozdigital.es/cadiz/20120219/sociedad/perico-tirabuzones-candelas-20120219.html?ref=https:%2F%2Fwww.google.com (accessed 20 January 2021).

Diego García, Emilio de (2009). 'El Mar en la Guerra de la Independencia' in *Cuadernos de Historia Contemporánea*, Extraordinary edition:59–70.

Diego García, Emilio de (2020). 'La Formación del Ejército de Andalucía', in *Revista Desperta Ferro/ Historia Moderna*, 45. Madrid.

Dufourcq, Charles-Emmanuel (1962). 'Un Officier de Murat en Catalogne. Le Baron Desvernois: sacarrière, safamille' in *Boletín de la Real Academia de Buenas Letras de Barcelona*, 29:319–44. Barcelona.

Esdaile, Charles, J. (1988). *The Spanish Army in the Peninsular War*. Manchester: Manchester University Press.

Esdaile, Charles, J. (2004). *Fighting Napoleon: Guerrillas, Bandits, and Adventurers in Spain, 1808–1814*. New Haven, CT: Yale University Press.

Esdaile, Charles, J. (2008). *Peninsular Eyewitnesses: The Experience of War in Spain and Portugal 1808–1813*. London: Pen & Sword.

Espinosa de los Monteros y Jaraquemada, José María (2014). *Milicia y política en la revolución liberal española. El General Carlos Espinosa de los Monteros y Ayerdi (1775–1847)*. Logroño: Universidad de La Rioja.

Espinosa de los Monteros y Jaraquemada, José María (2018). 'Los Prisioneros Bajo Palabra. Un caso singular durante la guerra de la Independencia' in *Revista Ejército*, 926.

Esteban Ribas, Alberto Raúl (2009a). 'La Derrota de la Fuerza de Maniobra de Cataluña. La Batalla de Valls' in *Revista de Historia Militar*. Madrid: Instituto de Historia y Cultura Militar.

Esteban Ribas, Alberto Raúl (2009b). 'La Batalla de Valls de 1809. El Punt de Vista Militar' in *A Carn!'* in *Publicacio electrònica d'Historia Militar Catalana*, 9.

Fernández Duro, Cesáreo (1903). *Armada Española desde la Unión de los Reinos de Castilla y Aragón*. Madrid: Sucesores de Rivadeneyra.

Fernández Fernández, José Carlos (2010). *Periplo Póstumo del XIV Duque de Alburquerque*. Comunicación presentada en el II Coloquio Internacional sobre la figura del XIV Duque de Alburquerque, celebrado en San Fernando (Cádiz) del 8–11 February 2010. Available at: http://milan2.es/AsDeGuia/AsDeGuia_Viaje_Postumo_Alburquerque.html (accessed 12 July 2020).

Fernández Grueso, Manuel (2014). *Franceses en Tarancón*. Tarancón.

Forcada Torres, Gonzalo (1966). *'Ingleses, españoles y franceses en los prolegómenos de la batalla de Tudela'* in *Príncipe de Viana*, 27(102–3). Pamplona.

Franco de Espés, Carlos (2019). *Los Enigmas de Valençay. La Corte Española en el Exilio (1808–1814)*. Zaragoza: Prensas de la Universidad de Zaragoza.

Fraser, Ronald (2008). *Napoleon's Cursed War: Popular Resistance in the Spanish Peninsular War, 1808–1814*. London: Verso Books.

Gálvez, Ana M. (2016). *La Batalla de Uclés*. Uclés: Ayuntamiento de Uclés.

García Fuertes, Arsenio (2006). 'Un poema épico de la Guerra de la Independencia: Los Cuadros de Alba de Tormes' in *Argutorio*, 16.

García Fuertes, Arsenio (2008). 'El Ejército Español en Campaña en los Comienzos de la Guerra de la Independencia, 1808–1809' in *Monte Buciero*, 13:101–66. (Dedicated to: La Guerra de la Independencia en Cantabria.)

García Fuertes, Arsenio (2016). *La Decisiva Participación de los 6° y 7° Ejércitos Españoles en el Triunfo Aliado en las Campañas de 1811 y 1812 durante la Guerra de la Independencia*. León: Facultad de Filosofía y Letras, Universidad de León.

Garcia Garcia, Jesús M. (2016). 'La Batalla de Alba de Tormes vista por los franceses'. Available at: https://www.salamancanapoleonica.com/pdf/LA_BATALLA_DE_ALBA_DE_TORMES_1809_VISTA.pdf (accessed 6 March 2023).

García González, Miguel José (2009). 'Ponferrada y el Bierzo al comienzo de la Guerra de la Independencia. 1808–1809', in *Estudios Bercianos*. Ponferrada.

García Prado, Justiniano (1947a). 'Los regimientos asturianos en la Guerra de la Independencia' in *Revista de la Universidad de Oviedo, Facultad de Filosofía y Letras VIII* (43–4):65–117. Oviedo.

García Prado, Justiniano (1947b): 'El Muy noble Ejército asturiano en 1808' in *Revista de la Universidad de Oviedo, Facultad de Filosofía y Letras VIII* (41–2):97–125. Oviedo.

Gil Novales, Alberto (2009). 'La Guerrilla de los Afrancesados: La Primera Guerra Civil' in *Spagna Contemporanea*, 36:67–80.

Goiogana, Iñaki (2013). *Lekeitio en guerra. 1812*. Available at: http://lekitxarrenartikuloak.blogspot.com/p/blog-page.html (accessed 10 January 2021).

Gómez de Arteche, José (1880). *Fernando VII en Valençay. Tentativas encaminadas a procurar su libertad*. Madrid: Manuel G. Hernández.

Gómez de Arteche y Moro, José (1883). *Guerra de la Independencia: Historia Militar de España de 1808 a 1814*. Vol. V. Madrid: Litografía del Depósito de Guerra.

Gómez de Arteche y Moro, José (1893). *Guerra de la Independencia: Historia Militar de España de 1808 a 1814*. Vol. VIII. Madrid: Litografía del Depósito de Guerra.

Gómez Rodrigo, Carmen (1976–7). 'Diez Meses en la Historia de Castro-Urdiales' in Altamira. *Revista del Centro de Estudios Montañeses*, XL. Santander.

González Lopo, Domingo L. (2010). 'El Águila Vencida: los Franceses en Galicia (1809)' in Fernando Martins and Francisco Vaz (eds), *O 'saque de Évora' no Contexto da Guerra Peninsular*. Évora: Publicaçoes de Cidehus.

González-Aller Hierro, José Ignacio (2005). 'La vida a bordo en la época de Trafalgar' in *Revista General de Marina*, 249(8–9):187–218.

Grahit i Grau, Josep (1959). *Partes Inéditos Sobre Gerona en 1809*. Gerona.

Guerrero Acosta, José Manuel (2011). 'El Duque de Alburquerque y la retirada del Ejército de Extremadura' in *Revista de Historia Militar*, Extraordinary volume:13–40. Madrid: Servicio de Publicaciones del Ministerio de Defensa.

Guzmán, Martín Luis (2003). *Mina el mozo: héroe de Navarra*. Txalaparta.

Van Halen, Juan (1814). *Restauración de las plazas de Lérida, Mequinenza y castillo de Monzón por medio de unas estratagemas: ocupación de estas por una de las divisiones del primer exército español en los días 13, 14 y 16 de febrero del año de 1814.*

Hamilton, Thomas (1813). *Annals of the Peninsular Campaigns from 1808 to 1814*. Vol. 1. London: Pickle Partner Publishing.

Herson, James P. Jr (1992). *For the Cause. Cadiz and the Peninsular War: Military and Siege Operations from 1808 to 1812*. Florida: Florida State University.

Hocquellet, Richard (2008). Resistencia y Revolución durante la Guerra de la Independencia. Zaragoza: Universitarias de Zaragoza.

Houdecek, François (2016). 'L'honneur instrumentalisé: le sort des généraux de Baylen (1808–1812)' in *Napoleonica. La Revue*, 1(25):142–61.

Hugo, Abel (1837). *France Militarie. Histoire des Armées Françaises de Terre et de la Mer de 1792 à 1837.* Vol. IV. Paris: Ed. de la France Pittoresque.

Iglesias Rogers, Graciela (2013). *British Liberators in the Age of Napoleon*. London: Bloomsbury.

Ilari, Virgilio (2004). *Le TruppeItaliane in Spagna*. Available at: http://www.centotredicesimo.org/wp-content/uploads/2015/11/Ilari-Le-truppe-italiane-in-Spagna-libre.pdf (accessed 12 June 2020).

Iribarren, José María (1942). *La batalla de Tudela*. Gobierno de Navarra: Institución Príncipe de Viana.

Juan y Ferragut, Mariano (2008). 'La Armada y el Factor Naval en la Guerra de la Independencia' in *Cátedra 'Jorge Juan': ciclo de conferencias: curso 2006–2007*/coord. por Adolfo Rey Seijo, pp. 111–34.

Junot, Laure (1835). *Mémoires de Madame la Duchesse d'Abrantès*, ed. L. Mame. París.

Lafon, Jean-Marc (2020). 'La Acción de Mengíbar y el cerco al ejército francés', in *Revista Desperta Ferro/Historia Moderna*, 45. Madrid.

Lievyns, A. et al. (1845). *Fastes de la Légion-d'Honneur. Biographie de tous les décorés, accompagnée de l'histoire législative et réglementaire de l'ordre*. Vol. 3. Paris.

Lievyns, A. et al. (1844). *Fastes de la Légion-d'Honneur. Biographie de tous les décorés, accompagnée de l'histoire législative et réglementaire de l'ordre*. Vol. 4. Paris.

Lievyns, A. et al. (1844). *Fastes de la Légion-d'Honneur. Biographie de tous les décorés, accompagnée de l'histoire législative et réglementaire de l'ordre*. Vol. 10. Paris.

Lión Valderrábano, Raúl (1973). 'El Regimiento de Húsares de Cantabria' en Altamira. *Revista del Centro de Estudios Montañeses*. Santander.

Lombroso, Giacomo (1843). *Vite dei primari Generali ed Ufficiali Italiani che si distinsero nelle guerre Napoleoniche dal 1796 al 1815*. Milán: Borroni e Scotti.

Longman et al. (1811). *The Edinburgh Annual Register for 1809*. Vol. 2. London: John Ballantyne.

Lores Altuve-Febres, Fernán (2007). 'Blas de Ostolaza, un apasionado de la fidelidad' in *Anales de la Fundación Francisco Elías de Tejada*, 13:141–63.

Marabel Matos, Jacinto J. (2016). 'Muerte y Simonía del Gobernador de Badajoz, el Excmo. Mariscal de Campo D. Rafael Menacho y Tutlló (I)' in *Revista de Estudios Extremeños*, LXXII(III):1,753–84.

Marcel, Nicolas (1814). Les Campagnes de Captain Marcel. Available at: http://web.science.mq.edu.au/~susanlaw/ninetyfive/marcel/marcelEpiF.htm (accessed 6 March 2023).

Martín Mas, Miguel Ángel (2008). 'Perez de Herrasti, Governor of Ciudad Rodrigo: the thumb breaks but does not bend', in *napoleon-series.org*. (accessed 1 July 2020).

Martín Roig, Gabriel (2010a). 'El cors a l'Empordà durant la Guerra del Francès' in *Revista del Baix Empordà*, 29:10–22.

Martín Roig, Gabriel (2010b). 'Les batalles de Palamós de 1810: l'assalt anglo-espanyol i la desfeta de Santa Llúcia' in *Revista del Baix Empordà*, 30:82–93.

Martín-Valdepeñas Yagüe, Elisa (2010). 'Mis Señoras Traidoras: las afrancesadas, una historia olvidada' in *Revista HMiC*, VIII.

Martínez Martínez, José Luis (2009). 'Algunas noticias sobre la guerra de la Independencia en la comarca Utiel-Requena. 1811–1812' in *Oleana: Cuadernos de Cultura Comarcal*. Ejemplar dedicado a: IV Congreso de Historia Comarcal. El alfoz en la época de auge y declive del absolutismo. Finales del siglo XVII a inicios del siglo XIX. Requena y Utiel, 6–8 November 2009, pp. 565–92.

Matrat, Gaeëlle (2015). 'Le traité de Valençay (1813): le séjour des princes d'Espagne à Valençay (1808–1814). Rétrospective d'une exposition historique' in *Le Courrier du Prince*, 7. Bulletin d'Information de l'Association Les Amis de Talleyrand.

Minali, Guillermo (1840). *Historia militar de Gerona, que comprende particularmente los dos sitios de 1808 y 1809*. Girona: A. Figaró.

Mira Gutiérrez, Vicente (no date). 'La Guerra de la Independencia en Cádiz'. Available at: http://www.islabahia.com/culturalia/01historia/laguerradelaindependenciaencadiz.asp (accessed 9 October 2020).

Miranda Rubio, Francisco (2018). 'Xavier Mina y su tiempo' in *Huarte de San Juan. Geografía e Historia*, 25:27–62.

Molero, Carlo (2020). '¿Sirvió un descendiente de Mahoma en las filas del Farnesio?' in the blog El Club de los Jinetes del Farnesio, 27 January 2020. Available at: https://regimientofarnesio.wordpress.com/2020/01/27/sirvio-un-descendiente-de-mahoma-en-las-filas-del-farnesio/ (accessed 1 December 2021).

Moliner Prada, Antonio (2005). 'La imagen de los soldados italianos en Cataluña en la Guerra del Francés' in *Revista HMiC: Història Moderna i Contemporània*, 3:225–48. Bellaterra: Universitat Autònoma de Barcelona.

Moliner Prada, Antonio (2008). 'De las Juntas a la Regencia. La Difícil Articulación del Poder en la España de 1808' in *Historia Mexicana*, LVIII(1):135-177. México D.F.

Moreno Alonso, Manuel (2012). 'Jovellanos y el colapso de la Junta Central en Sevilla' in *Boletín de la Real Academia Sevillana de Buenas Letras: Minervae Baeticae*, 40:349–84. Seville.

Mullié, Charles (1851). *Biographie des célébrités militaires des armées de terre et de mer de 1789 à 1850*. Vol. 2. Paris.

Murat, J. Joseph André (1897). *Murat, lieutenant de l'empereur en Espagne 1808: d'après sa correspondance inédite et des documents originaux*. [2nd edn.] Paris: Plon, Nourrit et cie.

Muriel Hernández, Manuel (2012). *Manuel Lorenzo. Militar y Gobernador de Santiago de Cuba*. Madrid: Facultad de Geografía e Historia. Universidad Complutense, doctoral thesis.

Murillo Galimany, Francesc (2006). *La batalla del Pont de Goi*. Valls: Institut d'Estudis Vallencs.

Murillo Galimany, Francesc (2011). 'La Defensa del Fuerte de la Oliva, mayo de 1811' in *A Carn!* Special number.

Napier, William Francis Patrick (1832). *History of the War in the Peninsula and in the South of France from the Year 1807 to the Year 1814*. Vol. 1. London: Thomas & William Boone.

Napier, William Francis Patrick (1834). *Histoire de la Guerre dans la Péninsule et dans le Midi de la France: depuis l'Année 1807 jusqu'à l'Année 1814*. Vol. 5. Paris: Treuttel & Würtz.

Napier, William Francis Patrick (1836). *History of the War in the Peninsula and in the South of France from the year 1807 to the year 1814*. Oxford: David Christy.

Oman, Charles (1903). *A History of the Peninsular War*. Vol. II (January–September 1809). Oxford: Clarendon Press.

Oman, Charles (1911). *A History of the Peninsular War*. Vol. IV. Oxford: Clarendon Press.

Osuna Rey, Juan Manuel and Osuna Carballeira, Daniel (1999). 'La Junta y Regimiento de Voluntarios de Lobeira' in *Minius. Revista do Departamento de Historia, Arte e Xeografía*, 7:75–96. Vigo: Universidad de Vigo.

Padín Portela, Bruno (2019). *La Traición en la Historia de España*. Madrid: Akal.

Palacio Ramos, Rafael (2008). 'Importancia estratégica de Cantabria durante la Guerra de la Independencia: vías de comunicación y plazas fuertes', *Monte Buciero*, 13:221–54. Santander.

Pardo Camacho, Ricardo (date?). *La Guerra de la Independencia en la Provincia de Castellón 1811*. Aula Militar 'Bermúdez de Castro'. Available at: http://www.aulamilitar.com/D08_14_1811.pdf?ID_SESION=HZPCFGBBZPJXWSHBQJCV (accessed 31 August 2020).

Parra López, Emilio La (2008). 'Fernando VII: impulso y freno a la sublevación de los españoles contra Napoleón' en *Mélanges de la Casa de Velázquez*, 38(1):33–52.

Parra López, Emilio La (2010). 'Los Hombres de Fernando VII en 1808', in Alberola-Romá, Armando and Larriba Árbol, Elisabel (eds), *Las élites y la «revolución de España» (1808–1814): Estudios en homenaje al profesor Gérard Dufour*. Alicante: Universitat d'Alacant/Universidad de Alicante, Servicio de Publicaciones.

Parra López, Emilio La (2013a). 'Los viajes de Fernando VII' in Emilio Soler Pascual and Francisco Sevillano Calero (eds), *Diarios de viaje de Fernando VII (1823 and 1827–1828)*. Alicante: Universitat dAlacant/Universidad de Alicante, Servicio de Publicaciones.

Parra López, Emilio La (2013b). 'La Titularidad de la Corona Española. Reacciones Europeas' in Cristina Borreguero Beltrán (coord.), *La Guerra de la Independencia en el Valle del Duero: los asedios de Ciudad Rodrigo y Almeida*. Valladolid: Fundación Siglo.

Parra López, Emilio La (2018). *Fernando VII. Un Rey Deseado y Detestado*. Booket Collection. Barcelona: Tusquets.

Patinaud, Michel (2017). *Les colonnes de prisonniersespagnols des guerres napoléoniennes à Saint Léonard (1810 à 1813): de la généalogie à la grande Histoire* … Available at: https://www.histoire-genealogie.com/Les-colonnes-de-prisonniers-espagnols-des-guerres-napoleoniennes-a-Saint-Leonard-1810-a-1813-de-la-genealogie-a-la-grande-Histoire?lang=fr (accessed 16 Nov. 2020).

Peltier, M. (1810). *L'Ambigu o Variétés Litéraires et Politiques*. Vol. XXVIII. Paris.

Pena García, José Manuel (2007). *Estradenses en la Guerra de la Independencia. Don Felipe Constenla y Garrido (1808–1810)*. Estrada: Museo do Pobo Estradense 'Manuel Reimóndez Portela'.

Pérez, Guillermo (2015). 'Los Coroneles del 'Villaviciosa': Barón De Armendáriz' in *Los Lanceros de Villaviciosa*. Available at: http://lancerosvillaviciosa.blogspot.com/2015/01/baron-de-armendariz.html (accessed 6 March 2023).

Pérez Francés, José Antonio (2011). *'Guerra y cuchillo' un grito por la Independencia y la Libertad*. Zaragoza: Asociación Cultural 'Los Sitios de Zaragoza'.

Pérez Francés, José Antonio (2017). *Entre las Ruinas de Santa Engracia*. Zaragoza: Asociación Cultural 'Los Sitios de Zaragoza'.

Pérez de Guzmán y Gallo, Juan (1908). *El Dos de Mayo de 1808 en Madrid*. Madrid: Real Academia de la Historia.

Pérez de Guzmán y Gallo, Juan (1909). 'Informe a Su Majestad el rey don Alfonso XIII acerca del capitán español D. Antonio Costa, de la expedición auxiliar del Marqués de la Romana al Norte y su sepulcro en Fredericia (Dinamarca)' in *Boletín de la Real Academia de la Historia*, 55:35–101.

Pérez-Reverte, Arturo (2007). 'Los presos de la Cárcel Real'. *El Semanal*, 9 December 2007.

Pintado I Simo-Monnè, Francesc (2013). *Tarragona 1811–13. Los Ejércitos Napoleónicos en la ciudad*. Madrid: Servicio de Publicaciones del Ministerio de Defensa.

Pitollet, Camille (1933). 'Sur les pas d'un officier d'état-major anglais en Portugal et en Espagne pendant la guerre de l'Indépendance' in *Bulletin Hispanique*, 35:209–86. Paris.

Planas Campos, Jorge and Grajal de Blas, Antonio (2020). *Officiers de Napoléon tués ou blessés pendant la Guerre d'Espagne (1808–1814)*. Vol. I. Madrid: Foro para el Estudio de la Historia Militar de España (FEHME).

Porras Castaño, Carlos (2012). 'Domingo Rico Villademoros: Condenado a muerte por las Cortes de Cádiz' in *Revista Hades*, 10. Madrid: Editorial Cemabasa.

Prats Pijoan, Joan de Déu (2010). *Historias y leyendas de Barcelona*. Barcelona: Marge Books.

Qadesh (2006/2017). *La expedición española a Dinamarca 1807–1808*. Foro El Gran Capitán. Article published 13 February 2006 and updated 21 December 2017.

Quintero Saravia, Gonzalo M. (2017). *Soldado de tierra y mar: Pablo Morillo el pacificador*. Madrid: Edaf.

Ramisa Verdaguer, Maties (2010). *La Batalla de Vic (1810). Un Episodi de la Invasió Napoleónica de Catalunya*. Available at: racocatala.cat (accessed 12 June 2020).

Reding von Biberegg, Theodor (1854). *Memorable Batalla de Bailen, y biografía del General Don T. Reding, Baron de Biberegg*. Madrid: Imprenta de la Esperanza.

Redondo Penas, Alfredo (2011). 'Los Regimientos que participaron en el Sitio Napoleónico de Tarragona' in *A Carn!* Special number.

Repullés (1842). *Historia de la vida y reinado de Fernando VII de España: con documentos justificados, órdenes reservadas y numerosas cartas del mismo monarca, Pio VII, Carlos IV, María Luisa, Napoleón, Luis XVIII, El Infante Don Carlos y otros personajes*. Vol. 2. Madrid: Repullés.

Rico Sánchez, Alberto (2009). 'La guerra en Monforte de Lemos (1808–1814)', in Emilio de Diego and José Luis Martínez Sanz (eds), *El comienzo de la Guerra de la Independencia*. Madrid: Editorial Actas.

Robertson Mendizábal, José Luis (2020). *Diego Joseph del Barco y de la Çendeja: Oriundo de Çierbena y Héroe de la Guerra de la Independencia*. Seville: Punto Rojo Libros.

Rodríguez Díez, Matías (1909). *Historia de la muy noble, leal y benemérita ciudad de Astorga*. Vol. I. Astorga: Porfirio López, pp. 416–31.

Rovira i Gómez, Salvador J. (2011). *Tarragona a la Guerra del Francès (1808–1813)*. Tarragona: Quaderns de l'Arxiu.

Rovira i Gómez, Salvador J. (2019). 'Tarragona a la Guerra del Francès (1808–1813)' in *Quaderns de l'Arxiu*, 6. Tarragona: Publicacions de la Universitat Rovira i Virgili.

Ruiz, José (2016). *El olvidado Batallón de Buenos Aires*. in *Revista Clío*. Available at: https://revista.elarcondeclio.com.ar/el-olvidado-batallon-de-buenos-aires-parte-i/ (accessed 30 June 2020).

Saint-Maurice Cabany, E. (1846). *Etude historique sur la capitulation de Baylen: renferment des documents authentiques et inédits, comprenant une narration détaillée de la campagne de 1808, en Andalousie*. Paris: Au Bureau du nécrologe universel du XIXe siècle/Chez Dauvin et Fontaine.

Salvadó Poy, Roc (2016). 'El bloqueig i l'evacuació de Tortosa i les seues consequüències (juliol de 1813–maig de 1814)' in *200 Anys de la Fi de la Guerra del Francès a les Terres de l'Ebre. Actes del Congrés d'Història i d'Arqueologia Tortosa, 16, 17 i 18 de maig de 2014*, edición a cargo de Roc Salvadó y Joan Martínez. Onada Edicions.

Sánchez García, Raquel (2008). 'El exilio de 1814' in *Ínsula: revista de letras y ciencias humanas*, 744:22–5.

Sañudo Bayón, Juan José (2009). 'Campaña y Batalla de Medellín. 1809' in *Actas de las Jornadas de Historia de las Vegas Altas: la Batalla de Medellín*, pp. 111–60.

Sañudo Bayón, Juan José (2011). 'La Batalla de Almonacid (11-VIII-1809)' in *Revista de Historia Militar*, 110:153–220. Madrid: Servicio de Publicaciones del Ministerio de Defensa.

Sañudo Bayón, Juan José (2013). 'La Batalla de Tamames' in *Revista de Historia Militar*, 113:213–54. Madrid: Servicio de Publicaciones del Ministerio de Defensa.

Sarmiento Pérez, José (2010). 'Biografía del Capitán General de Extremadura D. José Galluzo y Páez (1746–1817)' in *Revista de Estudios Extremeños*, LXVI(III):1,217–56.

Sorando, Luis (2010). *Unidades y Uniformes del Ejército Francés en los Sitios de Zaragoza*. Available at: napoleon-series.com (accessed 29 April 2020).

Southey, Robert (1825). *History of the Peninsular War*. Vol. 1. London: John Murray.

Stampa, Leopoldo (2011). *Pólvora, plata u boleros: memoria de embajadas, saqueos y pasatiempos relatados por testigos combatientes de la Guerra de la Independencia 1808–1814*. Marcial Pons Historia.

Stampa, Leopoldo (2012). *La Batalla de Almonacid 1809*. Wars and Battles Series. Madrid: Almena Ediciones.

Suchet, Louis Gabriel (1828). *Mémoires du Maréchal Suchet, sur ses campagnes en Espagne*. Vol. 1. Paris: Adolphe Bossange.

Thibaudeau, Antoine Clair (1835). *Le Consulatet l' Empire ou Histoire de Napoléon Bonaparte, de 1799 a 1815*. Vol. 7. Paris: Jules Renouard.

Thiers, Adolphe (1849). *Histoire du consulat et de l'Empire*. Vol. 9. Paris: Paulin.

Toreno, Count of (1838). Historia del Levantamiento, Guerra y Revolución de España. First edition. Paris: Librería Baudry.

Torrejón Chaves, Juan (2008). 'El Sitio Francés de la Isla de León (1810–1812)' in *Revista de General de la Marina*, 255:349–74. Madrid: Servicio de Publicaciones del Ministerio de Defensa.

Torrejón Chaves, Juan (2010a). 'Muerte a bordo del "León de Friedland": François Amable Ruffin, general de división del Primer Imperio Francés' in *Revista General de Marina*, 259:29–44. Madrid: Servicio de Publicaciones del Ministerio de Defensa.

Torrejón Chaves, Juan (2010b). 'El Bicentenario de la Muerte del General Sénarmont' en Diario de Cádiz, dated 6 November 2010. Available at: https://www.diariodecadiz.es/opinion/articulos/bicentenario-muerte-General-Senarmont_0_421458533.html.

Troncoso García-Cambón, Ricardo (2018). 'Los británicos en la reconquista de Vigo y Puente Sampayo: nuevos datos' in *Glaucopis*, 23:271–348. Vigo: Instituto de Estudios Vigueses.

Vaquero, Fernando (2010). 'El 6° Cuerpo a 15 de noviembre de 1808 y a mediados de ayo de 1809' in *Blog Galicia 1809. Guía uniformológica sobre el ejército francés en Galicia*. Entry for 1 March 2012. Available at: https://galicia1809.wordpress.com/2012/03/01/el-6o-cuerpo-a-15-de-noviembre-de-1808-y-a-mediados-de-mayo-de-1809/ (accessed 6 March 2023).

Vega Viguera, Enrique de la (1995). 'La singular vida de Tomás de Morla y Pacheco, militar político jerezano' in *Boletín de la Real Academia Sevillana de Buenas Letras: Minervae Baeticae*, 23:159–214. Seville.

Vidal Delgado, Rafael (2015). *Operaciones en torno a Bailén. La caída de los mitos*. Madrid: Edita Foro para la Paz en el Mediterráneo.

Villa Urrutia, Wenceslao Ramírez de (firmado como Marqués de Villa-Urrutia) (1922). *Fernando VII, rey constitucional: historia diplomática de España de 1820 a 1823*. Madrid: F. Beltrán.

Vinaixa Miró, Joan R. (2013). 'La Guerra del Francès a les Terres de l'Ebre' in Ramon Arnabat Mata (ed.), *La Guerra del Francès 200 anys després*. Tarragona: Publicacions de l'Universitat Rovira i Virgili.

VVAA (1815). *Mercurio de España. 1815*. Vol. II. Madrid: Imprenta Real.

VVAA (1820). *Victoires, Conquêtes, Désastres, Revers et Guerres Civiles des Français, de 1792 a 1815*. Vol. XVIII. Ed. C.L.F. Panckoucke. Paris.

Index